# HIGHER EDUCATION AND THE REAL WORLD: The Story of CAEL

# HIGHER EDUCATION AND THE REAL WORLD

## The Story of CAEL

by Zelda F. Gamson

Longwood Academic
Wolfeboro, New Hampshire

Published in 1989 by Longwood Academic, a division of Longwood Publishing Group, Inc., Wolfeboro, N.H. 03894-2069, U.S.A.

ISBN 0-89341-586-3 (cloth)
0-89341-587-1 (paper)

Printed in the United States of America

**Library of Congress Cataloging in Publication Data:**

Gamson, Zelda F.
Higher education and the real world : the story of CAEL / by Zelda F. Gamson.
p. cm.
Includes bibliographical references.
ISBN 0-89341-586-3 -- ISBN 0-89341-587-1 (pbk.)
1. Adult education—United States—Case studies. 2. Education, Higher—United States—Case studies. 3. Experiential learning—United States—Case studies. 4. Cooperative Assessment of Experiential Learning (Project)—History. 5. Council for the Advancement of Experiential Learning (U.S.)—History. 6. Council for Adult and Experiential Learning (U.S.)—History. I. Title.
LC 5251.G33 1989
374'.973--dc20 89-37670
CIP

# CONTENTS

CONTENTS

CONTENTS

# PREFACE

This is the story of an organization that set out to change a small part of higher education and ended up doing much more. The breadth of its reach tells us about the inventiveness of educators in this country. When colleges and universities are under siege, we have much to learn about how they change—and how they stay the same.

"CAEL" is the prism I will use to refract higher education. It is the name of an organization whose expanding sights were expressed in its name changes. The first CAEL, 1974-1977, was the Cooperative Assessment of Experiential Learning, a research and development project administered by the Educational Testing Service on the assessment of learning gained outside the classroom. The second CAEL, 1977-1984, was the Council for the Advancement of Experiential Learning, an independent organization which operated as an advocacy and diffusion center for all aspects of non-classroom learning. The Council for Adult and Experiential Learning, the CAEL that began in 1985, signaled CAEL's interest in almost all aspects of adult education.

CAEL is an organization whose fate, until very recently, depended almost entirely on foundations and federal agencies. Fast-moving, entrepreneurial, CAEL attracted people who were willing to do more. In many ways, it had the quality of a social movement. CAEL's adherents were bound together by friendship, the values they shared, and a leader who inspired devotion and loyalty. CAEL was also like a social movement in its looseness. While its central office was located in Columbia, Maryland, its regional representatives were spread across the country. A shifting group, these regional representatives carried the word of CAEL to all parts of the country.

CAEL succeeded in capturing the imagination of leaders in foundations, associations, and other organizations surrounding higher education—the Educational Testing Service, the

American Council on Education, the W.K. Kellogg Foundation, the Ford Foundation, the American College Testing Program, the Council for Postsecondary Accreditation, the Fund for the Improvement of Postsecondary Education, the Carnegie Corporation, the Lilly Endowment, and state educational agencies. It also drew into its orbit from time to time some of the leading commentators on higher education—Harold Hodgkinson, Alexander Astin, Virginia Smith, Cyril Houle, Arthur Chickering, Malcolm Knowles, K. Patricia Cross, Russell Edgerton.

CAEL thrived at a time when many other innovative organizations had to trim their sails—if they survived at all. CAEL was strikingly successful in financial terms. In the period covered by this book, its budget grew from a little over $600,000 a year in 1974 to $2.6 million in 1985.

What accounts for CAEL's ability to attract resources? How did it deploy these resources? To what effect? What does CAEL tell us about the openness to change in higher education more generally?

In the world of higher education, CAEL is known as "the responsible innovator." This is because it cultivated an image of moderation and deliberately sought relationships with a variety of organizations. It was optimistic, egalitarian, and individualistic in the great Yankee bootstrap tradition. CAEL was very different from the most prestigious colleges and universities whose faculty, especially in the humanities, set the tone for American academia. As establishments go, the academic one is among the least permeable. But this is not the whole story. There is a genuine conflict between CAEL and academia, and the conflict is more than stylistic. It is ideological as well. CAEL provokes several ideological polarities in education: "innovation" vs. "tradition," "process" vs. "content." Under these headlines lie considerably more complex world-views.

CAEL started with a view of colleges and universities as instructional and credentialling institutions. People know more than colleges and universities give them credit for, and more people are educable than are currently enrolled. Students are "learners" and learners come before everything else. Close attention must be paid to the individual differences among learners if all of them are to get a good education. A good education is one that recognizes and develops capacities in learners that help them become more effective in the world. A good "educator" pays as much, if not more, attention to how content is delivered as to the content itself.

In contrast, traditional academics start with a view of higher education as a special, even sacred, institution. Instruction and credentials are important, to be sure, but they are secondary to the search for truth. While people undoubtedly learn all the time, not all of this learning is appropriate for college. College learning requires some detachment from experience. Such detachment is best achieved in the worlds of learning created on campuses and in classrooms. In these settings, content must command more attention than pedagogy. It is well to pay attention to individual differences among students, but there is a practical limit to the capacity of the faculty to do so.

Which point of view is the correct one? Is there a way to draw on the best of each? These are questions that have vexed me in my own life as a student and a teacher. I thought CAEL would help me answer them. Instead, it has only deepened my ambivalence.

My own relationship to CAEL has been ambivalent. I had been aware of CAEL for years before embarking on this study. I had kept a file on it for a while at the University of Michigan when I taught a course on innovations. I taught another course on the college student that introduced me to the literature on adult development. I became acquainted with some of the important contributors to this literature, some of whom had connections to CAEL. Yet while I had been active in educational reform throughout the 1970s, I had no contact with CAEL.

When Morris Keeton, the president of CAEL, invited me

in 1983 to study his organization, I knew him by reputation and through our common bond with Antioch College. I was at a turning point in my work, and CAEL offered me the chance to study change in higher education from the angle of an organization unconnected to a college or university. I had one main concern, however. Accustomed, as most academics are, to working on self-initiated grants, I worried about working on a contract with the very organization I was studying. How much freedom would I have to poke into hidden recesses of CAEL? Would I run the danger of subtle censorship? Would I be expected to provide help and consultation that might compromise sources of information and interfere too much in what I was studying?

As it turned out, I had little to worry about on the issue of freedom and censorship. CAEL opened itself up in every imaginable way. Any CAEL file was available. Staff and regional representatives, former associates, and observers all made room for me as I barged into their lives. No one refused me time, however busy and harried they were. All along, I tested my ideas with key people and sent early drafts of the final manuscript. Many pointed out errors of fact, some argued with my interpretations, but no one suggested that I change what I wrote.

As "historian" for Project LEARN, a large program with funding from the W.K. Kellogg Foundation, I took up a substantial share of the monies allocated for an external evaluation of LEARN. I was expected not only to write a case study of CAEL but also to provide "formative" evaluation of the project as my work proceeded. Here I ran into some difficulties. Keeton was in the habit of drawing outsiders, especially visible outsiders, into CAEL events. At the time I began studying CAEL, I was a member of a national study group which issued the first in a series of reports on higher education. As a result of this report, I received many speaking invitations. In the natural course of events, CAEL would have invited me to speak. Indeed, I received several invitations to speak at CAEL conferences on topics unrelated to my role as CAEL historian. I accepted two such invitations but found them uncomfortable, even though my hosts and I explicitly agreed to keep the roles (and payment) separate.

As LEARN's historian, I spoke publicly about my emerging understanding of CAEL as I went along. I did not find this a problem, even though I later changed my mind about some of the things I said. I also provided formative feedback in interviews and other conversations about my reactions to CAEL's programs and organizational structure. People would often disagree, but again put no pressure on me to change my mind.

CAEL activists became accustomed to seeing me at conferences or to talking privately with me. While all were friendly, some were more open than others. Some took me on as an informant takes on an anthropologist—teaching me about their society, hoping I would see it from their point of view. I had to take care not to be captured by these people, some of whom became friends. While we did not become friends in this way, Morris Keeton and I did establish a close colleagueship. His long-standing leadership of CAEL, formidable memory, and personal appeal made him a key informant. It was difficult to resist becoming too attached to Keeton.

While I found CAEL a fascinating puzzle and an extraordinary achievement, I was never attracted personally to it. Something held me back, and I am not sure what it was. Too much niceness, perhaps, though it was a refreshing change from the contentious life of colleges and universities. Perhaps it was the continuous quest for the newest idea, a quest fueled by the constant need to raise money. Perhaps it was the notion of awarding college credit for learning gained outside an academic institution, an idea I never wholeheartedly accepted. Or finally, perhaps it was too much process and not enough content. Whatever the reason, with CAEL as a backdrop I became a traditional academic.

## PREFACE

Out of a need to keep my distance, I found myself at some points becoming impudent because I found the pace of change in the organization and the sheer energy of CAEL people overwhelming. I joked about CAEL as an association of "manic progressives." In the first draft of this manuscript, I wrote overly dramatic interpretations of several events which turned out to be unfounded.

The need to keep my distance abated in time. CAEL moved on to other things as I struggled slowly to complete the writing. As my understanding of CAEL deepened, I became more confident in my own interpretations and less anxious about having other viewpoints imposed on me. It helped, of course, to have solid data. In the course of the study, I formally interviewed on several occasions forty-five members of the CAEL staff, board members, regional representatives, project staff, and consultants, as well as a dozen foundation officers and practitioners in adult and experiential programs. Informally, I spoke to at least that many people. I reviewed minutes of the CAEL Board of Trustees, read proposals and final reports of all major CAEL projects, constructed data files on membership and conference attendance, and assembled information for lists of staff, publications, and members of the Board of Trustees. I attended more than a dozen CAEL conferences and meetings, and visited another dozen regional offices and member institutions.

Chapter One analyzes the context in which CAEL was founded. It looks at non-traditional education in the 1960s, especially experiential education and adult education, and argues that these two streams were unconnected to one another. Although a national infrastructure for change was being laid down in the late 1960s and early 1970s, the reform of higher education was scattered and *ad hoc*. While many innovations were being tried in the 1960s, their cumulative impact did not amount to much, compared to the dominant forces operating within higher education at the time.

# PREFACE

A number of forces came together in the early 1970s which led to the first CAEL: general social and economic shifts that brought more adults into higher education, the recognition that many colleges and universities would have to fill out their undergraduate enrollments with adults, and a series of prestigious reports calling for more flexibility for adult students. Chapter Two recounts the formation of the first CAEL project with the Educational Testing Service. It describes a series of conflicts that threatened to tear the project apart, the people involved in them, and their resolution. It presents in detail the various projects that were carried out, at the same time that an agenda for change was being articulated and an organization to advance the agenda was being created. The first CAEL was an enormously productive endeavor, and Chapter Two suggests why.

Chapter Three turns to CAEL's first three years as an independent organization. With a large grant from the W.K. Kellogg Foundation, CAEL carried out a series of projects, the most prominent being the Institutional Development Program, which attempted to institutionalize experiential learning in the nation's colleges and universities. This turned out to be a difficult task, despite some initial successes, and CAEL turned to other strategies for changing higher education. Its dependence on foundations, especially the W.K. Kellogg Foundation, shaped CAEL's strategies, as well as its development as an organization. It elaborated a regional system, expanded its cadres across the country, and tried to find a secure financial base.

After weathering a severe financial and leadership crisis at the end of this period, CAEL entered its third phase. By this time, it had accumulated a large number of committed adherents and operated on many fronts: not only within colleges and universities, but in national associations, state governments, the federal government, the military, non-profit organizations, labor unions, and business. With a series of new grants from the Kellogg Foundation, supplemented by money from other sources, CAEL spun out a series of overlapping circles of activity. This "national network of adult learner services," which was intended to lead to the "transformation of the learning system," was the fullest expression of CAEL's increasingly protean ambitions. Chapter Four examines these ambitions in the light of the maturing of CAEL as an organization and asks how they were achieved.

Chapter Five analyzes CAEL as a social movement. It looks at the ways in which CAEL defined its agenda, mobilized for action, developed a fitting organizational structure, and engaged in efforts to change higher education. It asks whether CAEL gained acceptance from influential people in higher education, won new advantages for adult learners, and increased the effectiveness of the larger movement for change in higher education. The book concludes that CAEL made important gains on all three fronts, in part by building on ideas and innovations that were well underway. It was an extraordinary organizational success in the social movement for change in higher education and has much to teach other reformers about how to do it better. At the same time, it has much to teach about the limits of change in higher education. In spite of its scale, its manifest productivity, its energy, and its intelligence, CAEL never penetrated the academic establishment. Its greatest impacts were on the periphery, a periphery that was fast growing into a structure parallel to traditional higher education.

## ACKNOWLEDGMENTS

Many people helped me understand CAEL by agreeing to be interviewed, providing materials, and reading drafts. Some did all three, most notably Morris Keeton and Diana Bamford-Rees. There is no way that I can express my gratitude to them. Always responsive, they were full colleagues in my tortured efforts to grasp what they had created.

The first footnote to Chapters Two, Three, and Four lists the people I interviewed. They were, without exception, informative and generous. I will not list them all here, but I wish to thank several especially for the extra time they took with me in reading drafts or assembling materials: Anne Bryant, Arthur Chickering, Mary Ellis, Kathy Gallay, Ellie Greenberg, Cyril Houle, Lois Lamdin, Winton Manning, George A. Pruitt, Pam Tate, John Valley, and Warren Willingham.

Gerald Grant, J.B. Hefferlin, Malcolm Knowles, Jack Lindquist, Jessica Lipnack, Charles Muscatine, William Neumann, Shulamit Reinharz, Frederick Rudolph, Janet Ruyle, Milton R. Stern, Martin Trow, and Steven Zeverling gave me useful advice on the manuscript at different points. William Gamson, Emily Schmeidler, and Mayer Zald helped me understand the perspective of social movements. Alexander Charters and Carolyn Davis of Syracuse University and Judy Pfeiffer of the American Council on Education helped with materials on adult education. Dissertations by James Hall on adult degree programs and by Judith Grove on the Center for the Study of Liberal Education for Adults were especially helpful.

I am grateful to Margaret Talburtt, a partner in Formative Evaluation Research Associates (FERA), who suggested that I study the Compact for Lifelong Educational Opportunities, which was affiliated with CAEL for a time. Talburtt then brought me to the attention of Morris Keeton.

The resources of FERA were at my disposal. FERA first introduced me to the word processor, covered telephone expenses, provided research assistance, and helped with preparing the manuscript. Kathryn Jones and Janet Wright helped me beyond the call of duty. Kim Weisberg, Candace Helms, Debbie Oberman, Debby Murphy, and Patrick Hill helped in the preparation of the manuscript. Laura Winters, Sandra Butcher, and Robin Halnon at CAEL sorted out various loose ends. Richard Edelstein, Josh Gamson, and Phyllis Greenwood shared their astute observations of CAEL in addition to performing specific research tasks. Thanks to them all.

# DEDICATION

To Bill, Jenny and Josh: My family of educators.

# LIST OF ACRONYMS

| | |
|---|---|
| AAAE | American Association for Adult Education |
| AACRAO | American Association of Collegiate Registrars and Admission Officers |
| AAHE | American Association for Higher Education |
| ACE | American Council on Education |
| ACT | American College Testing Program |
| CAPE | Coalition for Alternatives in Postsecondary Education |
| CCV | Community College of Vermont |
| CLEO | Compact for Lifelong Educational Opportunities |
| CLEP | College-Level Examination Program |
| COPA | Council on Postsecondary Accreditation |
| CNAA | Council for National Academic Awards (Great Britain) |
| CSLEA | Center for the Study of Liberal Education for Adults |
| CUOP | College and University Options Program |
| ETS | Educational Testing Service |
| FDP | Faculty Development Program |
| FERA | Formative Evaluation Research Associates |
| FEU | Further Education Unit (Great Britain) |
| FIPSE | Fund for the Improvement of Postsecondary Education |
| IDP | Institutional Development Program |
| LEARN | Lifelong Education, Assessment, and Referral Network |
| NDTC | National Development and Training Center |
| NIWL | National Institute for Work and Learning |
| NSIEE | National Society for Internships and Experiential Education |
| OECC | Office on Educational Credits and Credentials, American Council on Education |
| SIGI | System of Interactive Guidance Information |
| UAW | United Automobile Workers |

# LIST OF TABLES AND FIGURES

## CHAPTER ONE

# Origins: Experiential Education and Adults

> For a tradition to live it must constantly be destroyed. At the same time, destruction by itself clearly cannot create new cultural forms. There must be some other force which restrains destructive energy and prevents it from reducing all about it to havoc.[1]

CAEL arose at the transition from the sometimes reckless expansiveness of the 1960s to the more pinched realism of the 1970s. It became the crucible in which several important innovations of the 1960s were fired and tested for survival. By exploiting some of the tough-minded innovations of the 1970s, it extended the logic of these innovations to the education of adults.

## Point and Counterpoint in Higher Education during the 1960s

All of this was happening at the edges of higher education. The main force in higher education during the 1960s was the steady march of the academic disciplines through the institutions of higher learning. When Christopher Jencks and David Riesman published in 1968 their well-known anatomy of higher education, what they called "the academic revolution" was in full sway. Its victory had been a genteel and well-funded affair, under-

---

1. Quoted in the frontispiece to *Diversity By Design* (1973), the final report of the Commission on Non-Traditional Study, from *Katsura—Tradition and Creation in Japanese Architecture,* by Kenzo Tange.

written by enormous sums of money from the federal government.[2]

The bargaining power of the faculty was heightened considerably during the early 1960s, when there were not enough college professors to teach the advance guard of the baby boom generation, who were beginning to enter colleges and universities in increasing proportions. College faculties began to be recruited nationally according to performance in their disciplines. Given an essentially free hand to teach the subjects they wanted to teach in any way they wished, young Ph.D.s carried the values of the academic revolution from the leading graduate schools to regional state colleges and universities, church-related schools, liberal arts colleges, and community colleges. By the late 1960s, many faculty members even in small, unknown colleges had become specialists in a certain discipline, with specialized knowledge within a subfield of that discipline. Faculty who never again published anything after their Ph.D. dissertations (and the majority did not) nevertheless drew deeply from their disciplinary identities.

Faculty control over the curriculum was enhanced considerably during the 1960s, primarily through decisions made by disciplinary departments, the controlling academic unit of most colleges and universities. The model of the research university's college of liberal arts—high standards, meritocratic values, advanced scholarship—spread unevenly but took hold in many schools that had to fight hard to attract faculty in the early years of expansion. Feeling their oats and firmly in charge, the faculty could lay on more readings and harder assignments. Undergraduates, especially the most talented ones, were to be groomed for graduate school.

The academic revolution depended on enlarging existing

---

2. In 1950, government support for higher education was $524 million; by 1970, it was over $2,682 million (U.S. Bureau of the Census, 1975).

institutions and founding new ones to accommodate the expanding undergraduate enrollments of the 1960s. Typically, the students in the high times were well-prepared academically. During the period of student engagement in the civil rights and anti-war movements, some student activists turned their attention to educational issues. But while the often more academically gifted activists pressed for less competition, greater relevance, and fewer requirements, average students conformed to faculty expectations (Riesman, 1981). In any case, the very faculty who supported campus activists on off-campus political issues were not as likely to support them on campus academic issues.

There was one possible exception: access to higher education for minorities and working-class students. The populist surges of the late 1960s, open admissions, and the availability of financial aid brought more black, Hispanic and working-class white students to campuses across the country. These students did not usually live in circumstances that encouraged the leisurely pursuit of truth. Many commuted to school from families and jobs, studied part-time, dropped in and out. They tended to go to the less selective private and state colleges, community colleges and proprietary schools that had expanded most during the 1960s. Many of the "new students" came to college with poor academic skills; "school" did not evoke pleasant memories for them (Cross, 1971). And the faculty, even those who had supported their coming, did not know how to reach them.

### *Counterpoint: Innovation and Experiment*

Throughout the 1960s and even before, voices of resistance to the academic revolution were being raised. By the end of the decade, traditionalists like Jacques Barzun (1969) and Robert Nisbet (1971), and experimentalists like Harold Taylor (1969) and Robert Paul Wolff (1969), could agree on one point: the research university was inappropriate as a standard for the rest of higher education.

Alternatives were around for the asking; indeed, they were present in the very research universities under criticism. Cluster colleges, interdisciplinary programs, individualized study, and dozens of other experiments in undergraduate education were to be found everywhere—in the Ivy League, the Big Ten, and prominent liberal arts colleges; in regional state universities, community colleges, and obscure private colleges (Baskin, 1965; Cornell Center for Improvement in Undergraduate Education, 1974; Grant and Riesman, 1978; Hefferlin, 1969; Heiss, 1974; Riesman, Gusfield and Gamson, 1975). Typically supported with start-up money from foundations, government or special institutional funds, innovations tended not to be on the collective agenda of the discipline-based departments—although individual faculty members might introduce innovations in the privacy of their own classes or get together with other faculty to teach a new course now and then.

Innovations during the 1960s took place in new institutions or in non-conforming enclaves within older ones. They tended to be initiated by administrators, student services staff, marginal faculty, or faculty who became marginal by virtue of their involvement in an innovation. People in the same institution working on different innovations—and sometimes even similar ones—were frequently isolated from one another. Nationally, there were few venues which allowed innovators to get together. As a result, their efforts were scattered and invisible. Pragmatic and a-theoretical, there was little collective learning, and mistakes were repeated as new people re-invented the same thing again and again (Gamson, 1984; Gamson and Levey, 1977; Grant and Riesman, 1978; Peterson, 1978; Riesman, Gusfield, and Gamson, 1975).

**Experiential Education.** Re-invention and lack of theoretical grounding characterized the cluster of innovations called "experiential education." The term was applied to a range of activities. Experiential education put students in direct contact with the realities they were studying, and is typically associated with the "real world" rather than the "artificial world" of the classroom or the campus. But it can also take place in the classroom, as when students perform experiments or plays, study themselves or their class, participate in classroom simulations, or analyze case studies.

There is, in principle, no limitation on where and when experiential learning can take place. Indeed, it is the way most people in most places learn when they are not going to school (Keeton and Associates, 1976). If this is so, some educators reasoned, it should be possible to make use of this natural way of learning in the more artificial setting of the college or university. This idea was not invented in the 1960s. An ancient notion, its immediate roots lay in the educational philosophies of John Dewey and Alfred North Whitehead, and in the psychological theories of Kurt Lewin, Jean Piaget, and Jerome Bruner (Houle, 1984; Kolb, 1984). There were precursors in the experiential programs developed thirty years earlier at experimental colleges. Antioch College had pioneered a cooperative work-study program which required that all students spend as much time working at jobs around the country as studying in classes in Yellow Springs, Ohio. Bennington, Goddard, and Berea regularly sent students out into jobs for limited engagements with reality. Other schools like Kalamazoo College and a few universities provided their students with junior years abroad. Students in professional programs were regularly expected to make direct contact with the arenas they would be entering—education students with schools, business students with firms, medical students with hospitals. Graduate students, and undergraduate students in some colleges, could carry out original studies through independent reading courses before embarking on the more substantial research required for the Master's degree or the doctorate.

Colleges and universities in the 1960s took all this and extended it to new subject matters and to new students for more credit than ever before. In a survey of colleges and universities with non-traditional programs in the early 1970s, half said they gave credit toward the degree for a variety of activities outside the course. Work experience programs were the most popular; thirty-five percent reported that they granted credit to students for participating in such programs (Ruyle and Geiselman, 1974). Study-abroad programs spread rapidly beyond the elite colleges and flagship universities where they had grown up; in the 1960s the number of colleges and universities offering opportunities for study abroad doubled to more than 600 (Heiss, 1974). Institutions without programs of their own could draw on the growing number of consortia and independent organizations that offered opportunities to study abroad. Students could get "hands-on" experience not only in professional programs but in the liberal arts through practical apprenticeships, internships, field-study programs, science and language laboratories, game simulations, interpersonal process techniques, and case studies (Heiss, 1974).

A particular contribution of the 1960s to experiential education was community-based or service-learning. While earlier generations of students interested in tutoring children in poor neighborhoods or helping out in a mental hospital could go to special offices like Harvard's Phillips Brooks House or Yale's Dwight Hall, they did not ordinarily connect what they did to their academic programs. In the 1960s, academic activities related to social and political issues came into their own. The Peace Corps, VISTA, the poverty program, community organizations, and public interest groups offered ways for students to apply what they learned in courses and reading—and get credit for it.

Not all students sought academic credit for involvements of this sort—the majority probably did not—but enough did to give rise to new units and staff positions in colleges and universities whose job was to administer and assess community-based learning. These tended to be local and homegrown arrangements, different on every campus. There was, however, a national program, the University-Year-in-Action, which carried a full year of college credit for skills acquired in anti-poverty programs. A variety of institutions participated in the University Year, including the University of Nebraska, Pepperdine College, Howard University, and Pitzer College.

New institutions founded during the 1960s, especially those with a special innovative mission, often incorporated experiential education into their requirements. This seemed to be as characteristic of selective as of unselective schools. For example, New College in Sarasota, Florida, a selective liberal arts college founded in 1964, required that all of its students complete four independent studies and a senior thesis for the B.A.; a special office for off-campus study helped students meet these requirements in internships and study abroad. The University of Wisconsin at Green Bay, opened in 1969, focused its curriculum on ecology and emphasized first-hand research on environmental topics. At Justin Morrill College of Michigan State University, all students were required to spend one term away from campus in a field placement. The University of Texas at Permian Basin expected its students to plan and execute a program of experiential learning before they graduated.

Well-established institutions were also introducing experiential education. At the University of Michigan, for example, students in the 1960s could join hundreds of other students each semester to earn two ungraded credits a semester for approximately six hours of involvement each week working in schools, child care centers, community organizations, mental health centers, or geriatric programs. Other students could tutor black children and receive academic credit through special course numbers set aside in several social science departments. They could canoe down the streams of New England and attend town meetings with a small group of other students and a professor of English during the summer, while reading nineteenth-century American novels. In their majors, students could arrange internships with local theaters and orchestras. They could sign up for independent study courses to work on election campaigns, go on an archaeological dig, or conduct original research. They could choose from several study-abroad programs sponsored by the University of Michigan or other universities, or they could plan their own programs abroad.

When they noticed, faculty members in the departments tended to find these efforts suspect, even threatening. If education could take place anywhere, as proponents of experiential education claimed, what was the role of the faculty? Experiential programs shifted the attention from the teacher to the student. Such a shift required faculty to stop telling students what they wanted them to learn and begin helping students discover what they needed to know in order to understand the realities they had experienced directly. Not many faculty members knew how to teach this way. The people who administered experiential education programs, often student services staff members or junior faculty, may have known better how to teach in the new way, but they commanded neither the attention nor the respect of regular faculty. In any case, they were not trained to exploit the theoretical evidence for the legitimacy of their work (Kolb, 1984).

The variety of activities being carried out in its name, the precarious status of the faculty and staff working on it, and the lack of a vehicle to carry out a program of change, relegated experiential education to the margins of higher education in the 1960s. Most faculty refused to get involved in experiential education. Those who did often found the demands, usually added to a full load, were excessive and withdrew. Faculty who stayed with experiential education programs discovered that their efforts went unrecognized—even punished—in deliberations about their salaries and promotions.

The capacity of experiential programs to engage students, in particular minority students and adults who might have a hard time with the usual courses, received less attention than allegations about credit chiselers—students who got credit for falling in love or bumming around Europe. At the time, a cross-section of the faculty in universities ranked "emphasize undergraduate instruction" forty-fourth in importance on a list of forty-seven goals for universities (Gross and Grambsch, 1968). It is not a surprise, therefore, that some institutions closed down experiential programs before allowing their adherents the chance to answer the searching educational questions they were increasingly asking (Reinharz, 1977): How did hands-on experience lead to analysis and reflection? How did experiential education enhance book-learning? How did programs ensure that students, especially younger ones, actually carried out their plans of study? And, most urgent in the minds of critics and proponents alike: How to assess what students learned?

## Point and Counterpoint in Adult Education

Like traditional education, experiential education in the 1960s catered primarily to younger students. The absence of adults from the traditional and even the non-traditional streams of higher education in the 1960s was not new. The advent of compulsory elementary schooling in the nineteenth century and then of compulsory secondary schooling in the twentieth century brought age-based educational ladders—cohorts divided into narrow age groups that were to ascend the ladder together. This system was set up for children and adolescents. When higher education for the mass of Americans became a reality in the years after World War II, this system was extended to young adults. To the age-graded ladder was added the apparatus of standardized tests used to differentially allocate young people to institutions. Adults were outside this system (Houle, 1976).

Yet learning during adulthood has been seen as characteristic of Americans, from the Colonial era to the present. Much adult learning, like learning at all ages, occurs as a result of participation in other realms like the family or work. Explicitly educational programs for adults began before the republic. Ben Franklin organized the Junto in 1927 as a discussion club, which lasted in modified form for thirty years. The indomitable Franklin also founded the first library in 1735 as an outgrowth of the Junto; libraries with special educational programs open to the public spread rapidly in succeeding years. In the 1820s there were founded other organized educational programs for adults like mechanics' institutes and Lyceum discussion groups; and in the 1870s there flourished the Chautauqua movement of lectures, study circles, summer programs and correspondence courses. Voluntary associations like the YMCA, economic organizations like the National Association of Manufacturers, and trade unions like the International Ladies Garment Workers Union established educational programs in the nineteenth and early twentieth centuries (Harrington, 1981; Knowles, 1977).

As public education spread in the nineteenth century, school doors were opened in the evening for working youth. The great waves of immigration in the early twentieth century inundated the night schools (Knowles, 1977). Colleges and universities took in some of the promising young graduates of the night schools. The older immigrants—and natives as well—had to find their way to extension and correspondence programs.

Extension programs brought adults to campus or teachers to other locations in the evening for courses which generally did not carry academic credit. The first president of the University of Chicago, William Rainey Harper, was inspired by the Chautauqua movement to establish an extension division focused on academic subjects for adults as one of the five divisions of the university when it opened in 1892. A year earlier, extension divisions had been organized at the University of Kansas and the University of Wisconsin. These programs languished for several decades until the president of the University of Wisconsin, Charles R. Van Hise, broadened the scope of extension in the early 1900s to include practical subjects, most notably agriculture. Extension work in agriculture had already appeared in the 1880s at the land grant colleges and expanded rapidly when state and then federal money became available for agricultural extension. The Cooperative Extension Service, fairly well-established by the end of World War I, became the single largest adult education program in the history of American education (Knowles, 1977).

In 1915, the founding of the National University Extension Association signaled the emergence of specialized adult education workers. In later decades, national associations followed with other programs for adults, most notably the American Association for Adult Education, founded in 1926. The Carnegie Corporation provided generous support to this organization and to other programs for adults. Between 1924 and 1941, Carnegie spent close to $5 million and between 1942 and 1958 another $4 million on adult education. Other foundations also invested significant sums of money in adult education. The W.K. Kellogg Foundation subsidized the development of continuing education through grants totaling some $20 million between 1945 and 1959. Almost as soon as it was founded in 1950, the Ford Foundation established the Fund for Adult Education, which disbursed $47.5 million between 1951 and 1961 (Knowles, 1977).

Programs for adults outside of colleges and universities appeared in quickening pace from the 1920s onward in secondary schools, libraries, community groups, museums, workplaces, the armed forces, labor unions, voluntary groups, the media, religious institutions, and government. Within higher education, enrollments in extension programs grew, especially after World War II as the G.I. Bill brought veterans into colleges and universities in unprecedented numbers. Those who wanted degrees were expected to meet the same requirements and to attend the same classes as younger students, however inappropriate or inconvenient that might be.

The exception to this rule were the evening colleges, which swelled to accommodate veterans and other adult students. Administrators and faculty members in evening colleges and extension began to explore the possibility of special degree programs that would recognize the living circumstances and wider experience that adults brought to higher education. With encouragement and support from the Center for the Study of Liberal Education for Adults, which was funded by the Ford Foundation through the Fund for Adult Education, several institutions experimented with special baccalaureate programs. In 1954, Brooklyn College began an experimental project, which eventually became the Special Baccalaureate Degree Program for Adults. A carefully selected group of talented adults was allowed to complete requirements for the B.A. by taking special interdisciplinary seminars and by earning academic credit for learning from work and other life experiences. The Adult Continuing Education Program, founded in 1963 at Queens College, was modeled on the Brooklyn program. Two years later, Mundelein College introduced its Degree Completion Program, which adapted many of the features of the Brooklyn and Queens programs for mature women. In 1966, Roosevelt University opened the Bachelor of General Studies program, which allowed students to graduate when they completed special upper-level courses without having to take lower-level courses.

These programs met the different needs of adults in special seminars and in programs that granted credit for learning from experience, or they allowed students to bypass lower-level courses altogether. All, however, required that adult students come to campus on a regular basis to take courses. Several institutions experimented with this requirement as well. In the 1930s, Goddard College arranged for adults to come to campus for short, non-credit conferences; this program evolved in the early 1960s into the Adult Degree Program, a special baccalaureate program for adults which combined independent work with short, intensive seminars on campus. In 1961, the University of Oklahoma started the Bachelor of Liberal Studies program, which also brought students to campus in short bursts for residential seminars after periods of home study. Programs with varying content that also combined residence periods with independent study were founded in the middle 1960s at Syracuse University and the University of South Florida (Hall, 1975).

Staff members, as well as adjunct or moonlighting faculty in colleges and universities who worked in special adult degree programs, extension and continuing education, emerged as a distinct professional group separate from other faculty and staff in the early 1960s (Knowles, 1977). National associations and graduate programs in adult and continuing education both reflected and sponsored the professionalization of adult education as a field. It would not be too long before scholars turned their attention to adults and their development as well (Chickering, 1981; Knox, 1977).

Yet for all of their efforts, it is clear the proponents and practitioners of adult education had not penetrated the core of higher education. In the middle 1960s, faculty members in universities ranked "assist citizens through extension programs" thirty-sixth and "provide special adult training" thirty-eighth among forty-seven university goals (Gross and Grambsch, 1968). In spite of this lack of support from faculty, by the late 1960s adult education had become a rich potpourri of activities which operated under a variety of auspices. This had its advantages, but it also meant that, as Knowles put it, "adult education in this country is. . . a patternless mosaic of unrelated activities" (1977, p. viii).

# CHAPTER ONE

## *Counterpoint: Adults as Regular Students*

In 1952, 844,000 people were enrolled in extension programs; by 1972, there were 3.3 million (Knowles, 1977). Registration in non-credit adult education courses grew by 57% between 1967 and 1975, and adult registration in all forms of organized learning grew by 31% between 1969 and 1975 (Cross, 1981). In 1968, students over twenty-five years old comprised 17% of the undergraduate enrollments in colleges and universities; by 1975, older students accounted for one-quarter of the enrollments (National Center for Education Statistics, 1970 and 1976).

Something had happened to bring more adults into education during the early 1970s. If the 1950s and 1960s were the decades of great expansion for higher education in general, the 1970s and 1980s were the decades of expansion for adults. Several social forces, on both the supply and the demand side, came together at approximately the same time to produce this effect.

On the demand side, the populist movements of the 1960s had brought young black and other minority students to higher education; it was only a matter of time before they would also bring adults. The women's movement, in particular, legitimated college-going among older women who had dropped out to bring up families or who had never started—women who were beginning to join younger women in the labor force. Economic necessity drove adults to college, just as it had driven younger people there. In a society that was abandoning its industrial base for a technological and service economy, more employers required that employees hold college degrees (Berg, 1970; Collins, 1979). More states and professional associations were requiring that members of certain vocations and professions take additional courses in order to retain their licenses. People who were entering the labor market for the first time or looking for a better job were filling up employer-sponsored training and education programs, proprietary institutions, and colleges and universities. Increasingly, those who had lost their jobs or feared losing them were also impelled toward education and training programs.

The positive face on the centrality of higher education to the labor force began to be articulated in the early 1970s, especially in Europe. This perspective began to leave its mark on the supply of educational opportunity for adults. The Swedish notion of "recurrent education," the recognition by employers and governments that they should provide education and training for people of all ages, began to be picked up by the Organization for Economic Cooperation and Development, the International Labor Organization, and the United Nations Educational, Scientific and Cultural Organization. In 1971, Britain's Open University began operating after almost a decade of planning. The Open University attracted international attention through its rigorous degree program for adults, which exploited the potential of radio and television, independent study, and regional learning centers (Evans, 1981; Houle, 1973; McIntosh, 1976). Israel, Canada, Australia, India, France, Japan and Germany experimented with different approaches to "distance learning" for adults. All made use of technologies that traditional educators tended to spurn: television, radio, radio-assisted instruction, telephone, audio cassettes, and—somewhat later—video technologies and cable television (Feasley, 1983).

In the United States, "lifelong learning" began to be discussed not only among adult educators but among politicians and industrial leaders as well (Knowles, 1977; Vermilye, 1977). Several efforts were made to adapt the British Open University to the American landscape (Hartnett et al., 1974; Pifer, 1970). In 1976, the Lifelong Learning Bill was passed as an amendment to the Higher Education Act of 1965. This bill encouraged the development of lifelong learning opportunities and their planning, coordination and assessment. While funds for implementing the bill were not appropriated, legislation for dozens of other social programs benefited adult education (Knowles, 1977). Federal grants still favored younger students by requiring full-time enrollment in traditional programs. The 1972 amendments to the Higher Education Act of 1965, which provided for student aid, made inroads in these requirements by allowing students enrolled in non-traditional programs to receive aid from the U.S. government.

There were more such programs for adults around in the early 1970s. While it is true, as Patricia Cross asserts, that colleges and universities made only "minor concessions to accommodate adult learners in regular degree programs" in the early 1970s when adults began appearing in larger numbers, new efforts were appearing at the margins of institutions and in entirely new institutions (Cross, 1981, p. 36). Adults could continue to take courses through extension and evening programs, but now they could become regular students. Part-time study, intermittent enrollment, and open admissions began to become more common, especially in the struggling private colleges and regional state institutions that were beginning in the 1970s to experience a decline in the traditional college population. The ability to fill out their enrollments with adults meant survival for some of these colleges.

The pressure on higher education from legislatures and the public to become more accountable for its performance led to a variety of new ways of assessing what students learned. This approach emphasized what was learned rather than what was taught. It did not take much to see that some students could demonstrate that they already knew what colleges and universities wanted to teach them, and that the college degree could be "time-shortened" (Carnegie Commission on Higher Education, 1971a).

This reasoning benefited adult students. If they thought they had already met some college requirements, adult students could present themselves for assessment by a variety of new methods (Commission on Non-Traditional Study, 1973; Heiss, 1974; Knapp, 1977; Knapp and Sharon, 1975; Meyer, 1976; Vermilye, 1972). They could take standardized tests like the College-Level Examination Program (CLEP), which the College Board had begun administering in 1967, or they could take homegrown examinations designed by faculty members to test their knowledge of material covered by courses in departments (Vermilye, 1972). If they were in the military, they could take examinations through the United States Armed Services Institute, an outgrowth of the military's interest in assessment dating back to World War I (Grant, 1979). They could receive academic credit for courses they had taken in the military through the Office on Educational Credits and Credentials of the American Council on Education, which had been operating since 1945 (Peterson, 1979).

As a result of adaptations of assessment techniques developed in industry, adults could take performance tests, engage in simulations, be observed in action, or submit to interviews (Boyd and Shimberg, 1974; Crooks, 1974; Grant, 1979). They could present portfolios for academic credit. The portfolio was one of the innovations from the 1960s developed for younger students, especially in independent study and experiential learning programs, that was generalized to adults in the 1970s. Portfolios typically included an autobiographical account of experiences in work and other settings, the learning that these experiences fostered, a resume, a log of activities, evaluations from supervisors and other people, samples of achievements, and other evidence of learning (Heiss, 1974; Knapp, 1977; Knapp and Sharon, 1975; Meyer, 1976).

By the early 1970s, adults could imagine receiving a baccalaureate entirely through assessment. Beginning in 1971, they could earn a Bachelor's degree from a New York state college or university by passing examinations administered by the New York Regents External Degree Program. In 1973, they could earn a college degree at New Jersey's Thomas A. Edison State College by means of examinations, accrediting of job training programs, assessment of life experience, and transfer credit.

If they wished to study on a campus, adults in the early 1970s had much more choice than they did a decade before. They were more likely to find special counselors and "mentors" sensitive to the needs of adults, especially those of older returning women. If they lived in the right place, they could go for advice to educational "brokering" services and consortia outside of colleges and universities (Heffernan, Macy, and Vickers, 1976). They could earn a degree at one of the learning centers operated by Antioch College in several cities across the country, or they could go to a University Without Walls program at colleges and universities affiliated with the Union for Experimenting Colleges and Universities. They could find special baccalaureate arrangements like the one pioneered at Brooklyn College, combined residential and independent study programs like the University of Oklahoma's, or variations on a time-shortened degree like the one at Roosevelt University (Hall, 1974; Commission on Non-Traditional Study, 1973). They could take courses by newspaper and television, earn degrees at a weekend college like one at Wayne State University, or enroll in an external degree program (Houle, 1973; Sosdian, 1978).

They could also attend one of the new, innovative institutions founded primarily for adults in the early 1970s: Empire State College, Minnesota Metropolitan State College, the College of Public and Community Service at the University of Massachusetts-Boston, Florida International University, and the Community College of Vermont. While several schools serving adults, especially workers, were established in the early part of the century—Ruskin College, the Breadwinners' College, and the Rand School of Social Science—they were outside the established world of higher education at the time. The new colleges of the 1970s were hardly part of the establishment, but few would question their right to be part of the world of higher education.

It was clear that "non-traditional education," as the new programs for adults were called, was being taken seriously. The harsh realities of the 1970s were, paradoxically, conducive to the sort of "non-tradition" represented by the presence of adults. In what had rapidly become a buyer's market, many colleges and universities needed adults to survive. They needed adults for political support. Most important of all, higher education needed adults to demonstrate its importance to the economy.

## National Higher Education Policy-Makers Take Note

These matters were bound to draw the attention of national policy-making bodies for higher education—foundations, the higher education associations, the federal government and the media (Gamson, 1987). Change in higher education during the 1960s tended to be initiated on the campuses; policy-making bodies tended to follow, rather than lead, the campuses. In the 1970s, these bodies became more active in setting agendas for higher education. They were particularly prominent in the adult education scene.

The American Council on Education, the Association of American Colleges, the American Association for Community and Junior Colleges, the Council of Graduate Schools, and the Federation of Regional Commissions of Higher Education formed special groups to examine non-traditional education. The higher education magazine, *Change,* and Jossey-Bass, the pre-eminent higher education publishing house, published frequent accounts and critiques of non-traditional education throughout the 1970s. While they raised questions about the abuse of academic credits and "cut-rate" degrees (Hefferlin, 1974), on balance national policy-makers were sympathetic to the developments in education for adults.

The Carnegie Commission on Higher Education, which had been issuing reports on almost every aspect of higher education from the middle 1960s to the early 1970s, made several recommendations with implications for experiential education and adults. It argued that changes in the economy would force colleges and universities to recognize that "more jobs require some basic skills and knowledge and then a willingness to keep on learning. . . Thus it would seem wise to space formal education over one's lifetime, reducing the amount of time spent on it early in life, and spending additional time on formal education later in life. . . " (Carnegie Commission on Higher Education, 1974, p. 43).

*Less Time, More Options,* published by the Carnegie Commission in 1971, recommended that there be more service and other employment opportunities for students between high school and college, with stop-out points during the college years. It also urged that there be more opportunities for credit-bearing learning outside of formal institutions, such as work settings. It advocated that colleges and universities be more open to adult and part-time students by creating "alternative avenues by which students can earn degrees or complete a major portion of their work for a degree. . . for those to whom it is now unavailable because of work schedules, geographic location, or responsibilities in the home" (Carnegie Commission on Higher Education, 1974, p. 44). In *New Students and New Places* (1971b) and *The Fourth Revolution: Instructional Technology in Higher Education* (1972), the Carnegie Commission continued to argue for the need for greater flexibility and suggested that external degree systems and open universities be expanded.

A second prestigious group recommended even deeper changes in higher education to support experiential and adult education. A task force appointed by HEW Secretary Robert Finch and chaired by Frank Newman questioned the arbitrariness of many credit policies in higher education (Newman, 1971). It recommended that 2% of federal funds for work-study programs be devoted to upgrade the work portion into a significant learning experience. It pointed to the need for long-term support to evaluate the proficiencies required for success in various fields. And, most radical of all, it suggested that regional examining agencies be established to award credentials on the basis of proficiencies rather than credits accumulated (Newman, 1973).

## CAEL's Parentage: The Commission on Non-Traditional Study

While all of these ideas set the stage for the founding of CAEL, its existence depended most on the Commission on Non-Traditional Study. The Commission began its work in 1971 under the joint sponsorship of the Educational Testing Service (ETS) and the College Board. ETS had developed the College-Level Examination Program (CLEP) and was interested in other measures of learning acquired independently of formal schooling. It had begun tracking non-traditional education in 1971 through the Office of External Degree Plans, later named the Office of New Degree Programs. This office received over 700 letters of inquiry in its first year (Houle, 1973). John Valley, who headed the Office of External Degree Plans, and Jack Arbolino, program director of CLEP at the College Board, were excited about the momentum of the non-traditional education movement. In a presentation to a joint meeting of the officers of ETS and the College Board in 1970, they suggested that the two bodies support the development of a national university that would grant degrees strictly on the basis of assessment (Commission on Non-Traditional Study, 1973, Appendix A). While the officers rejected the idea of actively promoting such a university, they were intrigued by the potential of non-traditional education.

Alden Dunham, a program officer at the Carnegie Corporation who kept in close touch with senior staff at ETS and the College Board, had been watching developments in non-traditional education for several years. He had worked with the Carnegie Commission on Higher Education and had been responsible for several grants and conferences on non-traditional education. The Carnegie Corporation and the Education Foundation of America made a grant of approximately two million dollars for two years to ETS and the College Board for a Commission on Non-Traditional Study. This commission would study the current status, assess needs, and recommend directions for the future of non-traditional education.

The members of the commission were powerful people. Chairing it was Samuel B. Gould, former president of Antioch College, chancellor emeritus of the State University of New York, and vice-president at ETS. Among the members were five heads of institutions or state systems: Howard Bowen, chancellor of the Claremont University Center; Mary Bunting, president of Radcliffe College; Richard Gilman, president of Occidental College; Charles Le Maistre, chancellor of the University of Texas at Austin; and Clifton Wharton, president of Michigan State University. There were, however, more organizations represented on the commission from outside of higher education than from within it. A wide spectrum of organizations participated: EDUCOM, the Council on Library Resources, the American Association of University Professors, the AFL-CIO, the National Commission on Accrediting, the

American Council on Education, the National Catholic Educational Association, the Women's Bureau of the U.S. Department of Labor, the Corporation for Public Broadcasting, the Encyclopedia Brittanica Educational Foundation, the U.S. Office of Education, the International Council for Educational Development, the Southern Association of Schools and Colleges, and the Brookings Institution.

The commission ran surveys of adults to find out how interested they were in continuing education. It also asked selected colleges and universities to describe what they did to accommodate adult students. These surveys demonstrated a keen desire among adults for continued education (Carp, Peterson and Roelfs, 1974). All but about one-sixth of the institutions encouraged adults to enroll, especially in regular programs along with younger students (Ruyle and Geiselman, 1974).

Sixteen staff members from ETS and the College Board worked with the commission. They were enormously productive. Four books were published as a result of their work: *Diversity by Design*, the final report, published in 1973; *Explorations in Non-Traditional Study*, edited by Cyril O. Houle and published in 1973; and *Planning Non-Traditional Programs*, edited by Cross and Valley, and published in 1974.

The commission, one of the most influential in the history of higher education, stood on a pragmatic and moderate platform of defending the need of adults for flexibility. At the same time, it emphasized quality, especially in the assessment of experiential learning. Among its fifty-seven recommendations, two laid the groundwork for what would become CAEL. Recommendation 47 stated that "new devices and techniques should be perfected to measure the outcomes of many types of non-traditional study and to assess the educative effect of work experience and community service" (Commission on Non-Traditional Study, 1973, p. 125). Recommendation 48 added that "systems of quality control should be built into the instruction and evaluative aspects of non-traditional study whenever possible."

The innovations which flourished in the 1960s, including experiential education, did not add up to a coherent force for change in higher education. In part, this was because national policy-makers did not have a common agenda for change. In contrast, foundations, associations and the media supported non-traditional education for adults in the 1970s. It was possible that not only would it be accepted, but non-traditional education might influence the mainstream. But even so influential a body as the Commission on Non-Traditional Study could not ensure that non-traditional education would flow beyond the tributaries it inhabited. A vehicle was needed to perfect it and then carry it to colleges and universities across the country. This vehicle turned out to be CAEL.

CHAPTER TWO

# Defining the Collective Agenda: The First CAEL[1]

> CAEL says "Utopia is possible, and we're going for it." The view of human nature is that it is infinitely educable, the view of society is almost Candidian in its optimism about human perfectibility. Working hard and structuring are the most important elements of life, for both the individual and the institution. Striving, pushing ahead, not leaving anything to chance are essential (Greenwood, 1984, p. 3).

When the Commission on Non-Traditional Study ended its work in 1973, several people connected with it pressed to implement the recommendation that "new devices and techniques" be devised to measure the outcomes of study outside the traditional classroom. Doing so would "require not merely the talents of a theoretician of assessment but also the active and continuing collaboration of specialists whose work is far afield from traditional systems of schooling. The product may be no more than a manual of techniques, but it may also go beyond that to some new system of assessment" (Commission on Non-Traditional Study, 1973, p. 130).

Alden Dunham, the officer at the Carnegie Corporation who had backed the commission, thought it should have offered some guidance for the development of the "new devices and

---

1. Sources for this chapter incude the publications listed in Appendix B and interviews with the following people:

*George Ayers*, president of Chicago State University, member of the Steering Committee of the CAEL project, secretary in 1976-80 and chair in 1982-84 of the CAEL Board of Trustees.

*Neal Berte*, president of Birmingham Southern College, member of the Steer-

techniques" they had recommended. Perhaps in response to the commission, non-traditional programs were applying to the Carnegie Corporation for support. Dunham thought a joint effort of some sort would make more sense than funding a series of individual projects. What sort of joint effort? Who would carry it out? Dunham turned to the Educational Testing Service (ETS). This was natural for Dunham to do. He lived in Princeton, New Jersey—home of the ETS—having formerly served as Director of Admissions at Princeton University. Carnegie had funded many ETS projects in the past, and Dunham was friendly with some of the senior officers of ETS. On its side, ETS had been interested in developing examinations for learning acquired

---

ing Committee of the CAEL project, and member of the CAEL Board of Trustees, 1976-77.

*Diana Bamford-Rees,* director of training for joint ventures at CAEL, and staff to the original CAEL project at the Educational Testing Service.

*Laura Bornholdt,* special assistant to the president at the University of Chicago, former program officer at the Lilly Endowment.

*Harriet Cabell,* associate dean of New College and director of External Degree Programs at the University of Alabama, chair of the CAEL Board of Trustees, 1984-85.

*Arthur Chickering,* professor and director of the Center for the Study of Higher Education, Memphis State University, chair of the CAEL Board of Trustees, 1980-82.

*Diana Christopulos.* Vice-President for Planning and Human Resources at the American Heart Association, a member of the Faculty Development Program in the CAEL project.

*K. Patricia Cross,* professor, Harvard Graduate School of Education, member of the CAEL Board of Trustees, 1982-85.

*Aubrey Forrest,* director for instructional design and assessment at the American College Testing Program, chair of the Implementation Committee of the CAEL project, 1974-75.

*Sheila Gordon,* Associate Dean for Development at LaGuardia Community College, member of the Steering Committee of the CAEL project, member of the CAEL Board of Trustees, 1976-77.

*James Hall,* president of Empire State College, member of the CAEL Board

independently of formal schooling for a long time; its College-Level Examination Program (CLEP), for example, had begun operating in 1966.

After some discussion, William Turnbull, president of ETS, asked Winton Manning, senior vice-president for research and development, to think through a response to Dunham. Manning drew in Warren Willingham, a psychometrician who directed the research office in Manning's division, to write up a proposal.

Dunham pressed ETS to work with practitioners in non-traditional programs. The ground for this connection had already been worked by the Office of New Degree Programs, which had been jointly sponsored by ETS and the College Board since 1971. As head of the Office of New Degree Programs, John Valley had been keeping track of what was happening in non-traditional education across the country. He had formed relationships with many of the people working in this field and was an immediate connection to them. With Valley's contacts and

---

of Trustees, 1983-85.

*Harold Hodgkinson,* senior fellow at the Institute for Educational Leadership in Washington, evaluator of the first phase of LEARN.

*Cyril Houle,* senior program advisor at the Kellogg Foundation, member of the Steering Committee of the CAEL project.

*Morris Keeton,* president, Council for Adult and Experiential Learning, chair of the Steering Committee of the CAEL project and executive director, then president, of CAEL.

*Joan Knapp,* executive assistant at the Educational Testing Service, staff to the CAEL project at the Educational Testing Service, member of the CAEL Board of Trustees, 1981-84.

*Winton Manning,* Senior Scholar at ETS, Senior Vice-President for Research and Development at the time of the CAEL project, member of the Steering Committee.

*Larraine Matusak,* director of the Kellogg National Fellowship Program at the Kellogg Foundation, member of the CAEL Board of Trustees, 1976-80.

*Myrna Miller,* superintendent of the Marin Community College District, member of the Implementation Committee of the CAEL project in 1974-75,

Carnegie's money, ETS convened twenty-six representatives from some twenty-two institutions best known for their work with adults and prior learning, such as Empire State and Minnesota Metropolitan State, as well as those that were known for their work outside the classroom, such as Antioch and New College at the University of Alabama. An exploratory conference at ETS headquarters in Princeton was held in September, 1973. Also attending were representatives of educational associations, agencies, state higher education associations, researchers, and consultants. Many of the people at the conference were to become central to the history of CAEL in later years: Morris Keeton from Antioch College, Arthur Chickering from Empire State College, and Cyril Houle from the University of Chicago.

The official agenda of the conference was to talk about how to tackle the validation of non-traditional education, but the tacit agenda was to build a relationship between ETS and those who were engaged in such education. The meeting was not one that

---

member of the CAEL Board of Trustees, 1978-84.

*Robert Press*, coordinator of field experiences and professor of education at Governor's State College, member of the Faculty Development Program in the CAEL project.

*Peter Smith*, lieutenant governor of Vermont, secretary of the Steering Committee of the CAEL project, member of the CAEL Board of Trustees, 1976-80.

*John Valley*, independent consultant, staff to the original CAEL project, co-director of the Office of New Degree Programs and director of the College Level Placement and Equivalency Programs.

*Urban Whitaker*, regional manager at the CAEL Learning Center in San Francisco, vice-chair of the Implementation Committee of the CAEL project, 1974-75, member of the Faculty Development Program, member of the CAEL Board of Trustees, 1976-80.

*Warren Willingham*, vice-president for Program Research at the Educational Testing Service, executive director of the first CAEL project and executive director for Program Research at the Educational Testing Service.

people at ETS would forget. The practitioners asked questions that prefigured conflicts that would arise later in CAEL. Some suggested that ETS was interested in them because of the potential for selling evaluation and testing instruments in the new adult market, while others, vulnerable and exposed in their institutions, were afraid that standardized tests would be imposed upon them.

There were differences in style as well. The innovators were not used to the quiet comfort of places like the ETS offices in Princeton, or to elegant hotel rooms and fine business meals. Most of them dressed more casually. Several were used to more confrontational relationships than were the people at ETS. It was clear that ETS would need to win over the practitioners if its work on non-traditional education were to be accepted, but whether it would gain their support without compromising ETS' goals and reputation was an open question.

Things moved quickly. Two months after the September meeting, ETS used John Valley's contacts again and invited representatives from nine institutions to discuss an initial proposal drawn up by Willingham. These institutions, which later became the nucleus of the project, were a diverse lot. They included new and old schools; universities, colleges, and community colleges; large and small public and private schools; single institutions and multi-campus systems; and programs for adults as well as programs for younger students. The institutions were:

New College, University of Alabama
Antioch College
San Francisco State College, California
State University and Colleges
Thomas A. Edison College
El Paso Community College
Empire State College
Florida International University

# CHAPTER TWO

## Framingham State College, Massachusetts State College System
## Minnesota Metropolitan State College

ETS underscored the cooperative nature of the project. An agreement was reached to go ahead and, in December 1973, a formal proposal was submitted to the Carnegie Corporation for a three-year project. The name of the project, the "Cooperative Assessment of Experiential Learning," was first proposed by Winton Manning, vice-president for research and development, in an ETS meeting. The plan was for a cooperative project between ETS and the nine "Task Force" institutions which had attended the earlier meeting. The Task Force would try out new materials and make detailed studies on the nine campuses. Their work would be reviewed and discussed by a "Forum" representing a cross-section of some fifty other institutions also engaged in experiential learning. The proposal provided an illustrative list of institutions that operated field studies programs through the University Year for Action and another twenty institutions that operated individualized programs, many of them for adults, through various University Without Walls external degree programs.

The proposal requested $2.3 million for three years and four months, with $869,000 of that amount to be allocated to Task Force institutions and selected others. ETS would coordinate, provide the technical expertise, supervise and disseminate the work of the project, and the institutions would help develop and apply a variety of systematic approaches to assessment.

More than assessment was involved, however. The project was to take a "systems approach" to its work, which would proceed in three overlapping circles of activity: (1) the *development* of new methods other than conventional tests, based on a thorough review of current practices and needs; (2) the *validation* of the new methods and materials for their practicality, reliability, and validity; and (3) the *utilization* of the outcomes through cooperative activities, publications and training. The proposal underscored the need to pay attention to all three aspects of the project if experiential learning were to be woven into the "fabric" of institutions through "an existing structure of credit, academic guidelines, administrative relationships" ("Cooperative Assessment. . . ," p. 1, p. 9).

Aside from the use of portfolios, the work of the project could apply to non-classroom activities like internships and cooperative programs sponsored by institutions as well as to activities not sponsored by them. The proposal made a crucial conceptual breakthrough in calling all of these activities "experiential." Before the CAEL project, the two sides of nontraditional education had been separated linguistically. Activities which took place during enrollment in a college or university usually took their names from the activities themselves; they were called "internships" or "coop jobs" or "field studies." Activities which took place prior to enrollment were usually called "prior learning" or "life experience." The two forms of experiential learning applied to different sorts of students—therefore, to different parts of institutions—and drew on different personnel as well. "Prior learning" and "life experience" were directed almost exclusively to older students, while work outside of classrooms for enrolled students applied to students of all ages, but especially to younger ones.

The proposal also made an important contribution by insisting that it was interested in measuring and documenting the *learning* that resulted from experiential activities, not the activities themselves. This was not a trivial issue. For one thing, while serious practitioners in both kinds of experiential programs made a point of saying that they gave credit for reflecting on experience, not for the experience itself, they were more likely to use the term "experiential education." Shifting to "learning" had several advantages. First, it focused attention on the student. It asked what and how much the student had learned by whatever means that learning had been gained. This made the task of evaluation and testing a bit clearer. And it established an important symbolic point: CAEL was about learning and learners.

Although no positive word had yet come from Carnegie about the funding for the CAEL project until well into February, planning went ahead for the first meeting to take place at ETS on March 7th and 8th, 1974. Until the grant came through, ETS staff time was covered out of the ETS budget. (ETS had already agreed with the Carnegie Corporation to reduce its overhead rate for the project from 32% to 15%.)

In late February, the Carnegie Corporation made a grant of $821,000 for sixteen months, substantially less than had been requested. The project began anyway, with ten "Task Force" institutions: the original nine, plus the newly opened Community College of Vermont (CCV). K. Patricia Cross, who had played an important staff role on the Commission on Non-Traditional Study and ETS, had made a site visit at CCV for the Fund for the Improvement of Postsecondary Education, a new federal grants agency which had supported its creation. Cross reported that CCV, while promising, was chaotic and might improve by joining the CAEL project.

Such multi-institutional, collaborative projects have since become more common in higher education, but little has been written about them (Gamson, 1983). CAEL was not the first, but it was an early effort of this sort.[2] How did it work? ETS,

---

2. People who became involved in CAEL had been part of multi-institutional projects before. One of the earliest multi-institutional projects in the period immediately preceding the founding of CAEL was the Project on Student Development in Small Colleges, which ran from 1965 to 1970. Arthur Chickering, on the CAEL Steering Committee and a continuously active member throughout CAEL's history, headed this project. See his *Education and Identity* (1969) for the results of that project. A successor project,

a "Steering Committee," and an "Implementation Committee" formed the CAEL organizational structure—literally, a three-ring circus.

Conservatively calculated, about thirty people carried regular responsibilities on the project, and more than fifty worked on particular tasks as they arose. Task force institutions were funded in small and varying amounts by the project, but considerably more people were involved on their campuses without payment. Over the three years of its life, CAEL drew people from an additional 136 institutions on various special projects.[3]

At ETS, a core group of nine professional staff members from different departments, not all of them full-time on CAEL, were supported by six research, administrative and secretarial helpers and, as needed, by assorted vice-presidents and technical specialists.

On the assessment tasks, ETS was responsible for defining the issues, identifying people to work on them and keeping them moving, coordinating their efforts, and publishing the results. Warren Willingham directed CAEL. Richard Burns, a psychologist who directed college and university programs at ETS, served as associate director. John Valley and his assistant, Diana Bamford-Rees, who had worked on publications for the College Board, were in charge of the "associational" side of the project, such as conferences, newsletters, and publications. Joan Knapp, a doctoral candidate in educational psychology who had recently moved to ETS, became an increasingly important figure as she participated in many of the CAEL studies. Winton Manning watched over the project, as did several other vice-presidents

---

Strategies for Change and Knowledge Utilization, began in 1971 under the direction of Jack Lindquist, an early member of CAEL and later on the Board of Trustees. For the results of the Strategies for Change project, see Lindquist's book (1979).

3. See Appendix A for participants in various CAEL projects.

at ETS. Alden Dunham continued to be an important actor, mostly behind the scenes.

The Task Force institutions were represented by a president or vice-president (in the case of the California State and University Colleges, by a dean) on the Steering Committee. The latter also included Winton Manning from ETS and several at-large members from other institutions. This group was later augmented by additional people, typically deans or program directors, elected by members of what was to be called the

---

**FIGURE 1**

**The Structure of the First CAEL, 1974-1976**

---

ETS

Director: Warren Willingham
Administrative Staff: 6 people
Professional Staff: 9 people

STEERING COMMITTEE

Chair: Morris T. Keeton, Antioch
Vice-Chair: Jules Pagano, Florida International University
Secretary: Peter Smith, Community College of Vermont
ETS: 1 person
Task Force Institutions: 9 people
At-Large Members: 2 people
Assembly Representatives: 6 people

IMPLEMENTATION COMMITTEE*

ETS: 2 people
Task Force Institutions: 9 people

*Operated in 1974-75 only.

---

"Assembly." The Steering Committee met three times a year, its Executive Committee of seven members more frequently. In addition to setting general policy for the project, the Steering Committee reviewed plans for the assessment project and other activities and put its stamp on publications.

Also established was an eleven-member "Working Committee," whose name was soon changed to "Implementation Committee" (because of the implication that the Steering Committee did not work). Its members, staff members from nine of the ten Task Force institutions (Framingham State College essentially dropped out of the project), plus Willingham and Richard Burns from ETS, worked closely with the ETS staff on every phase of the project and coordinated project work on their campuses during 1974-75.

## Settling Early Conflicts

The complexity of the project, coupled with its ambitious goals, guaranteed considerable conflict. Confrontation about the motives of ETS continued, and several distinct issues sparked disagreement. The first was the question of money. Among Task Force institutions, presidents of two of the three new colleges for adult learners created in the early 1970s pointed out that they were not being compensated adequately for their work on the project. James Hall, president of Empire State College, in an early letter to ETS agreeing to allow Empire State to participate in the project, wrote that "[e]ach of the . . . institutions will be contributing a substantial amount of time to this project, involving a number of faculty, administrative staff, and support personnel. Because the institutional support indicated in the budget does not reflect the level of cost which we anticipate will be involved, I again request that further consideration be given to shifting the funding modestly to increase this support level'' (''Cooperative Assessment. . . ,'' 1973, p. 51). David Sweet, president of Minnesota Metropolitan State College, wrote: ''Institutions attempting to develop non-traditional programs, especially totally new kinds of institutions, require extraordinary time commitments from faculty and staff. At this time it would be very difficult for us to reallocate existing staff time to coordinate our part of the CAEL project. Resources are simply not available'' (''Cooperative Assessment. . . ,'' 1973, p. 59).

The question of money symbolized other concerns as well. Institutional representatives worried that the instruments developed in the project would not serve their own needs. They feared that ETS wanted to produce standardized tests, while they needed help in improving individualized assessment techniques for portfolios and learning contracts. Despite several statements in the original proposal to the contrary,[4] several members of the Task Force institutions did not believe ETS.

Why? There was some reason for their distrust, for alongside assurances about not relying on conventional tests, the proposal also argued that the need to validate experiential learning required the development of ''a sufficient sense of common procedures and understandable standards so that credit

4. Three examples: (1) ''This project will seek strategies for developing innovative measurement techniques, rather than straightforward application of traditional methods. It may prove desirable to develop some conventional tests, but they are not likely to constitute an important proportion of the total effort'' (''Cooperative Assessment. . . ,'' 1973, p. 13). (2) ''[I]nsofar as possible individuals will be assessed according to defined guidelines or standards rather than simply on a competitive basis. Such guidelines should be based upon an array of examples. . . '' (''Cooperative Assessment. . .,'' 1973, p. 15). (3) ''[A]ssessment measures that are developed are more likely to consist of procedures, guidelines, and supporting materials than what might be regarded as an 'instrument''' (''Cooperative Assessment. . .,'' 1973, p. 16).

based upon experiential learning is transportable from one institution to another'' (''Cooperative Assessment. . . ,'' 1973, p. 9). While the practitioners wanted to legitimate experiential learning, they did not want ETS to determine what the ''common procedures'' and ''understandable standards'' should be.

This reflected not only tension between practitioners and testers, but a more fundamental difference between the certification function of assessment and its educational value. The Carnegie Corporation and the Commission on Non-Traditional Study wanted to shore up the academic currency system against abuses in the awarding of credit. Hence, their attention to assessment was based upon concerns about certification and validation. The practitioners were animated by a desire to increase the credibility of their programs. If assessment could help them achieve that, then they were all for it.

The point of drawing in practitioners was precisely to overcome their criticisms, but even here ETS' intentions were suspect. ''Cooperative,''' as the members of the Task Force institutions saw the situation, read more like ''cooptive.'' From their viewpoint, the Carnegie grant subsidized ETS to exploit practitioners in order to develop instruments that they would sell later. As one member of the Implementation Committee put it, ''ETS was waiting to pick our brains. We all felt like holders of secret information. They would use this information to enhance their reputations. *We* were the people in the trenches, but when the project ended *they* would get the credit.''

There was another difference between the practitioners and the ETS people—their attitudes toward research. Like practitioners in many other fields, the college and university people did not think researchers could possibly understand the subtleties of what they did without experiencing them directly. This argument takes on greater force when the subject under investigation is experiential learning! How could Warren Willingham and the other ETS staff members assigned to the

CAEL project understand the problems of experiential learning without engaging in it themselves? Perhaps psychometricians were temperamentally unable to accept the ambiguities of experiential education, ambiguities that the practitioners willingly embraced, even enjoyed. Warren Willingham—soft-spoken, detached—seemed to several members of the Steering Committee to be the wrong man for the job.

Before the first meeting of the Steering Committee, David Sweet called other members to organize a caucus. A vituperative and blunt man, Sweet was able to convince only one other member of the Steering Committee to join him. Others, however, agreed with several of his criticisms. "Messianic, pure, greedy, selfish," as one of the participants described himself and his colleagues a dozen years later, they threatened to leave the project if ETS did not respond to them.

At its first meeting at ETS in March, 1974, the Steering Committee asserted its agenda for the project. First, it took control over the use of language. It was responsible for the aforementioned switch from "Working Committee" to "Implementation Committee," and it called the "Forum" the "Assembly." It also made specific plans for a membership organization, with dues set at $250 a year, and directed ETS staff to begin working on the membership of the Assembly.

The Steering Committee also challenged the ETS people on the matter of institutional support from the Carnegie grant. The cuts in the original grant left only $150,000 for all institutions. The Steering Committee set up a special subcommittee to decide how to allocate the funds to Task Force institutions and members of the Assembly on a 50-50 basis.

Then, it selected Morris Keeton of Antioch as chair of the Steering Committee. Arthur Chickering, Vice-President for Academic Affairs at Empire State College, took an active role behind the scenes. A psychologist with a national reputation as a researcher in higher education, it was Chickering who suggested Keeton as chair and Jules Pagano, Dean of Program Development and Evaluation at Florida International University, as vice-chair.

Chickering was also responsible for the creation of a subcommittee which drafted seven principles enunciating the practitioners' attitudes toward assessment and laying out the direction of the project:

> The priorities for the processes, methods, and criteria used for assessing and crediting the outcomes of prior and ongoing learning should conform to the following propositions:
>
> a. Learning occurs within formal educational settings and in the community at large.
> b. Each individual has different needs, prior experiences, and objectives.
> c. Individual learning and aspirations should be fostered.
> d. Individual acceptance of responsibility for learning should be reinforced.
> e. Criteria for assessment should rest upon individual goals or upon institutions or external requirements, or upon both, as appropriate.
> f. The array of processes, methods, and criteria used for assessment should meet the needs of persons not now being served.
> g. The results of assessment should give substantive information about the knowledge, competence, attitudes, values, and other dimensions of personal development which the individual has demonstrated in relation to his or her goals.[5]

Everyone—ETS and institutional participants alike—agreed that machine-scorable paper-and-pencil tests would not result

5. Minutes of CAEL Steering Committee Meeting, March 7-8, ETS, Princeton, N.J., pp. 3-4.

from the project. Rather, it would focus on the assessment *process*, in particular the use of expert judgment about how to assess learning from experience. CAEL would lay out the assessment principles "that need to be understood and applied, the procedural steps that are normally useful, and the prototype materials and documents that could be locally adapted to particular situations and types of learning" (Willingham, Valley, and Keeton, 1977, p. 14).

Focusing on the assessment process meant that the CAEL project would not have much to contribute to the certification of experiential learning. There were certain benefits in not attempting to do so. Emphasizing process brought a measure of peace among the warring parties in the project. It allied ETS with a group of innovative educators whose work would bring the testing company to the cutting edge of new practices in higher education. Whether or not this happened, the project was likely to help in the development of general principles of assessment not only for experiential education but for higher education generally. Willingham and the ETS staff who worked with him were practical people who had little patience with research that sat on shelves. He was as interested in having an impact as the practitioners were.

David Sweet was not happy with the compromises struck after the first Steering Committee meeting, particularly on the issue of how much money the institutions would receive and who would control the budget. Soon after the meeting, he wrote to Alden Dunham asking for a new beginning. Dunham replied to the whole Steering Committee in no uncertain terms:

> It is highly unlikely that Carnegie Corporation will agree to any major change in the project. The grant was made on the basis of what was spelled out in the proposal. The proposal itself was the result of planning sessions attended by representatives from the cooperating institutions. Most

if not all the issues raised by David Sweet, who did not attend the planning sessions, were discussed in the preparation of the proposal. Letters of endorsement of the proposal were submitted by each of the cooperating institutions, including MMSC [Sweet's institution]. . .

The principal purpose of the project has never been to provide funds to each cooperating college to develop and refine its own assessment procedures, nor has the principal purpose been to enable ETS to develop just another standardized test. . .

The planning sessions and the proposal itself reflect many difficult questions of process and substance. The endorsement of the proposal by the cooperating institutions led Carnegie Corporation to conclude that despite the difficulties the institutions felt that the importance of the project warranted their support of the proposal as written. Moreover, the cooperating colleges recognized at the second planning session the need for very close and open relationships among the group. *That being the case, if other institutions now have second thoughts about their endorsement of the proposal and share the views of David Sweet, they should consider withdrawing from the project prior to the next meeting of the Steering Committee. Depending upon the extent of the withdrawal, Carnegie Corporation will decide whether to cancel the grant.* Needless to say, we hope that this step will not be necessary. Impressed with the significance of the project, the quality of the people and the institutions involved, we want CAEL to move forward.[6]

Sweet withdrew from the Steering Committee at this point, but kept his institution in the project. George Ayers, his vice-president and later to become chair of the CAEL Board of Directors, took Sweet's place. "Torn," as Winton Manning put it, "between a desire to participate in a prestigious, well-

6. Letter from Alden Dunham to the CAEL Steering Committee, March 22, 1974, pp. 1-2, emphasis added.

funded project and a fear that ETS would run over them. . . the other members of the Steering Committee decided to remain.''[7]

The conflicts between the Steering Committee and ETS were mirrored in the attitudes of the Implementation Committee not only towards ETS but toward the Steering Committee as well. Members of the Implementation Committee challenged the right of the ETS staff and the Steering Committee to define agendas, insisting that they should have more say in setting the direction of the project. These tensions cross-cut others between those who were seen as conservative (though they were hardly so within their own institutions) and those who were seen as liberal. Whatever the accuracy of these labels, representatives of the large, older institutions like San Francisco State and the University of Alabama had more political experience than people from newer institutions.

A special meeting was called on April 4th, 1974 to hammer out agreements about the proper role of the three groups in CAEL. Operating procedures for the Implementation Committee were developed, which clearly limited its powers and access to the Steering Committee. These agreements were written up in a document which asserted that ETS, not the Steering Committee, was the fiscally responsible party for CAEL. The Steering Committee, however, was ceded authority over almost all substantive and organizational aspects of the project, including coordinating closely with the ETS staff.[8]

The task of pulling all this off fell to Morris Keeton as chair of the Steering Committee. The choice of Keeton as chair of the Steering Committee was fateful, because it laid down the character of CAEL. Keeton was not likely to be rattled by the disputes in CAEL. He came to Antioch in 1947 as college pastor

---

7. Letter from Winton Manning to the author, June 7, 1984, p. 2.

8. ''Basic Assumptions Concerning CAEL Project Roles and Responsibilities,'' April 4, 1974, p. 1.

after several years with the American Friends Service Committee. Dean in 1963 and then provost in 1973, Keeton helped create a number of Antioch outposts across the country. His administrative career at Antioch spanned its most tempestuous period, when long-time faculty colleagues fought bitterly and students were on the verge of a war on the college.

At the time he joined CAEL, Keeton was gaining a national reputation. He had just published several books—on off-campus programs, the reform of higher education, and liberal arts colleges—sponsored by the American Association for Higher Education and the Carnegie Commission on Higher Education.[9] A *Change* magazine survey of 400 college and university presidents, foundation executives, journalists and government officials carried out a few months after the CAEL project began cited Keeton as one of the forty-four most important people in American higher education. This judgment put him in the company of prominent people like Clark Kerr, former president of the University of California, and U.S. Representative John Brademas, chair of the House select subcommittee on education. The citation for Keeton in the article entitled "Who's Who in Higher Education" focused on Keeton's credentials as a force for change in higher education: "He is largely responsible for Antioch's growing roster of network institutions and is a leader in the experiential education movement. An educational philosopher of considerable depth, Keeton is currently devoting much effort to the rational development of nontraditional learning" (*Change,* 1975, p. 29).

---

9. Keeton wrote (with Conrad Hilberry) *Struggle and Promise: A Future for Colleges* (1969); *Models and Mavericks: A Profile of Private Liberal Arts Colleges* (1971a), sponsored by the Carnegie Commission on Higher Education; *Shared Authority on Campus* (1971b); and "Dilemmas in Accrediting Off-Campus Learning" (1972).

## CHAPTER TWO
## Getting to Work

Early debate in the Steering Committee centered around the definition and rationale for experiential learning. In a series of commissioned papers, Virginia Smith (director of the Fund for the Improvement of Postsecondary Education and former associate director of the Carnegie Commission on Higher Education), James Coleman (professor of sociology at the University of Chicago), and Melvin Tumin (professor of sociology and anthropology at Princeton University) discussed the educational and social implications of CAEL. They presented their talks to the first CAEL Assembly. Their papers were edited by Morris Keeton as a working paper and were included two years later in the book *Experiential Learning: Rationale, Characteristics, and Assessment* (Keeton, 1975; Keeton, 1976).

Experiential learning provoked questions very quickly about the way academics went about their business, questions that are still unresolved today: If academic credit was to be assigned to learning that took place outside of the classroom, then one would want to equate it to learning that resulted from studying inside the classroom. CAEL addressed learning that could not be associated with any particular course or even discipline; it talked about such things as interpersonal skills and work competences (Willingham and Associates, *The CAEL Validation Report*, 1976). Courses in colleges and universities are organized around subject matters based on academic disciplines or professional practice. While faculty often claim that students acquire certain competences and skills in their disciplines, they do not usually teach them explicitly. Examinations and other course requirements do not systematically test to find out if students do, in fact, acquire the assumed competences and skills.

CAEL saw, and later documented in its various studies, that there was little agreement among faculty from different colleges and universities, even in the same discipline, about what skills and competences characterize college-level learning. It was this fact that led Morris Keeton to write early in the project that "[t]ruth in labeling is surely the victim of this nonsystem" (Keeton, 1975, p. 3). When claims to benefits such as problem-solving ability or ability to communicate are made but not demonstrated, as Virginia Smith put it, then "much of higher education sounds like some sort of shell game. Ostensibly, students may be spending their time learning about economics or history, but we are told that they are really learning analytical ability" (Keeton, 1975, p. 17).

CAEL also raised questions about the social inequality that resulted from unequal access to higher education and, therefore, to valued and well-paid jobs. "This is done on the assumption that the traditional lines of access are blocked, or unfriendly, or not in tune with the life orientations of large numbers of people of all ages" (Keeton, 1975, p. 43). CAEL hoped that allowing adults who did not have college degrees to get academic credit for learning outside of school settings would reduce inequality. After years of studying class and stratification in the United States, Melvin Tumin doubted that this would happen (Keeton, 1975).

"They could talk philosophy all day," Aubrey Forrest, the psychometrician who chaired the Implementation Committee, said ten years later, "but someone would have to bite the bullet and get some work done." This remark expressed what became a characteristic CAEL style. The Steering Committee decided to focus on four priority areas, areas that reflected problems preoccupying practitioners of experiential learning at the time. These were: (1) assessing the achievement of interpersonal skills, (2) using portfolios in assessing nonsponsored learning, (3) assessing the learning outcomes of work experience, and (4) improving expert judgment in assessing learning outcomes.

The first task was to find out what practices were going

on in experiential learning programs. The group proceeded inductively. Willingham listened to discussions among members of the Implementation Committee in order to draw out specific practices, and wrote down detailed descriptions of what people said. ETS staff and the Implementation Committee sent out questionnaires and made site visits to hundreds of campuses across the country. CAEL also uncovered a variety of measurement techniques in use outside of higher education that were appropriate to assessing experiential learning, such as performance tests, simulations, interviews, ratings, and product assessments (Knapp and Sharon, 1975).

In addition to the Task Force institutions, other colleges and universities were drawn into the work of the project from the very beginning, either as participants in special institutional projects or as testers of CAEL materials.[10] Twenty institutions carried out special projects in each of the four priority areas; five of these were published as institutional reports and distributed to members of the CAEL assembly for experimental use [Lewis et al., 1975 (Antioch College); Tatzel and Lamdin, 1975 (Empire State College); Permaul et al., 1975 (UCLA); Spitzer and Smock, 1975 (Wayne State University); Christensen, 1975 (William Rainey Harper College)]. In assessing interpersonal skills, for example, Kurt Spitzer and Sue Smock at Wayne State University described the development of a performance checklist they used in a social work field-work practicum. Frank Christensen of William Rainey Harper College described portfolio procedures for assessing nonsponsored experiential learning among applicants to a new associates degree in liberal studies.

By the end of the first year, CAEL had produced ten working papers, five institutional reports, fifteen special project reports, two tape/slide presentations, a resource book, and three newsletters. A guide for the systematic use of portfolios was

10. See Appendix A for participants in various CAEL projects.

prepared for faculty and staff, and another, more popularly written one, was directed to students (Forrest, 1975). Three other faculty and staff guides (Breen, Donlon, and Whitaker, 1975a; Sharon, 1975; Reilly et al., 1975) and two other student guides were produced (Breen, Donlon, and Whitaker, 1975b, and Forrest, 1975).[11]

Even judged more than ten years later, these publications are impressive. They looked good. Like all of CAEL's publications and stationery, their covers were made of heavy ivory paper, with printing and design details in blue and olive. While the colors conveyed dignity and tradition, the logo was more quirky: "cael" in lower-case letters, with the "e" on a slant.

The substance of CAEL's work also carried the message of quality and inventiveness. Painstakingly thorough in their coverage, the handbooks, guides and other materials demonstrated "a genuine effort to embrace originality of thought and freshness of approach" (Greenwood, 1984, p. 1). They were obviously meant to be used, and therefore were presented in compact and practical packages. Whether they were used by the faculty, students and staff members to whom they were directed—and used in the ways intended—is another question.

## The Money Rolls In

Besides coping with the conflicts at the beginning and running the various CAEL projects, Warren Willingham, with help from Morris Keeton, frantically wrote proposals to continue the project beyond the sixteen months of Carnegie funding. They could appeal to foundations on several grounds: the unusual combination of researchers with practitioners; the prestige of

11. For a complete listing of CAEL's publications from 1975 to 1985, see Appendix B.

ETS; the separateness of the various aspects of the project, which allowed foundations to take credit for particular parts of the project; the logic of the overall plan, which multiplied the effect of any one part; the fact that Carnegie had bet a substantial amount of money on the project already; and, perhaps most important, the demonstrated productivity of the project.

By early summer 1975, money had come through for the additional two years needed to complete the project. The Carnegie Corporation gave an additional $203,000; the Ford Foundation and the Lilly Endowment gave $200,000 each; and the Fund for the Improvement of Postsecondary Education approved $375,000. Combined with the original Carnegie grant and income from publications, workshops, and assemblies, these grants brought the total CAEL budget from March 1974 to June 1977 to a little over $2 million.

The prospect of large amounts of money brought up yet again the question about how much would go to ETS and how much to Task Force institutions. This time, at the suggestion of Arthur Chickering, the Steering Committee set up a budget committee to review CAEL budgets and suggest changes in them. ETS saw this as a challenge to its fiscal responsibilities and as a breach of earlier agreements with the CAEL Steering Committee. Given the hard-won *modus vivendi* between ETS and the institutions, ETS officials worried in an internal document that "the revisionist nature of this development" could "backfire. . . because of persistent comments we hear concerning ETS rip-off, brain-picking, copyright on materials, etc."[12] ETS did not have "a strong political base—nor much understanding—among the diverse individuals who are interested in CAEL. Many of these people do not come from the more traditional ETS constituencies. They tend to be on the periphery

---

12. Memorandum from Richard Burns and Warren Willingham to David Brodsky, Winton Manning, Robert Solomon, and John Summerskill, May 15, 1975.

of the educational establishment, are opposed to mass standardized testing, etc., etc.''[13]

The issue required delicate handling. ETS invited members of the budget subcommittee of the CAEL Steering Committee, which included Arthur Chickering, to a meeting in Princeton on June 6, 1975. Before the meeting, Chickering asked for a detailed accounting of the money already spent as well as the projected expenditures for the new components of CAEL. He also requested information on the training and experience of the ETS staff members involved in CAEL, as well as their assignments, time allocations, and performance. ETS' strategy was to inundate the committee with information. Reports were presented on income and expenses for the past year, anticipated income, publications income and expenses, assembly expenses and income, and budgets submitted to Ford, Carnegie, FIPSE, and Lilly. The budget subcommittee concluded, after reviewing the mountain of material, that the projects were not overstaffed.[14] In the end, the Task Force institutions and the other colleges and universities that participated in various projects received $850,000 over the life of CAEL, slightly over 40% of total income.

## Validating Expert Judgment

The project had spun into existence four separate but intersecting realms, each with its own rhythm and temperament. Intense, hard-driving, the Steering Committee served as a forum for senior administrators. The Implementation Committee

13. Memorandum from John Summerskill to Richard Burns, Winton Manning, Robert Solomon, John Valley, and Warren Willingham, May 21 1975.

14. Summary of CAEL Budget Committee Meeting, June 6, 1975, p. 2

despite resentments about its subordinate role, had much to do and soon set about doing it. The ETS staff had its jobs and pursued them systematically. And the Assembly became a world of excitement and goodwill. As the project gathered momentum and the conflicts got settled, these different worlds intersected more. CAEL began to invent its own language, "CAELic."

After the first year of collecting information, CAEL materials were ready to be tried out and validated. The Implementation Committee, a source of friction with the Steering Committee, was disbanded for a series of *ad hoc* groups focused on specific tasks. The Validation Study announced that Assembly members could apply to participate in three, increasingly demanding ways: some could do critical reviews of the CAEL materials and treat them as a basis for discussion and planning in their own institutions; others could use the student and faculty guides experimentally; and still others could become field research sites to validate their use. Eighty institutions signed up to try out the materials, and twenty-four were selected as research sites.[15] The study drew in more than 1000 faculty members and students. In addition to six Task Force institutions, among the institutions in the field research was a mix of private liberal arts colleges and universities, state colleges, community colleges, and research universities. Each received between $2,000 and $3,500, depending on how many activities they joined.

Ten validation studies were carried out in the four priority areas—the assessment of interpersonal skills, the use of portfolios, the assessment of the learning outcomes of work experience, and the use of expert judgment in assessing learning outcomes. ETS staff designed studies to test the assumptions underlying the assessment of experiential learning: that faculty could agree on the types of learning that were worthy of

15. See Appendix A for the eighty try-out institutions and the twenty-four research sites.

academic credit and that they could agree on how much academic credit to award. They also conducted studies of certain key practices; for instance, to find out if faculty members were consistent in how they awarded credit for learning described in portfolios.

It was not easy to gather reliable data from the twenty-four institutions, whose time perspectives and daily struggles continued to diverge from those of the people at ETS. Nevertheless, ETS staff succeeded in getting faculty to assess students through interviews, role-playing, portfolios, and ratings.

The results were mixed. When faculty members in the same institution were asked to decide how much credit to give students on the basis of work presented in illustrative portfolios, they agreed fairly well. But there was substantial disagreement across institutions about what they thought should be counted as college-level work and how much credit they would assign for the same learning. For example, faculty in one college said they would give no credit at all for "knows the function and application of standard metal fabricating machines," while faculty in a second college said they would give lower-division credit, and faculty in a third college said they would award upper-division credit. Reviewing the same set of portfolios, faculty in one institution awarded an average of forty credits, while faculty in other institutions awarded twenty-five, ten, or even eight credits (Willingham, Valley, and Keeton, 1977 and Willingham and Associates, 1976).

These findings raised problems for the assessment of credentials based on experiential learning. Even more, they opened up the fundamental question of what constituted college-level work—the "truth in labeling" issue raised at the outset by Morris Keeton. While this problem was to come up again and again in CAEL's history, it always resisted taking it on directly. In 1976, the Steering Committee and ETS staff took to the Assembly the question of whether the CAEL guides should take a position on what constituted college-level learning. Concerned about their own freedom to decide what counted as college-level work, the members recommended that CAEL not prescribe the same definitions of college-level learning for all colleges and universities.

## Utilization and Implementation

While CAEL would not tackle the question of college-level learning in general, it could try to figure out how to help faculty members in individual institutions reach consensus about what constituted creditable learning at their institutions, apply sound assessment methods for finding out if it occurred, and gain institutional support for the effort. The Operational Models project, funded by the Fund for the Improvement of Post-secondary Education, and the Faculty Development Program, supported by a grant from the Lilly Endowment, were devoted to these questions.

Like all CAEL projects, the Operational Models project and the Faculty Development Program were to be joint efforts. The Operational Models project struggled with the tension between the need for some uniformity and the need for flexibility in dealing with the differences among participating colleges and universities. The project tried to answer questions about responses of organizations to innovation, appropriate administrative structures, the allocation of resources, and institutional politics. Twelve institutions, representing different implementation problems, were selected as participants. They were given quite a bit of autonomy in defining their work, which was to be guided by three orienting "themes": (1) the "systems" approach, outlined initially in the first CAEL proposal, should look at the assessment of experiential learning in the context of institutional policies, procedures, and administrative structures; (2) a commitment to articulate a "model" of implementation should be generalizable to other institutions; and (3) particular attention should be paid either to standards or to costs.

Twelve different models resulted. Two of the projects were at new programs at traditional institutions, and two were at older programs at non-traditional institutions; two were concerned with financing assessment programs, two with the coordination of assessment within a multi-campus system, and two with assessing broad educational competences. There were some practical results as well. Union College, Memphis State University, a consortium from California, and San Francisco State University, for example, worked on designing documents and procedures for their programs. Florida International University discovered that its use of negotiated learning contracts carried certain unrecognized latent standards. The Community College of Vermont dealt with ways to balance the autonomy of local review committees with consistency across committees. There was wide dissemination of these models in print, at an assembly, and in regional workshops (Nesbitt and Willingham, 1976).

In their discussion of the Operational Models project, Willingham, Valley and Keeton (1977) concluded that implementing clear standards for student performance continued to be a thorny problem. The project seemed, however, to have made some headway in sorting out some of the issues involved in financing the assessment of experiential learning, an area that until then had received little attention. The most subtle and far-reaching implications had to do with effects on faculty. "Revelation is not enough," as they put it (1977, p. 44). Faculty must go through the process of discovering the meaning of new approaches like experiential learning in their own settings. The Operational Models project helped faculty go through this discovery process. A "community of interest" and "common values" emerged among faculty: "a commitment to facilitating competence, a concern for students, an interest in instruction, a willingness to mold programs to educational needs. . . , a central concern with *learning* as opposed to other priorities of college faculties" (1977, p. 45).

The Faculty Development Program capitalized on these common values by making them a central focus. Its main goal was to prepare faculty to understand, implement, and disseminate experiential learning. It turned out to be "a graduate program of doctoral or postdoctoral level in the design, conduct, and assessment of experiential learning" (Willingham, Valley, and Keeton, 1977, p. 48). The Faculty Development Program became, in fact, a CAEL within CAEL. The original proposal had talked about the need for faculty development in the utilization phase of CAEL. As it unfolded, the Faculty Development Program developed a stronger identity than the other projects did. The way it was organized, and the spirit it engendered among its participants, was to a large extent responsible for the grassroots tinge of CAEL. Joan Knapp, the ETS staff member responsible for the program, worked closely with Urban Whitaker, a specialist in international relations and Dean of Undergraduate Studies at San Francisco State University, who was active in CAEL on almost every front. As dean, he freed resources at San Francisco State for CAEL activities.

The program tried to produce "ripple effects." A first generation of people were trained; they in turn were expected to train a second generation; the second generation would train a third generation; and so on. Twenty-three people from twelve institutions attended three intensive workshops on different aspects of experiential learning. In addition to using CAEL materials and documents, the program also created special materials and exercises using simulations, role-playing, case studies, and tape/slide shows on institutional politics, the assessment of field experience and portfolios, and how to put on an effective workshop. Faculty, for example, were asked to participate in an imaginary university committee that was considering how to credit experiential learning. They role-played a variety of assessment situations, making use of simulated portfolios and field experience programs.

Participants received assignments between workshops. After the first workshop, trainees were asked to write an account of their involvement with a faculty member with an experiential learning assessment case, to develop a strategy that could be used to promote adoption of an experiential learning program on their campuses, compile a list of items for a bibliography, create a presentation on one technical problem concerning the assessment of experiential learning, and develop plans for a workshop at their own institutions.

The Faculty Development Program had great impact. Ten years later, participants still talked about the excitement of the workshops and the pleasure of working with people like themselves from different institutions. Many of them were located in peripheral and unrecognized programs. The Faculty Development Program gave them recognition and the chance to meet with people like themselves from other institutions. It also gave them the tools and the backing of CAEL as a whole.

When they completed their workshops, the twenty-three trainees then became trainers in workshops held regionally across the country. They could draw on a loose-leaf notebook where training exercises were collected, along with scripts for slide/tape presentations. More institutions requested training than could be accommodated in some of the workshops. Altogether, 250 people attended thirteen workshops. Of those who attended, 60% were faculty members, another 22% were administrators, and 17% combined administration with teaching. Like the first group of trainees, many worked in innovative programs within their institutions.

## CHAPTER TWO

# CAEL as an Organization

Meanwhile, the organization-building side of the project was moving forward. John Valley and Diana Bamford-Rees corresponded with administrators and faculty members in hundreds of colleges and universities, as well as with officials in higher education associations and agencies and an occasional private organization. In 1976 their files showed letters to almost 250 correspondents; two-thirds were addressed by their first names.

Membership in CAEL exceeded all expectations. Invitations to join were sent to all undergraduate colleges and universities in the spring of 1974, as well as to other agencies and associations. The original proposal for CAEL mentioned a membership of about fifty institutions. Within two months after the invitations were issued, however, a total of 140 institutions had joined. By the end of the project, membership had grown to 270, the majority being colleges and universities, with a scattering of consortia, state systems, governing boards, state agencies, and private organizations. CAEL member schools were distributed across the range of higher education, although compared to national averages they tended to be drawn from the public sector, to be larger, have graduate programs, to be average in the competitiveness of their admissions, and to have somewhat fewer part-time students.[16]

CAEL held six assemblies between 1974 and 1977. Attendance ran between 215 people in 1974 and over 300 in 1977. Between assemblies, members were kept informed by means of newsletters—six- to twelve-page circulars in the CAEL colors which appeared two to three times a year. The news-

16. See Appendix C for membership information and assembly attendance from 1974 to 1986.

letters, which often included photographs and other visual material, described the latest CAEL activities in some detail, discussed literature and events relevant to experiential learning, and reported on selected member institutions.

The attention to detail that was characteristic of the way CAEL did its other business extended to the assemblies. The assemblies, which turned out to be crucial to CAEL's continuation when its connection with ETS ended, were at once highly structured and personal. Valley and Bamford-Rees sent letters to everyone who proposed a session, even when the proposal was not accepted. Each presenter on the program received instructions ahead of time about how to proceed. The program allowed time for informal conversation in addition to the prepared presentations on subjects deemed important by CAEL people. The assembly also became one of the most important ways to disseminate CAEL's products. In workshops, new materials could be presented and interested users identified.

In the first three years, assembly presentations closely paralleled the activities of the project. Assessment was the commanding issue. Certain subjects, which became more prominent in later years, began to appear on assembly programs as well: institutional issues, curriculum and pedagogy, national and state policy, matters affecting CAEL as an organization. The assembly topics took on a less defensive tone as time passed. At first, "there seemed to be an image being built, a sort of 'here's how to get faculty/administration to take you seriously' tone. The change looks like a change in confidence: in the beginning the tone seemed almost apologetic, like they weren't quite sure whether they really were quite legitimate" (J. Gamson, correspondence, p. 1).

As the assembly programs grew broader, the number of people making presentations grew steadily, from thirty-six in 1974 to ninety-three in 1976. In addition to featuring people from the Task Force as well as other cooperating institutions on programs, CAEL was able to attract some prominent people for keynote speeches: the psychotherapist and writer Carl Rogers; the educational psychologist K. Patricia Cross; and the editor of *Change,* George Bonham.

The various CAEL projects drew in a minimum of 137 different colleges and universities; about one-third participated in more than one activity. While we do not have a count of the individuals involved in CAEL projects, we can assume conservatively that an average of three people were involved in each CAEL project at each participating institution. A rough estimate of the number of individual participants is, therefore, about 700.[17]

How to capitalize on the energy unleashed by CAEL after it had ended? The future of CAEL was first broached publicly at the Spring assembly in 1975. By the fall, a special subcommittee of the Steering Committee came up with a proposal for an "Association for Experiential Learning," to continue after the project ended. A decision was made to keep the CAEL acronym but to change two of the words in it: from "Cooperative" to "Council," and from "Assessment" to "Advancement." In March 1976, the Executive Committee of the Steering Committee, with help from ETS lawyers in New York, formally applied for a charter from the Regents of the University of the State of New York.

This application and the proposed by-laws were distributed to participants in the Spring 1976 assembly, along with a questionnaire soliciting their reactions. The people were overwhelmingly in favor of CAEL's continuation as an independent organization, but they disagreed about what the organization's main focus should be. Some members urged that

---

17. See Appendix A for a count of the number of institutions that participated in the various CAEL projects. The estimate of 700 individual participants results from tripling 232, the total number of institutions involved in CAEL projects. This number includes institutions—and presumably individuals—who participated in more than one project.

CAEL deal with accrediting and regulatory bodies; others argued for continued development and application of approaches to experiential learning; still others advocated that CAEL try to influence national and state policy.

The Steering Committee was reconstituted as the Board of Trustees in the summer of 1976. Six new members and three holdovers from the Steering Committee were elected by the members; they joined the six holdovers from the Steering Committee who had served as incorporators. Once the by-laws were in effect, the Board of Trustees could hire, fire, and supervise the CAEL staff, something they could not do before.

The October 1976 assembly was entitled "Institutionalizing Experiential Learning." Morris Keeton presented "Through a Glass Darkly," an analysis of the future of CAEL in the context of higher education as a whole. He proposed the following priorities for CAEL: that it improve the assessment of learning outcomes, promote wider use of mixes of experiential and theoretical learning in classroom and non-classroom settings, and become a "non-lobbying advocate" among learners, educators, administrators, and policy-makers.

A regional flavor was beginning to season CAEL. The Operational Models project had disseminated its work, in part, through workshops held locally. The Faculty Development Program was a full-blown regional effort. One of the sessions at the October 1976 assembly organized the participants into regional groups roughly matching the areas covered by the regional higher education accrediting associations. The groups explored the possibility of a regional organization for what was now being called "CAEL II." The issues they were asked to discuss anticipated arrangements that would become typical of the later CAEL, such as using the regions to put on programs, do research, work out cooperative arrangements, recruit members, and disseminate information.

As the plans evolved, it became clear that CAEL would

operate primarily as a membership organization. Funds would come from dues, fees, and publications. Membership would no longer be restricted to institutions, as in the first CAEL; individuals could join at a reduced rate as associate members. The Steering Committee disagreed about the scope of the new organization's activities. Some members pressed for maintaining the focus on assessment. Others, including Keeton and Chickering, wanted to broaden CAEL's purview to include anything having to do with experiential learning.

The latter group won. The New York Regents approved CAEL's charter in September, 1976 as a nonstock corporation organized for educational purposes. The charter application and the by-laws allowed for a good bit of leeway. In the words of the charter, CAEL exists ". . . to assist institutions of higher education to increase their ability to define, assess, credit, sponsor and evaluate experiential learning and experiential learning programs, including the specific purposes of:

> a. assisting institutions of higher education increase their capacity to use and carry out experiential learning effectively;
> b. assisting institutions of higher education improve assessment practices;
> c. providing a forum for a discussion of ideas; and
> d. providing an outlet for scholarly thought."[18]

---

18. Application for Absolute Charter for CAEL, Pursuant to the Education of Law, Regents of the University of the State of New York, 1976, pp. 1-2, (draft).

# CHAPTER TWO

## Accomplishments of the First CAEL

By the end of three years, the first CAEL had evolved into a sure-footed operation with a strong identity and a unique culture. It showed that it is possible to tackle an intractable problem in higher education in an intentional and systematic way. The problem it tackled turned out to be so robust that it carried implications for more than experiential learning. The CAEL projects had much to teach higher education about good assessment in general, outcomes, the problem of defining college-level work, and faculty development.

From the start, CAEL was more comprehensive than most improvement efforts in higher education. It drew equally on the perspectives of researchers and practitioners from an extraordinary variety of traditional and non-traditional institutions. It fastened its attention on every conceivable angle related to experiential learning—as a problem for measurement, product development, field testing, marketing, dissemination, political and organizational support, personal commitment, and professional development. CAEL's products also reflect this diversity. Its twenty-seven published and some fifty unpublished documents include handbooks and guides for students and faculty members, references, and institutional reports. It produced slide/tape presentations, ran workshops, put on conferences. Practitioners in experiential and adult programs across the country displayed the familiar ivory and blue reports from CAEL on their bookshelves. Several of the CAEL products are still popular today, in particular Willingham's *Principles of Good Practice in Assessing Experiential Learning* (1977), and a slide/tape presentation on the history and rationale of experiential learning.

In addition to the reports and materials it produced, CAEL was extraordinarily imaginative organizationally. There was a sense of congruence in CAEL between its purposes and its actions which, in the eyes of one observer, ought to be "bottled. In an almost complete departure from the usual mode of such organizations, this one *produced!* so much, and so clearly, and so definitively, and so. . . on-target" (Greenwood, 1984, p. 13).

CAEL set a standard for inter-institutional cooperation and for membership involvement. The use of teams drawn from a wide variety of colleges and universities working on a common problem, the array of workshop techniques, and the small groups used at assemblies were fresh contributions to the toolkit of educational innovators. Work on CAEL was reviewed widely by the staff and peers, and the results were discussed publicly at assemblies and other meetings.

Other efforts in higher education have much to learn from the first CAEL on the benefits of diversity. The differences between the innovators and ETS were a source of much conflict, but once the two groups entered into a working relationship, they were astonishingly productive. There is no question that the collaboration between ETS and the Task Force institutions was crucial, despite or perhaps because of the conflicts between ETS and the Steering Committee. Had CAEL just been an internal ETS project, it would not have been as imaginative as it turned out to be. Had CAEL been a product of the Task Force institutions, it would not have been as productive. ETS brought to the collaboration recognition and objectivity; the practitioners brought commitment to the value of experiential learning. ETS made an investment to see CAEL through, and it did everything possible to ensure that the work would be competent. The message that the tasks, while exceedingly ambitious, could be accomplished kept up the pressure for productivity. The Steering Committee's insistence that decisions and resources be shared with the practitioners forced attention onto the way things were done as well as to how much was accomplished. Their belief in flexibility and autonomy balanced the push for productivity and accountability.

These balances were exhibited in the close working relationship between Warren Willingham and Morris Keeton. Both Southerners; both highly intelligent, sometimes brilliant; both committed to the practical uses of the project; both endowed with deep reservoirs of energy; both given to a certain intellectual crispness and emotional restraint. They were natural partners. While they kept each other informed constantly about their part of the project, they divided up the territory. Willingham's strengths lay in planning, analysis, and organization. He specialized in orchestrating and administering CAEL. Keeton had a knack for identifying good ideas, reaching consensus, and putting them into words. He specialized in mediating conflicts between ETS and the practitioners and keeping people enthusiastic, even when they and their institutions were donating time and other resources.

On the whole, the CAEL projects succeeded in balancing systematic research with practical utility, an unusual combination under any circumstances and especially in higher education, where research and practice tend to be disconnected. CAEL's structure forced constant interaction between researchers and practitioners on everything from the budget to the definition of tasks. The researchers had to put themselves in the practitioners' shoes in order to understand the way they made judgments about experiential learning, judgments that were appropriate to their different institutional settings. While they were constantly searching for some common framework to unite the work of the project, they also recognized the absolute necessity of local adaptation in the preparation and dissemination of CAEL's products. On the other hand, in articulating to the researchers the basis for their judgments, the practitioners had to learn about the fundamental principles of assessment and the necessity to give public and rational accounts of what they did.

CAEL had the quality of a major campaign. The amount of money devoted to the CAEL projects, while not extravagant, was substantial. There were hidden subsidies from ETS and from the institutions that became involved in the various projects—most of all from the people at ETS and the institutions who carried out the work. CAEL capitalized on the intensity of people's commitment to experiential learning and the energy which that commitment generated. The commitment was contagious. ETS is a forty-hour-a-week sort of organization, but few ETS staff who worked with CAEL limited themselves to just forty hours. ETS staff who did not know much about experiential learning and hardly considered themselves innovators found themselves drawn into a spiral of upward involvement. For them, as for many of the other members of the Task Force institutions and other colleges that were drawn in, CAEL was one of the most important experiences of their careers. Despite the conflicts and the costs, it was probably one of the most productive projects in the recent history of ETS.

The holding power of CAEL was great. CAEL offered a name, a culture, a professional identity, and a home to those who worked in innovative but often invisible and marginal programs. CAEL provided the opportunity for a group of lively people to get together regularly in pleasant surroundings, to eat and drink, and to have a good time. As one of them said later, "this was the only nice thing that was happening to us. Outside of CAEL, we were fighting battles and pinching pennies. Inside of CAEL, we could talk and have fun." They were, in CAEL jargon, part of a "network." They received generous recognition for their contributions. CAEL publications routinely thanked participants by name. A reviewer of the CAEL publications concluded that "never was there a set of documents which so fully acknowledged, appreciated, included, and thanked" (Greenwood, 1984, p. 13). Quite a few of the people who were drawn into CAEL were able to use their CAEL currency for career advancement, some to senior administrative positions.

Several of the original participants reported lasting effects on their careers. Norman Sundberg, Professor of Psychology and Director of the Clinical/Community Psychology Program at the University of Oregon, wrote in 1984 that "CAEL had a profound influence in helping me to organize and improve my concepts of field learning. I have presented about 5 papers on field learning and ecological assessment and have published 3 or 4 articles or chapters. . . I continue to use CAEL concepts in teaching and other ways."[19] Robert Fox, Associate Professor at Metropolitan University in St. Paul, coordinator of the Chemical Dependency Competence Assessment Program and coordinator of the Police Officers Standards and Training Program, wrote at about the same time that "[o]ne of the major influences on my career was that this project enabled me to become integrated into the higher education community. From my previous training and experience as a lawyer, this project provided me with the impetus and resources for learning about assessing experiential learning and the relationship between experiential learning and that learning which is important to being an educated person. Not only did it develop my competence in this regard, but it developed my confidence. . . . It helped me learn and refine my skills in conducting, planning and evaluating workshops. These matters are now all second nature."[20]

Translating these personal effects into institutional ones was a more difficult task. After the projects ended, CAEL did not monitor its members' effects on their institutions. Some did not try to apply what they learned in their institutions, either because they were not in a position to effect change or because they left their institutions. Those who did make the effort found the

19. Norman Sundberg, response to questionnaire "The Lilly/CAEL Project—What Happened?", 1984.

20. Robert Fox, response to questionnaire "The Lilly/CAEL Project—What Happened?", 1984.

going tough. It was with precisely the question of how to get institutions to accept experiential learning that the second CAEL began.

## CHAPTER THREE

# Broadening the Scope of Action: The Second CAEL[1]

We intend. . . to "seed" the entire field of post-secondary education and thus to have a salutary effect upon the standard of good practice throughout American higher education.[2]

The above statement would seem presumptuous coming from a new organization. But the Council for the Advancement of Experiential Learning was not a new organization. It began with a membership of some 270 colleges, universities, state systems, and other organizations, and a dowry of $40,000 worth of publications from ETS. With a reputation for being innovative and productive, it already had a head-start.

According to the original plans, the new CAEL would operate primarily as a membership organization with a projected

1. Sources for this chapter include final reports on the Institutional Development Program submitted by CAEL to the Kellogg Foundation from 1978 to 1983; reports from external evaluators; newsletters from 1978 to 1983; minutes of meetings of the Board of Trustees from 1978 to 1982; and special reports and publications cited in the text. Interviews with the following people provided additional material:

*George Ayers* (See Footnote 1, Chapter 2).

*JoAnn Harris-Bowlsbey,* assistant vice-president, American College Testing Program, developer of DISCOVER, a computer-based counseling system.

*Alison Bernstein,* grant officer at the Ford Foundation, former staff member at the Fund for the Improvement of Postsecondary Education, vice-chair of

2. Proposal for the CAEL Institutional Development Program, quoted in "A Report to the Kellogg Foundation on the CAEL Institutional Development Program," 1978, p. I-2.

income of about $85,000 a year. It was thought that CAEL would not need a large staff. Morris Keeton was prepared to direct the organization on a one-third time basis while continuing at Antioch. When it turned out that he was not selected as president of Antioch after serving as acting president in 1976-77, Keeton became available for a larger commitment to CAEL. He had already spent a good deal of time during 1976-77 contacting foundations for support. What was needed now, he argued, was a way to institutionalize experiential learning. The Operational Models Project had begun this task. Materials were ready; there were procedures for disseminating them; an organization was primed to carry them out.

With encouragement from Cyril Houle, a professor of adult education at the University of Chicago and a member of the

---

the CAEL Board of Trustees, 1981-82.

*John Duley,* professor emeritus at Michigan State University, member of the Steering Committee of the CAEL project, member of the CAEL Board of Trustees, 1976-81.

*Hugh F. Cline,* director of the Program in Educational Technology at the Educational Testing Service.

*Arlon Elser,* program director at the W.K. Kellogg Foundation, responsible for educational programs, including monitoring CAEL.

*Norman Evans,* director of Learning from Experience Trust, London.

*Harold Hodgkinson* (See Footnote 1, Chapter 2).

*Cyril Houle* (See Footnote 1, Chapter 2).

*Martin Katz,* senior research scientist at the Educational Testing Service and main designer of the System of Interactive Guidance Information (SIGI).

*Joseph Keller,* Dean of Instructional Development, Brevard Community College, CAEL regional manager, 1978-, for the South Coastal region.

*Morris Keeton* (See Footnote 1, Chapter 2).

*Robert Kinsinger,* retired vice-president at the W.K. Kellogg Foundation.

*Winton Manning* (See Footnote 1, Chapter 2).

*Larraine Matusak* (See Footnote 1, Chapter 2).

*Jerry W. Miller,* president of the Association of Independent Colleges and

Steering Committee of the first CAEL, Keeton left Antioch to become the full-time Executive Director of the new CAEL. Diana Bamford-Rees left ETS to become Executive Associate. Keeton and Bamford-Rees set up offices a few blocks away from Keeton's home in Columbia, Maryland, where a satellite campus of Antioch had been established a few years before.

Around the same time, Cyril Houle retired from the University of Chicago and became a senior advisor to the W.K. Kellogg Foundation. Distancing himself immediately, he resigned from the CAEL Board of Trustees. While he refused to play an active role on CAEL's behalf within the foundation, his inside view of the first CAEL undoubtedly enhanced the new organization's standing with Kellogg. Arlon Elser, the former vice-chancellor at the University of Pittsburgh who came to Kellogg as a program officer in 1975, recommended that the foundation support CAEL.

---

Schools.

*Anita Palsgrove*, former CAEL staff member who worked closely with the Learner Services Program.

*Jane Szutu Permaul*, director of field studies, University of California at Los Angeles, former member of the CAEL Board of Trustees, 1977-81.

*George Pruitt*, president of Thomas A. Edison State College, vice-president of CAEL, August 1981-December 1982, member of the CAEL Board of Trustees.

*John Strange*, professor at the College of Public and Community Service, University of Massachusetts-Boston, senior executive of CAEL, 1978-1981.

*Pamela Tate*, director of Joint Ventures at CAEL, Editor-in-Chief of the New Directions in Experiential Learning series, member of the CAEL Board of Trustees, 1983-85.

*Urban Whitaker* (See Footnote 1, Chapter 2).

## CHAPTER THREE

## The Institutional Development Program

The W.K. Kellogg Foundation granted CAEL $975,000 for a project called the Institutional Development Program (IDP). The first in a series of grants from Kellogg, which totaled $7 million by 1985, the IDP grant defined CAEL as an organization.

IDP extended many of the techniques pioneered by the original CAEL, especially the Faculty Development Program, but it also introduced new approaches. IDP began with the belief that the key to institutional development was to get the commitment of institutional leaders to a plan of action. These leaders would then support already committed faculty members or would encourage faculty members not yet committed to carry out the plan. With the help of IDP, these faculty members would work with consultants and receive training in the assessment of portfolios or other experiential learning techniques perfected in the original CAEL project. Some of them, in turn, would become consultants and trainers.

The IDP proposal called for three levels of participation: (1) *Task Force* institutions would take responsibility for coordinating a group of other institutions in addition to participating in the program; (2) *Participating* institutions would submit a plan to CAEL and, with its help, implement it; and (3) *Critic-Observer* institutions would sit in on IDP programs and prepare to become a Participant or Task Force institution later. Task Force and Participating institutions would receive $1250 to cover the costs of consultants. Drawing on participants from the first CAEL, as well as new people who turned up in the early days of IDP, CAEL could mobilize a large group to serve as consultants and trainers.

The original proposal projected sixty-five participants in the first year, with a total of 200 over three years. In an echo of the response to the original CAEL project three years earlier, many more institutions responded. Within six weeks after the Kellogg grant was announced, even before the project was organized, more than twice the number expected for the first year had registered as participants. By June 1, 1978, there were 189 active participants and 47 critic-observers.[3]

In what was to become a habit, CAEL constantly kept extending IDP's goals. IDP was originally to have involved 200 institutions by the third year; at the end of the first year, this number ws raised to 500. IDP was to have conducted 2500 "person days" of training through its five years; just in its first year, more than 3400 days of training had been achieved in the regions and nationally.[4] In the second year, the number of training days was increased to 10,000, and in the third year to 20,000. Even this latter goal was too small by the time the project ended.

IDP introduced several new procedures, and some turned into enduring structures. Each institution participating in IDP, including critic-observers, was to be represented by a "liaison" person, someone with whom CAEL would communicate and who would take responsibility for coordinating IDP activities on campus. If the liaison person was not the chief academic or administrative officer, an officer had to approve the institution's commitment to IDP in writing. By the end of the first year, virtually all institutions in IDP had appointed a liaison person.

Another innovation, which evolved into a regional system, was the clustering of institutions. The original proposal discussed the possibility of grouping institutions in geographic proximity to one another so that they could work on a common problem.

3. The distinction between Task Force and Participant institutions was dropped when the project began.

4. A "person day" is a minimum of six hours of training time or consultant time.

During the first year, forty-four such "clusters" came together, ranging from single institutions, to several institutions, state systems, whole states, and several states. Grouping institutions regionally made it possible to bring participants together for workshops and training, thus saving travel money and using it instead to pay for CAEL materials, consultants, and conference expenses. Nominally responsible for the clusters were volunteer "cluster coordinators," people who usually held administrative positions in the special kinds of programs to which CAEL continued to appeal: experimental or alternative or non-traditional programs, individualized studies, assessment centers, cooperative programs.

The cluster coordinators themselves needed coordinating, and it was clear that Morris Keeton and Diana Bamford-Rees, an administrative associate working on another project, and seven office staff could not do the job themselves. In a brilliant illustration of the old proverb, necessity became the mother of invention. The Operational Models project had disseminated some of its work in regional meetings, and the Faculty Development Program conducted most of its workshops regionally. In perpetual motion around the country, Morris Keeton met people who seemed to be ripe for something like CAEL. Some had been involved in the first CAEL; others had just materialized. Some were firmly planted within a college or university; others were in a variety of organizations and projects in and around higher education.

During the first year of IDP, Keeton invited ten people to become "regional managers" of CAEL. At first, they did this as volunteers. Within a year, however, Kellogg made a supplemental grant of $457,000 to increase the number of institutions in IDP to 500. Out of this supplement, each regional manager received $12,000 for 1979-80 and then smaller amounts each succeeding year. This funding plan was based on the assumption that the regional managers would raise additional money from fees, grants, and other sources. It was hoped that they would be self-supporting by the time IDP ended in 1982.

Extended and elaborated, the regional system set up in IDP has continued throughout CAEL's life. So did several of the original regional managers. Of the original ten, two went on to become members of the CAEL Board of Trustees, one became a vice-president, and two continued to serve as regional managers into 1984. Entrepreneurs, salespeople, change agents, the regional managers became the face of CAEL across the country. They were often the only contact some colleges, universities, and other organizations ever had with CAEL.

## Continuing Activities: Publications, Membership, and Assemblies

As soon as IDP began, CAEL embarked on a major publications program with the Jossey-Bass publishing house. Since the early 1970s, Jossey-Bass had been publishing inexpensive, quarterly "sourcebooks," often sponsored by an association in higher education such as the Association for Institutional Research. The several "sourcebook" series consisted of short and practical paperbound books designed to reach senior administrators and faculty members, as well as staff in student services, institutional research, and personnel in community colleges.

With large guaranteed sales to CAEL at a substantial discount, Jossey-Bass began publishing New Directions in Experiential Learning in 1978 and continued to do so until 1983. The sourcebooks covered a range of topics in both sponsored and prior experiential learning—the characteristics of students, issues of costs and standards, program development, professional and graduate education, and work with sectors outside of higher education. The series provided CAEL with an outlet for systematic writing on many of its preoccupations over the period in which it was published, and it broadcast some of CAEL's agendas for the future. Under the overall editorship of Morris Keeton and Pamela Tate, whose time was covered out of IDP funding, it was also a way of bringing CAEL activists into the public eye and drawing people into CAEL's world. Through the life of the series, over twenty-five different people edited twenty issues and more than 150 wrote chapters.[5]

The staff in Columbia, under the supervision of Diana Bamford-Rees, was also carrying out CAEL's membership activities. In 1977-78, 313 colleges and universities belonged to CAEL. In 1978, CAEL introduced a new membership category, the "professional subscriber," at a cost of $35 for individuals. Institutions had a choice of joining for a yearly membership fee of $250 or $350 for additional benefits from IDP. CAEL's membership shot up in 1979-80 to a total of 329 institutional and 205 individual members, representing 447 different schools and other organizations. In subsequent years, institutional memberships declined while individual memberships either increased or held steady.

CAEL members seemed to be dropping in and out of the organization as it changed.[6] Administrators, particularly those with mid-level positions in admissions, innovative academic programs, and continuing education or extension programs, predominated among rank-and-file CAEL members. Six to seven percent of CAEL's members were drawn from college faculties, a smaller percentage than those who were senior

---

5. For a yearly listing of the editors and titles of the sourcebooks, see Appendix B.

6. For a biennial review of CAEL membership from 1974 to 1986, see Appendix C1. Forty percent of the colleges and universities were members for only one year in the six measured years, while five percent were members each measured year.

administrators.[7] This is not unusual in associations in higher education, whose membership fees and conference expenses can be picked up out of administrative budgets. Faculty members, who have limited access to such budgets, are more likely to join disciplinary associations. CAEL's skew to administrators meant that the faculty members and junior staff, who worked in field studies programs and other sponsored experiential learning programs, did not become as involved in CAEL as those in programs for adults.

CAEL's institutional members were quite representative nationally, although a higher proportion were public, large universities. CAEL did not draw members from the most competitive universities and colleges in the country, which in any case are a small percentage of the total number of institutions of higher learning in the United States. Rather, CAEL institutions came from the mainstream of higher education—institutions that exercise limited control over student selection. Surprisingly, CAEL institutions have enrolled a lower proportion of part-time students than is the case nationally.[8]

As it had in 1976 and 1977, CAEL put on two national assemblies in 1977-1978. Starting in 1979, it dropped to one national assembly and a series of regional ones each year. Attendance at the national assemblies in the early years of the new CAEL ran to over 300; then it declined for several years to under 250 before rising again. Regional assemblies drew twice the number who attended the national assembly.[9]

## Facing the Intractability of Higher Education

"Institutional change is the ultimate agenda of the CAEL IDP," Morris Keeton wrote in his first annual report on IDP

7. See Appendix C2 for associate (individual) members' positions.

8. See Appendix C3-8 for characteristics of institutional members.

9. For biennial attendance at national assemblies, see Appendix C1.

to the Kellogg Foundation. He continued, "It is also the most difficult. . ."[10] The IDP staff was finding it close to impossible to get institutions to submit the work plans required for their participation. Getting the work plans was something like "punching a feather mattress," Keeton wrote. IDP's original notion that leaders of institutions participating in IDP would develop a long-range plan and then get training for those who would carry out the plans did not work out. "Things did not happen so sensibly," Keeton observed. He sketched a more common scenario:

> The institution is urged by an activist faculty member in experiential learning. . . to join the CAEL IDP. The academic vice-president approves membership, and permits the activist to report to CAEL. . . a three-year institutional plan. The plan for the first year includes sending four faculty members plus the activist to an orientation workshop provided by the CAEL cluster. They return to campus "fired up" and "rarin' to go," but encounter misgivings and resistance from fellow faculty members and key department heads. The academic vice-president withholds further support until a consensus can be reached.[11]

Keeton concluded that acceptance of experiential learning would take "months or even more than a year." CAEL would be required not only to provide the technical and moral support to activists within institutions; it would also have to develop a practical theory about change in higher education. Over the next year, Keeton struggled to articulate a theory of change which could direct IDP and CAEL more generally.

Keeton focused, first, on key actors inside colleges and universities. In the beginning there are usually a few committed

10. "A Report. . .", 1978, p. I-19.

11. "A Report. . .", 1978, pp. I-15 and I-16.

people who give their time and energy to an innovation. Then, an administrator with authority begins to see the value of the innovation. At this point, the key actors try to build broader support. This is a critical moment, when CAEL could play an important validating role: "Technical assistance for assuring quality can make the difference for institutions between remaining an interested bystander or. . . becoming actively and effectively involved in ongoing program development."[12]

Keeton began to see institutional development as occurring in four stages, each with different implications for the way IDP should operate. The first stage, heightened interest, can also generate heightened opposition to experiential learning. CAEL's role was to try to overcome opposition through training and development. The second stage, experimentation, implements a program on a trial basis. Unusual caution at this point signals the absence of strong political support. "Too small a scale of 'experiment' may fail to be cost effective or to generate the appropriate 'market'. 'Faint heart never won. . . '"[13] The third stage is one of expansion and refinement. More people are involved, modifications are made, and demands on staff become greater. As in the heightened-interest stage, this stage benefits from training programs. Finally, the fourth stage of institutionalization brings the impulse to export the innovation and train others to use it.

As CAEL continued to work with institutions under IDP, Keeton began to recognize the variations in their responses:

> In some complex institutions with many colleges and programs, the successful program is quickly adapted and

---

12. "A Report. . .", 1978, p. I-17.

13. "The Maturing of the CAEL Institutional Development Program, A Report to the Kellogg Foundation on Progress During 1978-1979", 1979, p. I-5.

> adopted in colleges other than the one or two leading the innovation. In others, however, the innovation pervades the initiating college, but is walled off from others. In some institutions with successful. . . programs, there is a strong sense that much remains to be learned. . . so faculty and administrators seek help in training, consultation, and sharing of ideas. . . In other institutions, the innovation becomes dogma, and the achievement is seen as completed; so such institutions may drop out of CAEL, feel no further need for innovation. . ., and see themselves as superior to the struggling practitioners in other places. . . . [A]n institution may sometimes depend almost entirely upon the energy. . . of one or two individuals for the acceptance. . . of its experiential learning programs. In other places. . . the developers may have elicited a pervasive appreciation of, and competence in, experiential education.[14]

These complexities were frustrating to Keeton and the CAEL cadres. Change was much slower "than would seem warranted or possible." Accustomed to fast action and tangible results, Keeton proposed that CAEL "re-examine carefully what strategies, techniques, resources, or other factors would result in a significant increase in the rate of needed development. . . The enormity of the problem. . . dramatically exceeds what we would have predicted earlier."[15]

By 1979, Keeton was saying that even the ample support of the W.K. Kellogg Foundation would not "change the character of institutions in the way we advocate," especially in a period of retrenchment.[16] He put a dollar figure on the situation. Assuming an average of 400 institutions for each of

---

14. "The Maturing. . .", 1979, pp. I-16 and I-17.

15. "The Maturing. . .", 1979, p. I-18.

16. Morris Keeton, Report to the 10th National CAEL Assembly, Minneapolis, Minn., November 8, 1979. In *Proceedings: CAEL National Assembly,* p. 22.

the five years of IDP, the average amount of money spent per institution came to just over $716 per year. This was a rough and ready figure which spread the total Kellogg grant, which at that time came to $1,432,000 with various additions, over five years. Kellogg eventually granted close to $2 million for IDP, and fewer than 400 institutions participated each year, so Keeton's figures underestimate the potential expenditure for each institution. In fact, IDP allocated a median of $435 to participating institutions in the first year; in the second year, allocations went up to $1500; in the third year, down to $947.

Difficulties in securing written plans led CAEL to drop it as a requirement by the end of the second year of IDP. The original goal of 200 institutions as full participants over three years or more, and its subsequent expansion to 500, also turned out to be somewhat unrealistic. While many more than 500 people were trained in IDP workshops and conferences, 481 different institutions were participants in the original IDP design in the first three years. Of these, 139 joined the program in its first year and stayed with it for all three years; another 111 participated for two of the three years; 231 participated for only one year.[17]

It was probably inevitable that not all institutions would stay with IDP for three years, given competing demands and the marginality of experiential learning. There were also reasons internal to CAEL that interfered with the continuity of IDP. To carry out its work with hundreds of colleges and universities, CAEL developed a regional system. Operating essentially as volunteers, the regional representatives were given the freedom to carry out the program pretty much as they wished. Some worked with individual institutions; others worked with clusters. Some offered a varied menu of activities; others helped institutions develop coherent plans. This flexibility, a hallmark of

17. For a list of the participating institutions in IDP from 1977 to 1980, see Appendix D.

CAEL—and required in any case by the variety of institutions, actors, and regional representatives involved—undermined the impact of IDP.

## Trying out New Arenas

The give-and-take between IDP's original goals and the realities of institutional change, as well as developments within CAEL itself, forced CAEL to look to different arenas for advancing its agenda. In part, this was a matter of survival. One of the intentions of the original IDP proposal was to help CAEL become financially self-sufficient. Colleges and universities interested in experiential learning were unlikely to provide a solid enough financial base for CAEL. Indeed, some of them had become spoiled by CAEL's success in raising money; they expected CAEL to pay them for participating in its projects. In its search for an effective base, CAEL spun out between 1977 and 1982 ten other projects and countless other activities besides IDP: computer-based counseling, international contacts, national and state policy, telecommunications, portfolio assessment for the military, information services for adults, professional development, the outcomes of higher education, an evaluation of black colleges, and alternative ways to assess the potential for college. These projects clarified the fact that, while CAEL existed to advance experiential learning in colleges and universities, it also saw itself as an advocate for learners. CAEL's constituency could potentially encompass the whole population, because only a fraction of those engaged in lifelong learning were doing so within colleges and universities.

The idea of reaching beyond colleges and universities received a boost with the arrival of John Strange as Associate Executive Director of CAEL, whose primary task was to direct

IDP. Keeton needed someone to work with the regional managers. He had met John Strange on one of his trips to New England, and they had hit it off almost instantly. For a while, Strange served as a regional manager. With the additional support from the Kellogg Foundation for the regional system and several other grants, Morris Keeton expanded the central staff from ten in 1977-78 to fifteen in 1978-1979, and to eighteen in 1979 through 1981. John Strange came with this expansion.

He was the man of the hour. A Southerner with a doctorate in political science from Princeton, Strange had taught at Livingston College in the late 1960s, when it opened at Rutgers University as a new college committed to social change. In 1972, he moved to the University of Massachusetts at Boston as the founding dean of a new college for older working adults, the College of Public and Community Service. Strange and Keeton were a study in contrasting styles. Keeton was never without a tie; Strange was hardly ever with one. Strange loved conflict; Keeton avoided it. Perhaps twenty years younger than Keeton, Strange seemed two generations younger. Yet the two men had much in common: a need for challenge, supreme energy, and a passion for making deals.

For the three years he served on the staff of CAEL, "Strange became like a Pied Piper," as one associate put it several years later. Travelling the country to visit the regional managers, he created a sense of excitement wherever he went. Before Strange's arrival, the regional managers did not identify much with one another. He funneled money to them for workshops, set up formal meetings, gave parties, created rituals. While Strange was at CAEL, and even for a while after he left, the regional managers became a cohesive presence within CAEL, in some respects more loyal to Strange than to Keeton.

Keeton's disappointment with the slowness of change in colleges and universities contrasted with Strange's excitement about developments outside of higher education. Strange was particularly taken with the growth of computers and video-disks, but he was also struck by the potential for CAEL of the expansion of organizations outside of traditional colleges and universities either providing or seeking educational services. CAEL itself had already been approached by the American Heart Association and several other organizations about the assessment of prior learning. Strange encouraged Keeton, who was already well-disposed, to respond to these developments.

CAEL would have to develop alliances "with new partners who share our visions and with whom we can work out mutually reinforcing agendas," such as accrediting bodies, employers, and other associations. Keeton fixed on the state level as an important arena, in which alliances would not only be "paper agreements," as they often are, but "negotiation of plans of work, state by state, in which CAEL and its new partners pool resources, work out shared. . . objectives, and define a set of specific activities which we will jointly undertake."[18] He could point to two examples. A CAEL pilot project stimulated the state of Pennsylvania to allocate additional money to community colleges for enrollment earned through the recognition of prior learning. In Florida, the State Department of Education, which participated in IDP from the beginning, was using funds allocated for vocational and technical education to disseminate program mapping, one of CAEL's enduring concerns.[19]

### *Project LEARN: Computer-Based Counseling*

Project LEARN, whose main activity was to develop and disseminate computer-based counseling to adults, first brought CAEL in touch with the "new partners" with "reinforcing

18. Morris Keeton, Report to the 10th Annual National CAEL Assembly, 1979, p. 22.

19. See Marvin Cook (1978a; 1978b; 1980; 1981) for a description of program mapping.

agendas" that Strange and Keeton sought. The route was a difficult and circuitous one that went back to the first CAEL. From the very beginning, Keeton and others recognized that the use of portfolios for assessing experiential learning was a costly, labor-intensive affair.[20] These costs stood in the way of its widespread adoption. In conversations with a neighbor in Columbia, Larry Fedewa of Control Data Corporation, Keeton had come up with the idea of using the computer to lower costs. Would it be possible, Fedewa and Keeton wondered, to develop computer software that would help adults organize their experiences in order to make claims for credit for prior learning? Keeton called Winton Manning, the vice-president at ETS who had worked most closely with the first CAEL, for help.

Manning suggested that ETS and CAEL join forces. ETS had a computerized career guidance system for minicomputer, the System of Interactive Guidance Information (SIGI), that it wanted to adapt for microcomputer. Many years in the making with support from the Carnegie Corporation, the National Science Foundation, and ETS overhead funds, SIGI was the handiwork of Martin Katz, a respected theorist of guidance and counseling, and his associate Warren Chapman. ETS contacted Kellogg for funding to adapt SIGI, but the foundation's staff was reluctant to put more money into SIGI. Concerned about dissemination and use, Arlon Elser suggested that ETS get together with CAEL.

CAEL and ETS entered into a series of negotiations about their mutual interests. SIGI had been developed for younger students; CAEL wanted to make sure that adults could use it. At this point, the logic of Keeton and Fedewa's idea began to unravel. Martin Katz did not think it would be a simple matter to adapt the software for CAEL's purposes. He insisted that

20. For discussions of the costs of assessing experiential learning, see the chapter by Weathersby and Henault in Keeton (1976), Knapp (1981), and MacTaggart (1983).

SIGI be used in a particular order, and that it be used to help individuals clarify their values before providing educational and occupational guidance. CAEL, on the other hand, wished to allow for a variety of paths through the program, as well as the opportunity for users not only to examine values but also to inventory interests, skills and prior learning.[21]

In spite of these disagreements, Keeton submitted a proposal to Kellogg for what would become Project LEARN (Lifelong Education, Assessment, and Referral Network). Negotiations among Kellogg, CAEL and ETS were protracted. Finally, in October 1979 Kellogg selected CAEL as the fiscal agent for LEARN. A two-year $1 million grant would support ETS for adapting SIGI to microcomputer and, under subcontract with CAEL, for the development of software for adults. CAEL would deploy its regional system to market computer-based counseling for adults. Five clusters, led by regional managers, were to operate in Michigan, Ohio and Kentucky, California, Florida, and Oregon.

This arrangement, which put its offspring, CAEL, in the driver's seat, was hardly agreeable to ETS. By the time the grant came through, Katz and his staff had taken on another large project and could not work on the development of software for adults. CAEL did not want to wait that long. John Strange suggested that CAEL turn to JoAnn Harris-Bowlsbey, a counseling psychologist from Towson State University who had designed a computerized guidance program for younger students called DISCOVER. Harris-Bowlsbey signed a contract with CAEL to develop ENCORE for adults along the lines that Keeton had intended in his first conversations with ETS.

While the sparks continued to fly between CAEL and ETS over the conception of the project, money, and the selection of Harris-Bowlsbey, Strange and Keeton saw computer-based

---

21. See *Counseling Psychology*, vol. 11, no. 3, 1983 for a full issue devoted to computer-based counseling.

counseling as an opportunity for CAEL to raise money. According to the original IDP proposal, CAEL was to generate $215,000 a year in unrestricted monies by 1981-1982. Yet only approximately $125,000 had been produced from membership fees, assembly registration fees, and the sale of publications and other materials. John Strange came up with the idea of selling a "CAEL Box," a micro-computer manufactured by On-Line Computers, to go with ENCORE and other computer packages. CAEL purchased seven computers and trained the regional managers to use them with SIGI and DISCOVER while the adult versions of both programs were being developed.

Several of the regional managers resisted LEARN. They could not understand how computer-based counseling would advance CAEL's agenda, nor did they feel prepared to deal with the new technology and carry it to their regions. As time passed, however, much of the resistance dissipated. The cooperation of the regional representatives was critical for the implementation of LEARN. A system of regional conferences and workshops offered training in computer-assisted assessment, guidance and technology. This training reached beyond colleges and universities to other sectors. In Ohio, for instance, a CAEL representative trained employees of the Cleveland Clinic Foundation, a large specialty health care organization, in the use of SIGI for career development within the company.

### *International Contacts*

CAEL also began developing connections with people interested in experiential learning outside the United States. Nine Canadian colleges and universities participated in IDP, five of them (Georgian College, Lambton College, Mohawk College, St. Clair College, and Sault College in Ontario) for three years. While Canadian educators were familiar with sponsored experiential learning activities like internships, they were less acquainted with the assessment of prior learning. There was a natural connection, however, with "distance learning," which was common in some rural regions of Canada.

CAEL offices regularly received visitors from Western Europe and Australia. Close connections with Great Britain began to develop in the early years of IDP through Norman Evans, a graduate of Cambridge University and former Principal of Bishop Lonsdale College of Education. First at the Cambridge Institute of Education and then at the Policy Studies Institute in London, Evans had been trying to find ways to increase access to higher education in Britain, especially for adults. Well-connected to political, industrial and educational leaders, Evans saw improved educational opportunities for adults as a way to solve some of the social and economic problems facing his country.

He began to publish articles in *The Times* of London and was working on a book on the connections between education and work (Evans, 1981) when he paid a visit to the United States to look into programs for adults. Quite fortuitously, he found out about CAEL and met John Strange. He and Strange became friendly, and they began talking about how to gain acceptance for the assessment of experiential learning in Great Britain. It did not seem far-fetched to think that they could be successful, perhaps more successful than CAEL. In contrast to the United States, England has a centralized educational system with a developed adult and technical sector and—most importantly—a well-elaborated assessment system separated from instruction. Given its economic problems, Great Britain could be more ripe for CAEL's approach than the United States.

The Kellogg Foundation awarded CAEL $25,000 in 1980 to cover some of Evans' activities in Britain and to bring influential educators and policy-makers to the United States for visits to institutions and programs for adults, in particular those that assessed prior learning. In turn, U.S. educators and policymakers would visit Great Britain to learn about quality control and accountability.

What became known as "British CAEL" moved quickly. By the time IDP ended, two national agencies with the greatest relevance to adult learners—the Council for National Academic Awards (CNAA), a degree-granting governmental body that establishes standards for non-university courses and programs, and the Further Education Unit (FEU)—were on their way to endorsing the assessment of prior learning for adults. Several polytechnics and colleges had agreed to run pilot projects in the assessment of prior learning for CNAA, which was to publish a review of institutional procedures for the admission of "unqualified" applicants. FEU published *Curriculum Opportunity*, a description of opportunities for the accreditation of experiential learning. Goldsmiths' College of the University of London and Thames Polytechnic had established programs in the accreditation of prior learning, and several other colleges were designing assessment courses. Heriot-Watt University was developing a way to identify the skills and knowledge for civil engineering at the graduate and professional level. The Commission for Racial Equality and the Inner London Education Authority were planning to run programs on experience and learning in several colleges, and another program was being planned for unemployed blacks in London.

### *State and Federal Policy*

CAEL's involvement in the policy arena dates back to 1978. The Coalition for Alternatives in Postsecondary Education (CAPE), an organization of seventeen non-traditional organizations, grew out of several meetings with other reform organizations convened by CAEL. CAEL had heard that ETS was attempting to undermine its standing with other reformers by describing CAEL as an interloper. In an effort to counter this view, CAEL helped CAPE's organizers financially and organizationally. CAEL's own role, as distinct from CAPE's, was not to lobby but to help CAPE with its joint projects and policy papers, and provide assistance to governmental and other agencies.[22] CAEL wanted to influence policy, but within careful limits. Within those limits, CAEL provided organizational advice and supported some people who were active in CAPE by commissioning papers and setting up task groups. CAEL contributed significantly more money than any of the other members of CAPE, but cut back its financial support in 1981.

Robert Sexton, active in CAEL from the beginning and a member of the Board of Trustees from 1976 to 1981, served as General Secretary of CAPE. In a series of working papers, CAPE worked out several revisions of the Higher Education Act of 1965, which would be coming up for reauthorization in 1980. Of particular concern to CAPE and CAEL were requirements that limited students' access to federal financial aid if they were enrolled for less than half-time, did not study for a standard degree, or were enrolled in non-traditional institutions or programs. CAPE also lobbied for changes in legislation that would support life-long learning, a more meaningful educational definition of the federal work-study program, support for experiential education in the Fund for the Improvement of Postsecondary Education's charter, an Urban Grant Universities program, and extensions of cooperative education. Several of CAPE's proposals were included in both the House and Senate versions of the Higher Education Reauthorization Bill, particularly the matter of financial aid for part-time students.

22. Ken Fischer, "Prospectus: To create a 'Washington Presence' for the Reform Movement in Postsecondary Education," 1978, p. 1. See also memorandum from Morris Keeton to the CAEL Executive Committee, May 4, 1978, p. 1.

A key figure linking CAPE to CAEL's later public policy activity was Michael Goldstein, an attorney who was Vice-President for Community Affairs at the University of Illinois at Chicago Circle. Goldstein was active in groups promoting sponsored experiential learning. He was also in the founding group of CAPE. Goldstein subsequently became CAEL's attorney and spearheaded CAEL's activities in Washington and the states.

Just as CAPE was winding down, Keeton began talking to Jerry Miller, head of the Institutional Relations and Academic Affairs office of the American Council on Education (ACE), under which the Office on Educational Credit and Credentials was located. Miller had served for a short time on the Steering Committee of the original CAEL and remained CAEL's principal liaison and supporter at ACE. Miller urged ACE to pay more attention to the interests of adult learners. The governmental relations office of ACE at first opposed asking Congress for financial aid for part-time learners, the key issue in CAPE's platform, because it feared it might pit colleges and universities with many part-time students against those with few. It also feared that pushing support for part-time students might jeopardize financial aid for full-time students. Keeton and CAPE argued against these positions. Eventually, the argument that support for adults—who comprised the majority of part-time students—promised economic payoffs for the nation convinced the governmental relations office, and it changed its position.

This was a great victory for CAEL, CAPE, and other advocates like Miller within higher education associations. While there are many specialized higher education organizations, ACE is the organization that speaks for higher education as a whole.[23] Largely because of Miller's advocacy, ACE decided to establish the Commission on Higher Education and the Adult Learner.

23. See Bloland (1985) for a discussion of higher education associations.

With contributed staff time from ACE and $25,000 from the Kellogg Foundation in a supplement to IDP, Keeton became chair of the commission in 1981 and Goldstein its policy coordinator. The commission would represent the interests and needs of adult learners when amendments to the Higher Education Act were being considered. With the access and expertise provided by the governmental relations staff of ACE, the commission worked with regional leaders in education, labor, business, and government. CAEL provided the leadership of Keeton, and soon after the University of Maryland's University College loaned William Warren, a former colleague of Keeton's from Antioch, as the day-to-day coordinator of the commission. The regional organization was deployed to disseminate a series of public policy papers and organize regional conferences.

*Telecommunications*

The Ohio regional managers, Betty Menson and Barry Heermann, were especially adept at capitalizing on the sophisticated media technology at Ohio University. In 1982, CAEL and Ohio University co-sponsored a national teleconference transmitted by satellite to more than ten cities on the theme, "New Connections for Learning in the 80's," focusing on alliances among educators, business, and labor. Representatives of the various sectors were interviewed on television for an hour. The subject was then discussed in gatherings across the country, followed by an hour of telephone inquiries. Four hundred seventy-seven people took part in the program.

## *Portfolio Assessment for the Military*

One of the regional managers, Tom Little, was the prime mover in CAEL's developing relationship with the military. Since World War II, the military had administered a program of examinations for college credit that members of the armed services could take on a wide range of subjects. More recently ACE made credit recommendations for military training courses. The unit which administered these programs, the Defense Activity for Non-Traditional Education Support, had heard about CAEL's work and issued a report in 1981 recommending that the assessment of prior learning by CAEL member institutions be recognized. This opened the door for the use of portfolios and other non-examination assessment of experiential learning in the military.

## *Information Services for Adults*

In 1979, on John Strange's initiative, CAEL began for the first time to deliver services directly to learners. With a two-year grant from the Fund for the Improvement of Postsecondary Education for $136,728, CAEL began a program called the CAEL Learner Services. This program disseminated information about experiential learning programs available to adults. Directories of opportunities for prior learning credit were compiled and distributed. A toll-free telephone number, which operated at its height for twelve hours on weekdays, connected callers with CAEL staff in Columbia, who provided information to anyone who called. They shared much more than information. Callers often received coaching about how to deal with institutions and how to present their needs for the assessment of prior learning.

The program brought much media coverage for CAEL, particularly among women. *Good Housekeeping* and *Woman's*

*Day*, for example, published short informational announcements about the program, describing how women ''who never started college or who dropped out'' could have their life experiences assessed for credit toward a B.A. at colleges CAEL could recommend in their area. CAEL's number and calling hours were listed, and a copy of a college profile from CAEL's *Directory of Opportunities for Prior Learning* was offered free. These articles generated thousands of calls. The Learner Services Program was a great stimulant and source of stories to the CAEL staff, who could see the significance of what they were doing every day through the lives of the callers—something that could not be said for the slow, indirect effects of IDP. By the time Learner Services ended in February 1982, CAEL had dealt with 16,000 people.

### *Professional Development*

A grant of $80,000 for one year from the Fund for the Improvement of Postsecondary Education enabled CAEL to work directly with faculty members and administrators in experiential programs to develop learning contracts for their professional development similar to those they would use with students. It turned out that the most likely participants were reluctant to participate in the program, in part out of fear that they might be penalized by their institutions for not carrying out their learning contracts. The program was adapted to allow faculty and staff to use the program materials privately.[24]

### *The Outcomes of Higher Education*

A $110,000 grant for two years from the Lilly Endowment permitted CAEL to continue struggling with the question which

24. See discussion in ''The Maturing. . .'', 1979, p. I-7 and Mark Cheren (1979).

had animated the original CAEL project—how to clarify the outcomes of traditional as well as non-traditional education. This project had its greatest impact in Florida.

*An Evaluation of Black Colleges*

Morris Keeton was commissioned independently to evaluate the Ford Foundation's program of grants to private black colleges from 1972-1979. With CAEL as fiscal agent, he received a grant of $337,000 for fees, administration, and expenses over a three-year period.

*Alternative Ways of Assessing Potential for College*

Keeton's work with black colleges led to the Student Potential Program. An initial grant of $25,000 from the Lilly Endowment and an additional $25,000 from the Ford Foundation enabled CAEL to explore new ways to assess the potential for college among those who would not qualify on the usual grounds.

## Relationships with Other Organizations

CAEL's ability to raise substantial amounts of money from foundations and win support from ACE demonstrated Keeton's success with mainstream organizations. The second CAEL continued to represent quality in the assessment of experiential learning. It disseminated Willingham's *Principles of Good Practice in Assessing Experiential Learning* and other CAEL materials, and it trained faculty and program administrators in their use. This was particularly important as CAEL ran into opposition to credit for prior learning from three powerful groups—accrediting associations, graduate schools, and registrars.

A flurry of articles in the national press about cheap "credit for experience" led several influential people, including Kenneth Young, the head of the Council on Postsecondary Accreditation (COPA), a newly-formed accreditation watchdog, to "view with alarm" the whole movement which had given rise to CAEL. Morris Keeton responded immediately with an offer to discuss the matter. In making his argument, Keeton walked a tightrope. On the one hand, CAEL was not an accrediting body, nor did it want to be one. Yet some institutions were using the CAEL name to attract older students and to give legitimacy to their prior learning programs. When such incidents came up, Keeton wrote stern letters to the offenders and to the appropriate accrediting organizations about CAEL's displeasure. He could not control how schools granted credit, experiential or otherwise. If, however, he could enlist the accrediting associations to endorse CAEL's approach to the assessment of prior learning, it would strengthen his position.

At the end of IDP's first year, CAEL set up an advisory board on quality assurance with fifteen members—a mix of college presidents and other senior administrators, deans, and faculty members. It also appointed a task force with representatives from the organizations most likely to influence accreditation decisions: the regional accrediting associations, ETS, the American College Testing Program, ACE, the Education Commission of the States, and COPA. If he did not know them already, Keeton contacted key people in the major accrediting associations personally to convince them of CAEL's seriousness about quality. He developed a particularly cordial relationship with Kay Anderson, the head of the Western Association of Schools and Colleges; in 1978 he spoke to its conference on standards, and CAEL continued to work with that association in later years.

A jointly sponsored task group on the transcribing and transfer of credit with the American Association of Collegiate Registrars and Admissions Officers (AACRAO) looked into ways of recording experiential learning on transcripts, which led eventually to endorsement by the non-traditional programs subcommittee of AACRAO. Within a year, the negative statements from COPA had been replaced with endorsements of CAEL's *Principles of Good Practice.*[25] The new head of COPA, Richard Millard, agreed to work with CAEL to reach state regulatory agencies, regional accrediting bodies, and institutions state by state to promote quality in experiential learning programs.

The Council of Graduate Deans had issued a statement opposing credit for prior learning at the graduate level and discouraging the use of sponsored experiential learning as well. After more than two years of work, CAEL organized an invitational conference jointly with ETS and Harvard's Institute for the Management of Lifelong Education in 1981 for sixty-six leaders in graduate education. By means of original case briefs and historical and policy papers, the question of experiential education was put in the context of trends in graduate education. Some of the papers were published in 1980 as a New Directions book entitled *Expanding the Missions of Graduate and Professional Education;* it was edited by Frederic Jacobs, chairman of the Harvard program, and Richard Allen, former director of the Division of Arts and Sciences at the Johns Hopkins University Evening College.

Even after one or two years as an independent organization, CAEL's access to some of the most important organizations in higher education was extraordinary. The connection with ETS, despite the conflict over computer-assisted counseling, remained basic. CAEL had almost instant lines to foundations and federal agencies. Contacts with ACE began early. Even

25. See Silverman and Tate (1980).

before CAEL became an independent organization, Morris Keeton and Jerry Miller, former head of the Office on Educational Credit and Credentials, had a close relationship. Miller and his successor, Henry Spille, were advocates for CAEL in the higher councils of ACE.

CAEL's ties to other organizations were often structured through "task groups," which it defined, organized, and supported from its various grants. The task groups followed a characteristic pattern: they were often set up in response to problems that people in the field would ask CAEL to tackle. The task groups, little think-tanks composed of representatives from most of the major sectors and organizations in higher education, were asked to suggest solutions. Their work would often appear sometime later in a CAEL publication, a new project, or a policy statement. Invariably, individuals would turn up who might become involved in other CAEL work.

In 1978-1979, for example, CAEL set up task groups on cross-cultural education and experiential learning. Another CAEL task group worked with ETS on computer-assisted services; a second on experiential education for health professions; and a third on the financial aid needs of adult and part-time learners. A task group was being prepared to work, jointly with several national unions, on higher education and labor, while another was being set up to explore alliances between employers and institutions.

CAEL also had a continuous, if ambivalent, relationship with organizations outside the mainstream in higher education. These organizations fell into two general types: those concerned with the education of adults and those concerned with experiential education. Relationships were tense with some of them because some of CAEL's activities competed with theirs. CAEL trod lightly among the dozens of organizations speaking for adults—organizations representing college and university extension programs, continuing education, adult development, adult literacy, distance learning, education and training groups outside of higher education, and specialized continuing education groups. From time to time, CAEL worked with one or another of these organizations, most notably the National University Continuing Education Organization and the American Society for Training and Development. But relations between CAEL and practitioners in adult education have been distant overall.

Relationships between CAEL and the dominant experiential education organization, the National Society for Internships and Experiential Education (NSIEE), have been closer. Led by younger people, NSIEE is a grassroots association of practitioners who are more likely than CAEL members to work directly with students located in or near academic departments. In contrast to CAEL, it has not succeeded in raising large amounts of grant money. It has a small central staff, and is strongly oriented to the needs of its members. As a former NSIEE president who knows both organizations described the differences between the two, "CAEL is a powerhouse fueled by one person, Morris Keeton. NSIEE is a participatory democracy with all its slowness and lack of focus."

CAEL has drawn several NSIEE activists into its orbit and contributed others from its own ranks. Pamela Tate, co-editor with Morris Keeton of the New Directions in Experiential Learning series, a member of CAEL's Board of Trustees, and a moving force in CAEL's later work with unions, came to Keeton's attention through her work in sponsored experiential learning. A former president of the Society for Field Experience Education, NSIEE's predecessor, Tate's connections with sponsored experiential learning guaranteed a balanced representation of topics and authors from both sides of experiential learning. Jane Permaul of UCLA, Urban Whitaker of San Francisco State, and John Duley of Michigan State University, all active in the original CAEL project and all members of the board, also came from the world of internships and other campus-based programs.

CAEL and NSIEE have worked together intermittently over the years. In 1980, Tom Little, a regional manager who has been active in NSIEE as well, secured a $120,000 grant from FIPSE for a joint project on institutionalizing sponsored experiential learning programs. NSIEE and CAEL have coordinated their policy activities through Michael Goldstein, legal counsel to both.

NSIEE has constantly pressed CAEL and Morris Keeton to do more in sponsored experiential learning. There was also a concerted effort from within CAEL to make sponsored experiential learning a central item on its agenda. In 1979, a task force on sponsored learning argued that the distinction between sponsored and prior experiential learning be dropped, on the grounds that it was confusing and unnecessarily divisive. Instead, they wanted CAEL to include experiential learning in all curricula. The Task Force made sixteen suggestions for bringing more attention to sponsored experiential learning. In 1981, Jane Permaul, John Duley, and Robert Sexton retired from the board. CAEL continued to try to cover sponsored experiential learning after their departure, although not to the extent that they and NSIEE wished.

## Enter the Board

In 1979, the Board of Trustees changed Morris Keeton's title from Executive Director to President and John Strange's title from Associate Executive Director to Vice-President. They also shifted CAEL's statute of incorporation from New York to Washington, D.C. This occasioned changes in CAEL's by-laws, whereby terms of board members were more limited than they had been originally. This was a way of opening up what was fast becoming an insiders' group. The colleagueship that came with serving on the CAEL board was important to those who served, most of whom came from the sectors in higher education to which CAEL most appealed: programs for adults and experiential learning in non-elite institutions. CAEL gave them a sense of being in on something worthy and exciting, especially as the money poured in.

Through their involvement on the board and as consultants and workshop leaders, several CAEL activists moved on to major administrative positions. This was especially true for women and minority group members. Larraine Matusak, for example, moved from the University of Evansville, where she was dean of alternative programs when she joined CAEL, to the presidency of Thomas A. Edison State College a few years later. George Ayers, the black Academic Vice-President from Metropolitan State who substituted for David Sweet on the Steering Committee of the original CAEL project and later became chair of the Board of Trustees, moved to the presidency of Chicago State University.

In the early years, the board was more than willing to give Keeton his head. The board met only once a year, and events in the fast-moving world in which CAEL traveled happened more quickly than that. Under Arthur Chickering, who became chair in 1980, the board began to press Keeton, Strange, and the regional managers for greater clarity about CAEL's mission. Some members asked questions about CAEL's scope and the need to set priorities among its many options. At a special meeting in June 1979 backed up by questions raised by external evaluators of IDP, the board debated whether CAEL served institutions or individuals:

> On the question of audiences, John Duley suggested that we need attention to both institutions and individuals. . . He asks whether we can serve individual learners and also develop new alliances and work effectively without diffusion. . . Art

> [Chickering] recalled 1974 discussions on whom we would serve, with a focus on improved services to students and helping a diverse group of students to articulate with institutions. . . Myrna [Miller] felt that we had not been directly involved with students, but had. . . become our own quality assurance program, with a thrust primarily through institutions. Morris [Keeton] suggested that students were the primary concern, but that the persons directly involved with CAEL were teaching professionals, measurement specialists and educational administrators. . . A question also raised was whether the term "institution" includes only colleges and universities, or whether it should also include corporations, the military, etc., in alliance or in alternate roles.[26]

Related to the question of focusing on institutions vs. individuals was the matter of computer-assisted services. When Project LEARN appeared without their knowledge, several members of the board exploded. Was CAEL turning into a money-grubbing operation? Would it take attention away from experiential learning? Would there be a loss of CAEL's human touch? Was CAEL running too far ahead of its members on campuses? There was some general anxiety that the regional managers, who were accountable to Morris Keeton and John Strange, and not to the board, were moving faster than their campus constituencies.

The question for the board was what kind of organization CAEL should be. Was it a membership organization, a think-tank, a research and development center, or a general improvement organization like FIPSE? One underlying issue was how much attention the CAEL staff should pay to the needs of members.

---

26. Minutes of the Board of Trustees meeting, June 18-20, 1979, p. 9.

> Bud [Hodgkinson, the external evaluator of IDP and LEARN] noted that we are staffed with very bright and entrepreneurial people, both at the staff and regional level and are moving rapidly, while the on-campus people are confronting the day-to-day problems and may feel that management is far in front of the membership. Bob Sexton related this concern to CCAS [CAEL Computer-Assisted Services] and further concerns on starting without institutional commitment.[27]

The board agreed that service to institutions and to members of CAEL must be maintained, but it did not say what the staff should give up in order to do this. There was a fundamental ambivalence here. Essentially, the regional managers, Keeton, and Strange were free to pursue their various projects as long as the staff back home in Columbia took care of the members. Work on LEARN went ahead, despite the misgivings of several board members and regional managers. After all, who could argue with success? CAEL's success was their success.

But so was CAEL's failure their failure. The bubble burst in 1980-1981. This was the year when both IDP and LEARN were ending and several grant applications had been turned down. The regional system, which by the end of IDP was to be producing revenue, instead was still dependent on the Columbia office for funds. Memberships had declined, and publication sales were lagging. The board discussed the possibility of establishing a credit line at the Prudential Bank, so that loans of a minimum of $100,000 at a time could be taken out against orders for the CAEL Box. A proposal to do so was passed by a vote of eight for, two against, and three abstentions. Keeton, attuned to consensus, asked for an explanation from those who voted against or abstained:

> There was a brief discussion, the nays pointing out that the

27. Minutes of the Board of Trustees meeting, June 18-20, 1979, p. 11.

> proposal involves a major shift in CAEL's focus of activity, that it is not clearly within the field of experiential learning, and that it puts CAEL into the business of selling hardware for profit.[28]

It turned out that the CAEL Box was more expensive than comparable systems. ENCORE, the computerized guidance program for adults being developed under contract with JoAnn Harris-Bowlsbey, was not compatible with other hardware and was not being marketed well in the regions. Keeton and the board decided that CAEL could not improve the situation enough to make money from the sale of the CAEL Box and ENCORE software. While this was going on, Harris-Bowlsbey had begun negotiations about a job at the American College Testing Program (ACT). In the summer of 1982, CAEL contacted ACT to take over ENCORE. The arrangements were completed a few months later, after ACT agreed to incorporate ENCORE into a new version of DISCOVER, which would then be useful for adults. Some of the funding for the new DISCOVER came from a Kellogg grant to CAEL for JoAnn Harris-Bowlsbey, which went to ACT when she became an officer there.

The board was also concerned about the administration of CAEL. John Strange had returned to the University of Massachusetts-Boston, from which he had taken a leave to work with CAEL, and was no longer carrying major administrative responsibilities. A search for an executive vice-president in 1981 resulted in the appointment of George Pruitt, an experienced administrator who was vice-president at Tennessee State University. Pruitt arrived in August of 1981, on the assumption that CAEL had a promising future and a solid financial base. Quite soon after his arrival, CAEL ran into serious financial difficulties. Its reserves were too low to sustain the number of staff members it had acquired with IDP, LEARN and other

28. Minutes of the Board of Trustees meeting, July 10, 1981, p. 6.

programs. Without additional grant money, it was clear that CAEL would have to cut back drastically.

Pruitt reported the situation to the board, forcing it to look seriously at the way CAEL did its business. He presented them with a pared-down budget, which they accepted. He and Keeton cut the staff in Columbia from fourteen to eleven. By December 1982, the staff had dropped to nine. The hope of a large grant for an expansion of LEARN meant that CAEL could not reduce the staff too drastically while it was waiting to hear from Kellogg.

Just as the situation was beginning to settle down, Keeton was diagnosed as having ulcers, along with a kidney infection, flu, and general exhaustion. Heavily medicated, depressed, Keeton could not call on his usual reserve of energy to deal forcefully with CAEL's problems. The board reacted with shock to Keeton's vulnerability. As one of them put it later, "the magician had lost his power." Keeton was still ill when Pruitt reported to the board in the summer of 1982 that CAEL was "fragile and precarious, but marginally solvent."[29] In December, Pruitt resigned to take the presidency of Thomas A. Edison State College, a position vacated by CAEL board member Larraine Matusak when she moved to the W.K. Kellogg Foundation. Pruitt later served CAEL as a member and then as chair of the board.

## Accomplishments of the Second CAEL

Vice-President Robert Kinsinger of the W.K. Kellogg Foundation was a strong proponent of evaluation at the foundation at the time that IDP was approved. He insisted that

29. Minutes of the Board of Trustees meeting, June 27-29, p. 9.

CAEL, along with other organizations Kellogg funded, build in an extensive evaluation of its activities. This CAEL did on its own and with the help of a three-member external evaluating team headed by Harold Hodgkinson.

Keeton recognized that numbers were in CAEL's favor. When IDP ended, twenty New Directions sourcebooks had been published or were in process. Dozens of other publications were also produced—surveys of experiential learning opportunities around the country, regional directories of institutional programs, syllabi for faculty members and administrators engaged in experiential learning programs, learning materials, literature guides, modules, slide/tape shows, casebooks, and commissioned papers. By 1983, IDP had underwritten over 80,000 training days for faculty and staff. As the years passed, a large percentage of those who came to CAEL workshops were not members of CAEL, yet another indication that CAEL's reach was broad. Harold Hodgkinson, the external evaluator of IDP, set about to check on some of CAEL's claims and found that they were accurate. He concluded that CAEL was clearly a "quantitative success" which had left a formidable "paper residue," one that equaled the productivity of the original CAEL project.

The regional system was useful in disseminating new CAEL projects quickly. As LEARN, the Commission on Higher Education and the Adult Learner, the Student Potential Program, and other projects came along, the regional managers passed news of them through newsletters, workshops, conferences, and informal conversations. Regional managers actively shaped CAEL's agenda as well. Several programs bubbled up from the regions. Teleconferencing, which began in Ohio, took on a national reach. Work with the military, which began in Virginia, had the potential to lead to other projects. Projects with workers and employers in Philadelphia, Kansas City, and Great Britain held promise for future work with organizations outside of higher education.

The regional managers adapted CAEL's menu of activities to their local terrain and personal interests. For example, the regional manager in the Pacific Northwest region, Valerie McIntyre, put on workshops at a variety of colleges and universities in Oregon. While she found it difficult to get institutions to work together, she was instrumental in moving half of Oregon's 42 colleges and universities to award credit for prior learning. In contrast, the regional managers for the East Central states, Barry Heerman and Betty Menson, found in their home state of Ohio that there was a good deal of experience with cooperative education but less openness to awarding credit for prior learning. In the South Coastal region, Joseph Keller had quite a bit of success in linking CAEL's work on the assessment of prior learning and program mapping to pressure from state agencies in Florida on public institutions for accountability and for greater coordination between community colleges and universities.

By the early 1980s, the assessment and crediting of prior learning had expanded rapidly. In 1974, the original CAEL project had located just over forty prior learning assessment programs, a figure that was probably a bit low even at that time (Willingham, Burns, and Donlon, 1975). Four years later, Knapp and Davis (1978) turned up a total of 211, of which 143 used portfolio assessment. Materials collected for CAEL directories published in 1981 showed 525 programs. In 1980, the Office on Educational Credit and Credentials at ACE sent out a questionnaire to find out how colleges and universities were dealing with extra-institutional learning. Almost all of the more than 2000 institutions that responded awarded credit, most commonly by examination. Almost 1,100 said they had portfolio programs for prior learning assessment. Major research universities and selective liberal arts colleges were less likely to use portfolios than other types of institutions.[30]

In a survey commissioned by CAEL for the external evaluation of IDP, the American College Testing Program estimated that about 1.2 million quarter hours of college credit were awarded for prior learning during 1980-81, in contrast to approximately 690,000 quarter hour credits in 1973-74. About 12% of the credits awarded in 1973-74 were based on portfolios and other individualized approaches; by 1980-81, 31% were awarded in these ways.[31] Adults using individualized assessment of prior learning increased from some 4000 in 1974 to more than 30,000 in 1981. CAEL's publications publicized this finding, and CAEL took credit for what it called a "spectacular" success.[32]

CAEL could not claim full credit, however, for the rapid growth of prior learning assessment. Other forces brought adults into higher education during CAEL's existence—the efforts of other organizations to legitimate learning throughout life, a restructuring in the economy which required that workers be trained for new jobs, the entry of vast numbers of women into the job market, and the need on the part of many colleges and universities to attract adults to make up for declines in the traditional college-age population. With more adults came more pressure for recognizing what they had already learned. While it over-estimated its unique role, CAEL could legitimately take credit for a general awareness of the importance of this issue, and for individualized approaches to assessing experiential learning, the portfolio approach especially.

---

30. Office on Educational Credit and Credentials, American Council on Education, memorandum to the Committee on Educational Credit and Credentials, September 9, 1980. A re-analysis by Virginia Smith (1987) shows a breakdown of portfolio use by state and institutional type.

31. American College Testing Program, "Survey of Prior Learning Assessment Programs at American Colleges and Universities", 1982.

32. "The CAEL Institutional Development Program, 1980-1981: A Turning Point", 1981, p. 9 and p. 14.

Whatever the portion of credit CAEL deserved, it seemed fairly clear that IDP, and CAEL's programs generally, had important results for individual students, faculty and staff. CAEL's emphasis on outcomes and assessment was something new in higher education; Hodgkinson concluded that "it may be one of the most important things that CAEL has accomplished on college and university campuses."[33]

CAEL called on its regional network for vignettes and case studies for the external evaluation. This produced an impressive, if unsystematic, collection of accounts from adults in prior learning assessment programs, as well as case studies of four states and a variety of institutions. The most affecting accounts were from learners, especially women. In his report on IDP, Hodgkinson quoted from an account written by a fifty-year-old wife and mother:

> As a result of taking the lifelong learning program, I found a new appreciation of the value of my time. The portfolio preparation was not an easy feat. It required lots of hard work and many long hours. . . To realize that I wrote 150 pages in my "spare time" proved to me that I can really accomplish anything I want to if it means enough to me. The portfolio is tangible. I can hold it up in my hand and say, "See what you did, Miriam, when you made up your mind to do it". . . All the knowledge and insight I had obtained began to fall into place. I was recording this onto paper, and my portfolio was coming to life—it was my life.[34]

---

33. Hodgkinson, Harold L. "External Evaluation of CAEL's Institutional Development Program", July 1982, p. 3. For a general discussion of outcomes and assessment, see Grant (1979).

34. Hodgkinson, Harold L. "External Evaluation. . .", 1982, pp. 3-4.

CHAPTER THREE

## CAEL's Future

CAEL demonstrated, yet again, that it could tackle serious issues in higher education with energy and competence. Its regional structure, *ad hoc* task groups of prestigious members, and productivity established the second CAEL almost immediately as a formidable force for change in higher education. Freed from the constraints of the first CAEL, Morris Keeton created an organization that was a textbook case of an innovative organization—decentralized, collaborative, entrepreneurial, hard-working, flexible (Kanter, 1983; Peters and Waterman, 1982).

But Keeton's entrepreneurial talent was double-edged. On the one hand, it brought money and a reputation for imagination to CAEL, when both were in short supply in higher education. On the other hand, Keeton's success as a fund-raiser may have interfered with a serious attempt at achieving the original goals of IDP and, thus, of CAEL into the future. It is clear that Keeton, with strong encouragement from John Strange, had changed the strategy for institutional change sketched in the original proposal for IDP. It turned out that change in colleges and universities was a slow and tedious process of breaking down the resistance of faculty members, enlisting the often shaky support of administrators, and moving resources to programs and people at the margins.

This was hardly the sort of project that would bring CAEL to the margin which foundations and entrepreneurs find more interesting—the cutting edge. Keeton saw fairly soon that CAEL's fortunes as an organization and as an influence for change might lie in working with organizations outside of higher education. As IDP ended, Keeton was drawing into CAEL's orbit people who were already doing this. The Compact for

Lifelong Educational Opportunities (CLEO), a consortium of colleges and universities in Philadelphia, became allied with CAEL when its executive director, Lois Lamdin, and associate director, Pamela Tate, also became regional representatives of CAEL. CLEO acted as a broker, bringing area businesses in need of courses together with colleges and universities which could teach them. Another consortium which played a brokering role, the Kansas City Regional Council for Higher Education, was also drawn to CAEL as its president, Larry Rose, and vice-president, Russell Wilson, joined CAEL's regional network. In Great Britain, a consortium of institutions including the Council for National Academic Awards, Marks and Spencer, the National Coal Board, and a regional health authority were exploring the use of "academic brokerage" between corporations and educational institutions to accredit learning from work and employer-sponsored courses.

Harold Hodgkinson strongly endorsed this direction. On the basis of his own experience with educational programs in profit and non-profit companies, Hodgkinson argued that CAEL should do more with the corporate sector and non-profit organizations outside of higher education. Many of the organizations were already running their own education and training programs, and CAEL could help them as well as other organizations.

It was quite possible that this effort would eventually make CAEL self-sufficient financially, but in the meantime it would need support, and the most likely source was the W.K. Kellogg Foundation. Of the many foundations that have supported CAEL from its founding onwards, the Kellogg Foundation fits CAEL best. Since its establishment in 1930 by the breakfast cereal manufacturer, the Kellogg Foundation has been interested in innovation and its dissemination in agriculture, education and health. It supported the expansion of community colleges and university-based residential continuing education centers.

Kellogg was especially sympathetic to land grant universities and regional institutions.

The behavior of foundations, the Kellogg Foundation in particular, had a subtle effect on CAEL's decision to move into other, more glamorous projects. Foundation officers must justify to their colleagues and boards the projects they recommend for funding. IDP obviously gave a boost to the newly-independent organization, but IDP was based on the understanding that CAEL would become self-supporting. The W.K. Kellogg Foundation's support for CAEL was far from automatic. Foundations make a distinction between supporting a program and supporting an organization. When the proposal for the extension of LEARN was circulated at Kellogg, several officers asked whether CAEL was too dependent on the foundation for its existence.

Arlon Elser needed evidence that CAEL was having an impact. While it was obvious that CAEL was expending a good deal of energy training faculty and staff in experiential learning techniques, it was not clear that it was having an impact on institutions. Had CAEL stuck with its original IDP plan longer, would it have made more of a dent on colleges and universities? Probably not. There is a limit to the impact that an outside organization without much power can have on colleges and universities, even if it uses the full array of techniques in CAEL's repertoire. This reality, other allurements, and easier successes all conspired to push CAEL away from institutions. Instead, it sought its fortunes where it operated best: at the boundary between higher education and the larger society.

## CHAPTER FOUR

# Mobilizing for Action: The Third CAEL[1]

> CAEL's drive for infusing higher education with [its] concerns [has] a more significant purpose; viz., to transform the understanding and practice of collegiate and higher learning, within and outside of the academy, among adults of all ages. We mean to become the new establishment, not simply to co-exist with the old one (Keeton, 1984, p. 4).

In 1985, CAEL became the Council for Adult and Experiential Learning, signaling yet another phase in its short history. The breadth of ambition expressed in the change of name was the culmination of a period of frantic activity under a second phase of LEARN.

In the early winter of 1983, the W.K. Kellogg Foundation awarded CAEL a three-year grant. CAEL in Columbia and the regional offices, funded directly for the first time, would have $4 million to develop a "national network of adult learner services." Negotiations for the second LEARN occurred at a time of transition for the Kellogg Foundation. Vice-President Robert Kinsinger was retiring, and the foundation was assessing its own funding decisions. Despite their reservations about continuing to support CAEL and difficulties in understanding the project, Elser's colleagues at the foundation agreed to award the largest grant to an educational program ever given by the

1. Sources for this chapter include annual reports on the second phase of LEARN for 1983, 1984 and 1985; a variety of numerical summaries; final reports on the Student Potential Program and the College and University Options Program; programs and announcements of the Commission on Higher Education and the Adult Learner; training materials for the Student Potential Program, the College and Universities Options Program, and the Commission on Higher Education and the Adult Learner; and *CAEL News* from 1983 to

W.K. Kellogg Foundation. The grant for the second phase of LEARN was made, however, on the understanding that it would be the last to CAEL.

There was a direct connection between the first and second phases of LEARN, both philosophically and organizationally. Throughout the first LEARN, regional managers resisted marketing SIGI or DISCOVER. The imposition of a single agenda, whatever its content, went against CAEL's grain. From

---

1986. Interviews with the following people provided additional material:

*Diana Bamford-Rees* (See Footnote 1, Chapter 2)

*Barbara Bonner,* registrar, Center for Robotics Technology, regional manager for Chicago in 1983-84.

*JoAnn Harris-Bowlsbey* (See Footnote 1, Chapter 3).

*Anne Bryant,* executive director of the American Association of University Women, chair of the CAEL Board of Trustees, 1985-86.

*Harriet Cabell,* (See Footnote 1, Chapter 2).

*Ruth Chapman,* regional representative of CAEL in the Mountains and Plains region, 1982-86.

*John Duley* (See Footnote 1, Chapter 3).

*Mary Ellis,* vice-president of CAEL, 1985-.

*Arlon Elser* (See Footnote 1, Chapter 3).

*Thomas Emling,* staff member of the College for Lifelong Learning at Michigan State University, regional representative in the Great Lakes region, coordinator for Michigan of the College and University Options Program, 1984-85.

*Norman Evans* (See Footnote 1, Chapter 3).

*Kathleen Gallay,* Director of the Core Program at CAEL, former director of the Student Potential Program and CAEL Institutes, 1984-86.

*Elinor Greenberg,* regional manager for the Mountain and Plains region of CAEL and program administrator of the Pathways to the Future project involving Mountain Bell and the Communication Workers of America.

*Barry Heermann,* executive director of Higher Education Management Institute, regional manager for the Ohio/Kentucky region, 1978-85.

*Harold Hodgkinson* (See Footnote 1, Chapter 2).

*Cynthia Johnson,* associate professor, Department of Higher and Adult

the beginning, Morris Keeton could not demand that regional managers do his bidding, nor was it his style to make such a demand. Working for little or no pay, the regional managers had to be highly committed to CAEL and its aims. That commitment depended on being left to do what was appropriate in each of their regions.

The tension between the need for a coherent national

---

Education, Teachers College at Columbia University, director of the Counselor Training Component of LEARN.

*Morris Keeton* (See Footnote 1, Chapter 2).

*Joseph Keller* (See Footnote 1, Chapter 3).

*Joan Knapp* (See Footnote 1, Chapter 2).

*Lois Lamdin*, director of the Business Development and Training Center at Great Valley, former director of the Compact for Lifelong Educational Opportunities, regional manager for the Mid-Atlantic region, 1982-85.

*Thomas Little*, center manager, Richmond Technology Enterprise Center, regional manager for the Maryland, Virginia, and Carolinas region, 1979-85.

*Larraine Matusak* (See Footnote 1, Chapter 2).

*Valerie McIntyre*, president, Brightwater Associates, regional manager for the Pacific Northwest, 1978-85.

*Betty Menson*, regional manager for the East Central states, 1978-85.

*Myrna Miller* (See Footnote 1, Chapter 2).

*Jerry Miller* (See Footnote 1, Chapter 2).

*David Novicki*, associate professor and counselor at the Counseling Center, Michigan State University, regional representative of CAEL in the Great Lakes region, 1983-86.

*Maurice Oliver*, director of Special Programs, Division of Continuing Education, University of New Hampshire and long-time member of CAEL.

*Anita Palsgrove* (See Footnote 1, Chapter 3).

*Jane Szutu Permaul* (See Fotenote 1, Chapter 3).

*Robert Press* (See Footnote 1, Chapter 2).

*George Pruitt* (See Footnote 1, Chapter 3).

*Larry Rose*, president of the Kansas City Regional Council for Higher Education, regional manager for the Midwest region.

*Barry Sheckley*, assistant professor, Department of Higher, Technical and

program and the decentralized regional system was expressed in the design of the second LEARN. Each of LEARN's elements solved some problem either within the foundation or within CAEL. To deal with reluctance at the foundation to continue funding CAEL as an organization, the second phase of LEARN instead funded the regions directly, with "CAEL Central" as coordinator. Resistance of the regional managers to a uniform program meant that the project, if it were to succeed, would have to be broad enough to permit a variety of activities. The regional managers wrote and negotiated their own agreements with Kellogg. Yet it was not enough that they just be lined up side-by-side; they would need something to hold them together. The notion of a "national network" provided both conceptual and organizational coherence.

---

Adult Education, School of Education, University of Connecticut, regional manager for New England.

*Susan Simosko,* national network coordinator for Project LEARN at CAEL, former director of Testing and Assessment, Thomas A. Edison State College, former regional staff member in New Jersey.

*John Strange* (See Footnote 1, Chapter 3).

*Marilyn Stocker,* associate executive director for program development, Office of Continuing Education, University of Chicago, coordinator for the College and University Options Program in the Chicago area in 1984-85.

*Margaret Talburtt,* partner, Formative Evaluation Research Associates, Ann Arbor, Michigan, and evaluation consultant to the W.K. Kellogg Foundation.

*Pamela Tate* (See Footnote 1, Chapter 3).

*Clark Taylor,* professor at the College of Public and Community Service, University of Massachusetts-Boston, long-time member of CAEL.

*Raymond Vlasin,* professor of resource development, regional manager in the Great Lakes region, 1983-85.

*Urban Whitaker* (See Footnote 1, Chapter 2).

*Russell Wilson,* vice-president of the Kansas City Regional Council for Higher Education, regional representative of CAEL in the Midwest region.

*Jacque Wright,* director of Project LEARN at the Center for the Study of Higher Education, Memphis State University and regional manager for the middle South, 1981-85.

## CHAPTER FOUR

# The Second LEARN

Recovered from his bout of illness, Keeton bounced back in full force. He was no longer satisfied to see CAEL ''seed'' higher education, the metaphor with which he had launched the Institutional Development Program in 1977. By 1983, he meant CAEL to become the ''new establishment.'' What could this possibly mean? Was this a bit of hyperbole, the sort of exaggeration to which captains of innovation are often moved? Project LEARN would carry the weight of Keeton's ambitions.

LEARN began with three major goals. The first was ''increased and improved learner services.'' The second goal focused on the institutional developments within colleges, universities, and other organizations that were necessary to make those services possible. And the third goal, ''an altered system of adult learning which accommodates the enhanced services and revitalized institutions,'' would relate the various disparate efforts.[2]

The three goals had a series of sub-goals, thirty-three overall in the beginning, which in turn had their own sub-goals. Goal 1, improved learner services, included much of the work CAEL had already pioneered: information and advocacy services, prior learning assessment, sponsored experiential learning, and better ways of recognizing potential for college work. Several new items were added: continuing professional education, alternative credentialing systems, and informal learning.

---

2. Morris Keeton, ''Building a National Network,'' Document 2A-15, March 2, 1982, p. 1. Many of the ideas behind a transformed learning system built upon the work of Herman Niebuhr, founder of the Compact for Lifelong Educational Opportunities and good friend of Arlon Elser. Arguing for a ''new paradigm'' in education, Niebuhr lays out these ideas in *Revitalizing American Learning* (1984).

Sub-goals under the second goal of institutional development echoed old preoccupations: improved missions and assessment of services for adults in colleges and universities, greater cost effectiveness in learning options, better quality assurance, faculty development for the use of emerging technologies in education, the development of publicly stated minimum standards for degrees and "demonstrable value added," financial aid packages for adults, and participation by consortia and systems of colleges and universities. Newer, but still recognizable from the earlier CAEL, was helping to build alliances with employers, labor and voluntary associations by laying on training programs for administrators on ways to design such alliances in the areas of CAEL's expertise.

The sub-goals under the goal of an altered system of adult learning were more difficult to conceptualize than programs and practices. It was clear that Keeton was groping for a way to express the underlying motif of LEARN, which included changes in awareness, shifts in policy, and new configurations of organizations. "Awareness among learners of the importance and feasibility of *self-directed lifelong learning*" and "awareness of the paradigm shift in learning among individuals and institutions" were early expressions of the awareness aspect of the third goal. "[C]hanges in public policy, institutional development, professionals' commitments, and learners' expectations and patterns of learning" addressed the policy aspect. And "cooperation among educational associations, public and voluntary agencies, institutions of higher education, and business," along with "a model of a nationwide system of learner services for adults" compared to what was available in 1983 adumbrated the organizational aspect of the third goal.[3]

What did it mean to say that the second phase of LEARN would build a national network of services for adult learners?

---

3. Morris Keeton, "The Purposes and Goals of Project LEARN, Phase II," Document 5A-18, May 12, 1983.

How could such a task even be envisioned? It would take all of Morris Keeton's rhetorical skills to get across what this meant—and then, even regional managers who had worked in CAEL for several years would find it difficult to understand. It would be an even more difficult idea for less involved people. When it was understood, how could such an effort be carried out, especially by an organization as precarious as CAEL? It would take not only entrepreneurial energy, which CAEL had aplenty, but administrative know-how and political leverage, which were in shorter supply.

The second phase of LEARN was organized into twelve "clusters," which included Great Britain, a counselor training component, ETS, and CAEL Central. Funding for the regions went to the institutions where regional managers were already employed or could easily be located, or to CAEL Central when the manager was not at an institution. The institutions with regional offices included seven state universities, a private college, a community college, two higher education consortia, a policy research institute, and a regional educational laboratory.[4]

The main problem facing Keeton as conductor of this far-flung orchestra was how to get the players to harmonize. At first, he envisioned a rather conventional research and

---

4. Funding to the regions was as follows:

| | |
|---|---|
| CAEL Central | $999,600 |
| ETS | 629,284 |
| Counselor Training Component (Funding routed through the University of Maryland Foundation) | 228,535 |
| New England (Funding routed through the University of Connecticut | 105,000 |
| Middle Atlantic (Funding routed through the Compact for | 173,450 |

development operation, with CAEL Central as top management and the regions as workers. In an early memorandum, Keeton outlined what he called "the strategy of embedment," which consisted of six stages: choosing the innovation and assessing

---

| | |
|---|---|
| Lifelong Educational Opportunities) | |
| New Jersey (Funding routed through Thomas A. Edison State College) | 176,675 |
| Maryland, Virginia, and the Carolinas (Funding routed through Virginia State University Foundation) | 178,400 |
| Mid-South (Funding routed through Memphis State University) | 198,050 |
| South Coastal (Funding routed through Brevard Community College) | 258,500 |
| East Central States (Funding routed through Ohio University) | 260,000 |
| Great Lakes (Funding routed through Michigan State University) | 251,176 |
| Mid-West (Funding routed through Kansas City Regional Council for Higher Education) | 189,600 |
| Mountains and Plains (Funding routed through Loretto Heights College in Denver) | 135,000 |
| Pacific Northwest (Funding routed through the Northwest Regional Laboratory) | 146,500 |
| Far West (Funding routed through the San Francisco State Foundation) | 140,900 |
| Great Britain (Funding routed through the University of Maryland Foundation) | 50,000 |

its prospects, clarifying the core invention and generating working models, gaining legitimacy, technical development, dissemination, and orchestration.[5] CAEL Central would be responsible for choosing, clarifying and developing the innovations that would be part of LEARN, working with the regions in legitimating them, and orchestrating the whole effort. The regions would be largely responsible for implementation.

Recent writers on innovation have pointed out that the assumption of a clearly defined, simple innovation is not usually correct, especially when it comes to innovations in education (Munson and Pelz, 1981). LEARN collected dozens of innovations, from computer software to complex relationships among organizations. Writers on innovation (Munson and Pelz, 1981; Rogers, 1978) have also shown how even a single, relatively simple innovation is shaped and adapted by users. While all of the regional managers were expected to demonstrate and implement certain common innovations—SIGI and DISCOVER, for example—they adapted the way they were disseminated according to their local circumstances.

Innovation theorists have argued, further, that the view of innovation which sees it as emanating from the center to the periphery underplays the creativity, resistance, and adaptability of the periphery (Schon, 1971). The regions had already generated activities and projects that were picked up by CAEL as a whole. At the same time, even though they were expected to become increasingly self-sufficient they were dependent on CAEL Central for funding. The second LEARN changed this. While Morris Keeton advised the regional managers in their dealings with Kellogg and helped them write proposals, the grants were between them and Kellogg. With the additional money from Kellogg and the independence that came from direct funding, the regions were even more likely to spin off in their

5. Keeton, "The Strategies of Project LEARN," memo 5-19, January 18, 1983, p. 1.

own directions in the second phase of LEARN. Instead of clones, the regions became glosses on CAEL.

*The Regional Staff*

The glosses were fine, as long as they were on the same texts. What would these be? At first, confusion reigned. Almost anyone could propose a regional project for Morris Keeton to review. Keeton blanketed the regional managers with a blizzard of memos and loose-leaf binders of numbered goals, each with their numbered sub-goals and sub-sub-goals, deadlines, and responsible people. Between trips, conferences and office work, he issued papers on policy and strategy. The regional managers had to practice triage on their clamoring tasks; only a few were full-time on LEARN and even the ones with twenty-twenty vision could not read as fast as Keeton wrote.

Keeton made himself available to the regional managers days, nights, and weekends. He spent a good deal of time on the telephone with them. At first, he paid more attention to the communication between CAEL Central and the regions than to communication among the regions. Building social relationships among people had never been his forte; while he inspired great personal loyalty in the people with whom he worked, they were more likely to be committed to him than to others in CAEL. Without John Strange, who had built a sense of community among the regional managers when he was vice-president, the regional managers did not have as strong a sense of common identity in the second phase of LEARN as they had earlier.

Even a skilled organizer would have found the task daunting. By temperament and profession, the regional managers were an independent lot. There were more regional managers to bring together in the second phase of LEARN. Between 1981 and 1983, the number of regional representatives grew from twelve to nineteen. Most of the new regional managers and the people who worked with them had not been much involved with CAEL before. Their attachment to CAEL and to Morris Keeton, therefore, was lower and more instrumental compared to that of the older regional representatives. There was a perceptible, but not openly discussed, split between novice and veteran regional staff. Even though there were more new regional representatives in 1983 (eleven) than there were holdovers from two years before (eight), newcomers had a hard time getting integrated. As several of the newcomers noted, there seemed to be an "ingrown" quality about CAEL. Old-timers, on their side, talked about the newcomers the way older siblings talk about the new baby: "Where did *he* come from?" they would ask. "Morris has a new favorite now."

The cohesiveness among the regional managers that had existed earlier was becoming strained by differences within the group. The proportion of women increased from a third to a little over 40% from 1981 to 1983. In a group where people over forty predominated, the newcomers included some younger people. In 1981, half of the regional managers held tenure track or regular administrative appointments in colleges and universities; in 1983, a little over one-third did. This was due, in part, to an increase in the number of regional representatives who worked in consortia and other independent organizations.

Because it could not pay regional people for their time, CAEL was more a beggar than a chooser. Like the old-timers, the newcomers talked about how they had been drawn into CAEL accidentally. By this, they meant that they did not apply for a job; rather, they were recruited as if they were joining a social movement or a club. Some of the liveliest accounts from regional participants were about how they had become involved in CAEL. Some of their stories, in order of seniority:

**Joseph Keller** has been at Brevard Community College in Florida for more than twenty years. He represented his college at a meeting of the first CAEL project, where Keeton issued a request for proposals from clusters of institutions that wished to work with CAEL. Keller helped establish a cluster in Florida and, as CAEL became independent, his involvement escalated from representing CAEL in Florida to representing CAEL in other Southern states.

**Valerie McIntyre** had just completed a doctorate in higher education administration at the University of Oregon when she became a member of the Oregon State Board of Higher Education. She was directing a project on alternative delivery services for education when Morris Keeton called her to set up a meeting for him in the state about CAEL's work. He then asked her to become a regional manager for CAEL in 1978.

**Betty Menson** was working at Ohio University in student services when the original CAEL project was founded. She took a job with a project in Ohio on the assessment of prior learning and began going to CAEL events regularly. *Barry Heermann,* the head of business administration and then dean at Sinclair Community College, was consulting with Ohio University on the project Menson headed. Keeton invited Heermann to become a regional manager in 1979, and Heermann said he would do it if Menson would join him as a co-leader. Menson agreed, and she worked with Heermann until 1986.

**Thomas Little** was campus minister at James Madison University working on a volunteer program for students, which he left to run a state-wide internship in Virginia. He met John Strange at a conference for recipients of FIPSE grants at the time that they both had grants in 1978. Strange invited him to become a regional manager, and Little accepted.

**Elinor Greenberg** was doing assessment of prior learning in the University Without Walls program at Loretto Heights College even before CAEL existed. In 1979, she left Loretto Heights to work on her doctorate. About the same time, she wrote a proposal to the Fund for the Improvement of Post-secondary Education which involved CAEL and the Council for the Advancement of Small Colleges as co-sponsors. In the fall of 1979, John Strange invited her to become a regional manager after the resignation of the manager in her region.

**Larry Rose** was teaching philosophy at Baker University when he first heard about the assessment of prior learning from the regional manager in his area at the time, Frank Christensen. As the president of the Kansas City Regional Council for Higher Education, he came up with the idea of having a cooperative program for the assessment of prior learning. Christensen encouraged him to write up a proposal under LEARN. When Christensen left CAEL, Keeton asked Rose to take over.

*Regional Activities*

The regional managers developed their own program of activities under LEARN.

**New England.** An ambitious regional manager, Barry Sheckley, came to LEARN with a newly-minted doctorate in adult education from the School of Education at the University of Connecticut, where he had been appointed recently as an assistant professor. While his position was considerably strengthened by the connection with CAEL and the substantial grant from the Kellogg Foundation, Sheckley was under a great deal of pressure to publish if he wished to be promoted. Much of his action in the region can be understood in terms of this situation.

New England had seen two ambitious regional managers before Sheckley. Peter Smith, founding president of the Community College of Vermont and a member of the original Steering Committee for the CAEL project, and John Strange. A number of institutions in New England have strong programs for adults, several of which predate CAEL itself. Beyond these and other schools with substantial enrollments of adults, CAEL is not well-known in New England. Perhaps because of their strength, the schools in the region have not worked together much. Smith and Strange, both busy with other major responsibilities, did not put enough time into their volunteer positions as managers to develop the New England region. For a time, Smith tried out an "educational auditing" program, in which people in the region visited each other's institutions, but this fizzled.

Sheckley did not set himself the task of reaching learners directly. He did not run an office to which adults could go for counseling and information, nor did he market SIGI and DISCOVER. Rather, he focused on the large number of experienced providers of educational services for adults. Under LEARN, he co-sponsored or helped organize regional conferences and institutes on economic development and the adult learner, and on theories of adult development. Drawing in people who had been active in CAEL for several years, as well as others, he started a network, the New England Action Research Network, to exchange ideas and to do joint research.

**Mid-Atlantic Region.** This region, which includes New York, New Jersey, and Pennsylvania, was coordinated by Lois Lamdin, director of the Compact for Lifelong Educational Opportunities (CLEO), and Susan Simosko, director of Statewide Testing and Assessment at Thomas A. Edison State College. Both concentrated their efforts in their own states. New Jersey was especially fertile ground for LEARN, since it already offered considerable services for adults. A unique institution founded in 1972, Thomas A. Edison State College assesses adults' learning for credit and advises them on educational planning, but does not offer instruction. The college was one of the members of the original CAEL project and has been connected with CAEL continuously through its presidents and some staff members.

Another unique institution, CLEO was a consortium of thirty-four colleges and universities in the Philadelphia region which banded together to attract more adult learners and provide services for them. CLEO offered HOTLINE information on the courses and programs offered by its members, provided career and academic counseling, and ran a regional center for assessing prior learning. It also organized faculty and staff development programs, marketed members' courses, and pioneered projects with non-educational institutions by providing on-site college fairs and career development programs.[6]

Given Simosko's and Lamdin's interests and the contexts in which they were working, they concentrated especially on providing information and counseling directly to adults, making use of their respective organizations as well as SIGI and DISCOVER. Their region also became a center for trying out several approaches to working with employees and employers. The Employee Action Program offered life and career planning in the context of a broader understanding of the impact on workers of technological and other social changes. Lamdin later developed a center to provide training courses and cultural services for employees in companies located at the Great Valley Corporate Center, a new industrial park outside of Philadelphia. These experiences shaped the work of LEARN with institutions outside of higher education, particularly the UAW-Ford College and University Options Program described later in this chapter.

**Maryland-Virginia-Carolinas.** From his base at Virginia State University, a predominantly black institution, Thomas Little focused more of his attention, until LEARN came along, on sponsored experiential learning. Closely connected to the National Society for Internships and Experiential Education, he worked under two FIPSE grants to train faculty to supervise internships and with a number of colleges and universities to institutionalize experiential learning. He was also linked to CAEL through another FIPSE grant on helping black colleges serve adults, a long-standing interest of Morris Keeton's.

---

6. CLEO disbanded in 1985. For an account of CLEO, see Gamson (1984).

While the South has seen its share of unusual educational experiments for at least fifty years, these experiments have not translated easily into programs for adults. This situation shaped what regional managers in the South could do within their LEARN grants. In Little's case, working to develop programs for the military was a way of providing services for adult learners in his region as colleges and universities moved slowly to do more themselves. When he began working with CAEL, Little found perhaps ten schools with programs that assessed prior learning for adults. Six years later, about forty schools had them.

**Mid-South.** This large region, which included Alabama, Mississippi, Louisiana, Tennessee, Oklahoma and Texas, fell to Jacque Wright to pull together. A specialist in adult development, Wright used her connection with the Center for the Study of Higher Education at Memphis State University to build credibility. The center was headed by Arthur Chickering, a member of the Steering Committee of the original CAEL project and former chair of the board of trustees. The faculty and graduate students at the center were known for their workshops and conferences on issues pertaining to adult education.

Wright focused primarily on developing networks of people working with adults, although she did not limit herself to promoting the assessment of prior learning. Instead, she helped with conferences sponsored jointly with the center at Memphis State.

**South Coastal Region.** A regional manager and dean since the beginning of the regional system, Joseph Keller was one of the most secure among the regional managers. The conservatism about adults and the assessment of prior learning throughout the South does not carry over to the community colleges in Florida, which have received support from the state for the development and use of portfolio assessment techniques and other "acceleration mechanisms." The state, in general, has been interested in projects initiated by CAEL. Program mapping, which began soon after the original CAEL project, took hold in Florida as the state invested over $1 million to train faculty members in all twenty-eight public community colleges to use the technique.

Keller began promoting the Student Potential Program as an alternative to heavy-handed efforts to impose conventional tests for entry to the freshman and junior year in public colleges and universities in Florida. In addition, Florida State University received funds from the W.K. Kellogg Foundation to operate a clearinghouse for computer-assisted guidance systems to do research and evaluation of SIGI and DISCOVER and to disseminate information about them.

**East Central Region.** Betty Menson, who graduated from Ohio University as an older returning student herself, and Barry Heermann operated in a more propitious environment than the regional managers in the South. Sponsored experiential learning programs and programs for adults have both flourished in Ohio, in innovative institutions like Antioch College and in traditional institutions like Ohio University. The other states in the region have also been quite responsive to developing programs for adults.

Menson and Heermann were able to capitalize on this environment. While many of the other CAEL regions set up advisory committees of representatives from area colleges, universities, and other organizations, the East Central region probably had the most active group. LEARN helped support a WATS line to dispense information about CAEL and programs for adults. CAEL was seen as a force in the region, and other groups turned to Menson and Heermann for advice and initiative. The state Board of Regents in Ohio, for example, contributed $5,000 to a conference sponsored by the Commission on Higher Education and the Adult Learner. A consortium of colleges and universities in Ohio came to CAEL for help in faculty development.

The East Central region was best known for its work in new technologies. Not only was it closely involved in the marketing of SIGI and DISCOVER, but it experimented with telephone conferencing with its regional advisory committee and other groups. The region also became the center for CAEL's efforts in telecommunications. Using well-equipped studios at Ohio University, Menson and Heermann, with the addition of a new regional associate, Patricia Dewees, put on yearly national satellite video teleconferences beginning in 1983. They also produced three courses for television on adult learning and development.

**Midwest.** Larry Rose is the president and Russell Wilson the vice-president of the Kansas City Regional Council for Higher Education (KCRCHE), a consortium of fourteen colleges and universities founded in 1962. Their involvement with CAEL began with the second phase of LEARN. While their region spanned Iowa, Kansas, Missouri, and Nebraska, much of their activity under the LEARN grant was with their consortium's members.

KCRCHE provided an ideal base for the dissemination of CAEL's work and for the development of new services for adult learners. When LEARN began, about three or four of the member institutions of KCRCHE assessed prior learning, although a larger number had programs for adults. Rose and Wilson focused on supporting the institutions doing assessment of prior learning, as well as encouraging other members to try it by putting on workshops and making materials available. They did the same for SIGI and DISCOVER. In the course of LEARN, Rose and Wilson opened the Center for the Assessment of Prior Learning with five member institutions to share assessment and counseling costs. They also used LEARN to publicize services for adults at adult learner fairs at shopping centers and on radio and television. Like CLEO, they began acting as brokers between businesses and higher education. This work later came into play when KCRCHE became the coordinator for the Kansas City region of the UAW-Ford College and University Options Program.

**Great Lakes Region.** The boundaries of this region were in flux. It was not clear whether Indiana would be included in the Great Lakes or in the East Central region. At one point, Illinois was included but Chicago was not. Responsibility for the region was confused in the minds of regional participants. Raymond Vlasin at Michigan State University remembered learning that he was to be a regional manager for the Great Lakes when he attended the first meeting of LEARN and later discovered that Barbara Bonner at the National College of Education in Chicago was regional manager for Illinois.

For most of LEARN, responsibility for the region resided at Michigan State University, where Vlasin was Dean of the College for Lifelong Learning until 1985. David Novicki, a psychologist with appointments in the Counseling Center and the College for Lifelong Learning, and Thomas Emling, a staff member in the College for Lifelong Learning with a background in sponsored experiential learning, had worked on the first phase of LEARN. They continued on the second phase.

Novicki and Emling focused on raising the awareness of people in their region about the potential of adult education for solving some of the economic problems facing the industrial Midwest. Central Michigan University operated a large external degree program for adults that enrolled people from across the country; Wayne State University had the Weekend College; and community colleges in the region enrolled large numbers of adult learners. But in the eyes of state policy-makers, union and business leaders, many colleges and universities, and the general public, higher education was still for kids.

Emling and Novicki spent a good deal of time networking. They set up meetings and conferences for policy-makers and for people who worked with adults. Novicki, whose interest in computers and counseling made him a good representative of the first LEARN, continued to ply the routes he had developed for SIGI and DISCOVER. He also became involved in the use of computers for communication. As the UAW-Ford College and University Options Program took shape, Novicki and then Emling became central actors in the strategic and large territory of Michigan.

**Mountains and Plains Region.** Based in Colorado but operating since the middle 1970s in a region that also spanned North Dakota, South Dakota, Utah and Wyoming, Elinor Greenberg focused her attention primarily on her home state. When she joined CAEL, she was already well-known around the state as the founding director of the University Without Walls program and as an advocate for adult education and women.

"CAEL" continued to be a serviceable acronym. In the Mountains and Plains region, CAEL was known as "Careers, Adult Education, and Learning." At the center located first at Loretto Heights College, a small formerly Catholic college for women in Denver, then at Regis College, a Jesuit men's college, Greenberg worked with Ruth Chapman, a researcher who had been working at Abt Associates. The Colorado CAEL center offered direct services to adults—materials, other print resources, and access to SIGI and DISCOVER. Beyond setting up this office, Greenberg and Chapman concentrated their efforts on building joint programs between educational institutions and non-profit organizations, many of which served or employed women: the Girl Scouts, the Red Cross, the PTA, the League of Women Voters, and the Junior League. Between 1982 and 1985, they also organized symposia for policy-makers, administrators and faculty members, including seven for the Commission on Higher Education and the Adult Learner. Soon after, Greenberg directed a CAEL program for the Communication Workers of America and Mountain Bell.

**Pacific Northwest Region.** Another large region, the Pacific Northwest included Alaska, Montana, Oregon, Washington, and various provinces of Canada. It was headed by Valerie McIntyre. The University of Oregon, Linwood College, and then the Northwest Regional Educational Laboratory, a federally funded program in Portland, provided McIntyre bases for her CAEL activities. Under the LEARN grant, she continued to do what she had been doing all along: speaking with adults on the telephone about learning opportunities in the region; advertising opportunities for adults on radio, television, and newspapers; running seminars, workshops and courses for adult learners; and doing research on the activities and impacts of programs for adults. She also held conferences for policy-makers and faculty members in the region's colleges and universities on the assessment of prior learning and other topics related to adult education.

When McIntyre began with CAEL, no institution in Oregon offered evening courses or credit for prior learning. Seven years later, almost every institution in the state did something to assess prior learning, and the Oregon Board of Education had formally recognized CAEL's approach to the assessment of prior learning.

**Far West Region.** Urban Whitaker was a veteran of the first CAEL project when he became a CAEL regional manager in 1982 as he retired from San Francisco State University. California took most of his time, although his territory also included Arizona, New Mexico, and Nevada, as well as Hawaii and Guam. Operating out of the Learning Center, his own independent non-profit organization located near the San Francisco State campus, Whitaker focused his work with LEARN on networking and the development of materials.

Whitaker had long been interested in sponsored experiential learning and faculty development, and he used his resources as a regional manager to promote both. Jointly with members of the National Society for Internships and Experiential Education, Whitaker helped organize conferences on experiential learning. At the same time, he called meetings and communicated with people in the whole region who were interested in adult education; this included putting on conferences with the Commission on Higher Education and the Adult Learner.

Whitaker's long-standing interest in training materials and media led to a video tape for CAEL on experiential learning and to "Bridging the Career Gap," a computer-based program for assessing and learning skills transferable to careers.

**Great Britain.** Norman Evans' work in Great Britain to promote the assessment of prior learning was incorporated into LEARN by appointing him a LEARN "liaison" in 1983. He received some money from the W.K. Kellogg Foundation, first in a supplement to the Institutional Development Program and then under the first phase of LEARN. He continued his program with a grant in the second phase of LEARN.

Evans conducted three rounds of activities. The Scholars Exchange program brought together academics, senior people from state agencies, and politicians in the United States and Great Britain. The assessment of prior learning was their first concern, but as time passed policies affecting adult learners as well as a range of questions about the relationship between educational institutions and economic development began to be discussed.

The second set of activities extended Evans' networking activities with leaders of key educational and economic organizations in Great Britain: the Council for National Academic Awards, the Manpower Services Commission, the Department of Education and Science, the Further Education Unit, the Coal Board, IBM, British Telecom, and special training programs for unemployed workers.

Evans' third set of activities centered on establishing a core group of British academics, some of whom he brought on trips to the United States. Located primarily in polytechnics and teachers colleges, these people began carrying out CAEL-like programs in their own institutions. As this work gathered momentum, the university sector began to take notice.

**Computer-Assisted Counseling.** With a separate LEARN grant under the second phase from the W.K. Kellogg Foundation, ETS completed an adaptation of SIGI for adults called SIGI PLUS. A few months before, JoAnn Harris-Bowlsbey had completed an adaptation of DISCOVER for adults, which incorporated some of the software for ENCORE developed in the first phase of LEARN. Funding from the second phase of LEARN allowed "DISCOVER for ADULTS" to be field tested by some of the CAEL regions and to be marketed by the American College Testing Program.

**Counselor Training Component.** Cynthia Johnson, an assistant professor in counseling and personnel services in the School of Education at the University of Maryland, was responsible for the Counselor Training Component. At the time that the first LEARN was beginning, she was engaged in a project at the University of California at Irvine using computers in career planning, especially for re-entry women and minorities. During the first LEARN she designed a training program for computer-assisted counseling with adult learners, which she used in workshops with faculty members and student services staff under the second phase of LEARN. She also distributed publications, video tapes, and other materials about computer-assisted guidance and worked with associations of student services staff as well as colleges and universities.

*CAEL Central*

While the regional representatives were carrying out their activities under the second phase of LEARN, so was CAEL

Central. These fell into four main categories: the assessment of experiential learning, state and federal policy, alternative ways of assessing potential for college work, and partnerships between higher education and other sectors.

**Experiential Learning.** CAEL continued to work on diffusing the assessment of prior learning and training people to do it. The assessment system developed by Larry Rose and Russell Wilson in Kansas City for their institutions was an important boost to CAEL in this area. CAEL commissioned Susan Simosko's handbook for students, *Earn College Credit for What You Know* (1985), which advised adults on how to prepare portfolios. As it had from time to time in years past, CAEL also organized a consultants' service on prior learning.

Training continued as well. There were always some sessions devoted to the assessment of prior learning at yearly assemblies, although the fraction was considerably lower during LEARN than in earlier years. Regional managers offered workshops on prior learning from time to time. Institutes, residential workshops held in the spring and summer to help raise unrestricted funds, always included at least one on prior learning and its assessment. The UAW-Ford College and University Options Program also trained faculty and staff from participating colleges and universities in CAEL's approach to the assessment of prior learning. A three-year grant from FIPSE for $275,000 to help thirty black colleges and universities develop educational services for adults included a strong training component, although prior learning was not as attractive to these colleges as other approaches to adult education.

Interest in prior learning was coming from several new quarters. The National Guard, whose officers were being required for the first time to earn B.A.'s, was interested in ways of accumulating academic credit for prior learning. The large numbers of people involved, plus financial support from the National Guard and the GI Bill, opened a potentially lucrative market for CAEL.

Morris Keeton and Susan Simosko spent several days consulting with educational officials in Quebec, after the province had decreed that all general and technical colleges—institutions similar to community colleges in the United States—would include the assessment of prior learning.

Norman Evans was making progress in Great Britain, as he continued to bring English educators and policy-makers to the United States, and vice-versa. In the spring of 1986, the Council on National Academic Awards (CNAA) announced the Credit Accumulation and Transfer Scheme, which allowed adults to receive academic credit for "earlier academic experience in any relevant training or experience" at work (Evans, 1986). A variation on Thomas A. Edison State College in the United States, this program would allow people to receive degrees through a combination of assessment and courses at several institutions or through enrollment in a single institution. Under the present system in Great Britain, transfer from one institution to another is difficult. The institutions offering degrees which fell into CNAA's jurisdiction—polytechnics primarily—stood to gain from this arrangement. Some universities which were not under the supervision of CNAA—the Open University, the University of London, Manchester University, and the University of Hull—were especially interested in the new program. Employers like British Airways, Xerox, British Telecom International, and others were attracted to the new program as a way of recognizing training they already provided to their employees.

CAEL continued to monitor the diffusion of prior learning assessment. After a hiatus of four years after surveys of the use of the assessment of prior learning around the country had been conducted by the American Council on Education and by CAEL through the American College Testing Program, Valerie McIntyre carried out a mail survey of colleges and universities in 1984. She found that over two-thirds of the responding institutions said that they offered credit for prior learning. These programs typically served a small number of students for a small number of credits: 51% said fewer than twenty-five students had received credits the year before; 71% said they awarded fewer than fifteen credits per student. National standardized tests like the Defense Activity for Non-Traditional Education Support, the College-Level Examination Program, Advanced Placement tests, and ACE's Program on Non-collegiate Sponsored Instruction, were most commonly used.[7] Local examinations designed by faculty members—"Challenge Exams"—were also popular. Portfolios were used by 37% of the institutions.[8]

CAEL continued to support its other original interest: sponsored experiential learning. Urban Whitaker collaborated with Experiential Learning, a group of faculty members, student affairs staff, and administrators from the nine campuses of the University of California system. Under a FIPSE grant, Thomas Little worked with the National Society of Internships and Experiential Education to institutionalize experiential learning programs. A grant from the Lilly Endowment allowed CAEL and the National Collegiate Honors Council, whose members are faculty members and administrators in honors programs, to hold seven joint events in 1984 and 1985 on the theory and practice of experiential learning.

**State and Federal Policy: The Commission on Higher Education and the Adult Learner.** The Commission on Higher Education and the Adult Learner was established by the

7. ACE's Program on Non-collegiate Sponsored Instruction recommends designated amounts and types of academic credits for formal training programs sponsored by business, industry, labor unions, professional and voluntary associations, government agencies, and trade and technical schools.

8. From "1984 Prior Learning Assessment Survey." Questionnaires were mailed to all colleges and universities in the U.S. About half (1,493) responded.

American Council on Education and administered by CAEL. Keeton chaired the commission and William Warren managed it. The commission was funded from several sources. In addition to grants of $80,000 from FIPSE, $123,000 from the Arthur Vining Davis Foundation, and $220,000 plus the value of Warren's time from the University of Maryland, the commission received $150,000 in LEARN funds for Keeton's time, staff and office support, as well as additional funds for conferences in the regions. Between thirty-five and forty members served as national commission members. The majority were senior administrators in colleges and universities, although about a third were from business, labor, higher education associations, and the public sector. As the commission's work gained momentum, leaders of these different sectors were also represented on regional bodies.

By focusing on federal and state policies, public attitudes, and institutional behavior, the commission hoped to promote the "new paradigm" which fueled LEARN's third goal, the transformation of the learning system. The commission found support for its efforts among people who were beginning to talk and write about the changing economy. Arguing that industrial jobs were shrinking and that service and technical jobs were expanding in the United States, the economy would depend more on the knowledge and talents of its population than it had in the past. Education and training were key ingredients in the successful transition to a service and technological society, especially for the adults currently caught in the shifting occupational structure. The commission embarked on a national campaign to publicize the connection between education for adults and economic development.[9]

In a position paper entitled "Adult Learners: Key to the

9. CAEL was influenced by the work of Anthony Carnevale (1982), an economist with the American Society for Training and Development. See also Spenner (1983), Adler (1986), Hirschhorn (1984), and Office of

Nation's Future'' (1984), the commission argued that an aging population and a restructured economy required that educational policy address five tasks: (1) helping unemployed workers become employable; (2) developing skills needed to cope with technological change; (3) eliminating illiteracy among adults; (4) providing equal access to education; and (5) developing citizens appropriate to an information-based society. It called for ''*a new policy in the federal government, the 50 states, and in the corporations and educational institutions: that adults be enabled to continue learning—regardless of their financial resources, ethnic and socio-economic status, age, and sex—long enough and effectively enough to be competent in adult roles and to contribute productively to American life*'' (Commission on Higher Education and the Adult Learner, 1984, p. 5, italics in original).

Extending the work that Michael Goldstein, CAEL's counsel, had begun with the Coalition for Alternatives in Postsecondary Education a few years earlier, the commission under Goldstein's continuing advice pressed for federal support of adult learning. It urged that grants be authorized for FIPSE to stimulate experimentation in adult learning services and that other grants help institutions establish programs for adults. It asked for a tax credit of 10% of the cost for businesses when they sent their employees to a postsecondary institution for training. It recommended that individual tax deductions be expanded to include all educational expenses, not just those directly related to the maintenance of present job skills. It proposed that there be tax credits for training in critical areas of need to the nation and the individual, an educational maintenance account like the Individual Retirement Account,

---

Technology Assessment (1984), especially Chapter 6, ''Education, Training and Retraining Issues.'' Elements of the argument began appearing in the higher education press. For example, see ''Change in America'' (1986), Cleveland (1985), and Wegmann (1985).

direct grants to needy individuals, and tuition vouchers for unemployed workers. It also recommended that Congress pass new legislation requiring that adults facing structural unemployment receive financial aid for further education. Finally, it urged the federal government to support state and national information and counseling services for adult learners which would make use of telecommunications technologies.

It will be a long time before the federal government takes up all of these suggestions—if it ever does.[10] The commission's efforts began to pay off, however, in 1984, a year when reports criticizing higher education were beginning to appear. Senator Orrin Hatch of Utah introduced a bill, S. 2919, in the 98th Congress authorizing the "Secretary of Education to make grants to strengthen the capacity of postsecondary institutions to respond to the continuing education needs of adults, to link postsecondary resources more closely to the preparation and performance of the American workforce, and to enhance Federal policies affecting the development of the Nation's human resources." With provisions closely following the commission's recommendation, S. 2919 provided for the authorization of $50 million for fiscal 1985 and each succeeding year until 1990. Similar bills were introduced by Congressman Gunderson and Williams in the House. The bill that finally emerged from the House was more favorable to the commission's position than the bill from the Senate. Many of the commission's recommendations, in particular those dealing with financial aid for adult and part-time learners, found their way into the reauthorization of the Higher Education Act of 1965 ("The Higher Education Amendments of 1986," 1986; Stewart, 1986).

The commission saw the states as an increasingly important

10. See Hartle and Kutner (1980) for a discussion of federal policies and Powell (1980) and Cross and McCartan (1984) for state policies on adults and higher education before the Commission on Higher Education and the Adult Learner began its work.

arena for action. "Smart workers working smarter" had particular appeal as governors across the nation were competing to attract or keep industry, especially high tech companies. Most states were already regulating their public, and sometimes private, colleges and universities. The commission saw that adding attention to adult learners with the activity already going on in the states and connecting it to an economic agenda might not be too difficult.

One technique for reaching policy-makers was the short regional conference. Between 1983 and 1986, the commission co-sponsored with local organizations twenty-five conferences around the country. Approximately 4,000 people from some 600 government, business, labor and educational organizations attended. For example, an invitational conference entitled "Developing Human Capital: A Shared Responsibility" at North Carolina State University featured addresses by Governor James Hunt of North Carolina and Robert Scott, former governor of North Carolina. Another conference, co-sponsored with the New England Board of Higher Education, the New England Governor's Conference, the New England Congressional Caucus, the Caucus of New England State Legislatures, and the National Conference of State Legislatures, focused on the retraining needs of mid-career workers in New England. Governor Michael Dukakis of Massachusetts spoke, along with several other politicians, state economic development officers, and academics.

The responsibility for organizing these conferences fell to state and regional co-sponsors, usually mobilized by the regional offices of CAEL. The regional offices were less central in carrying out the commission's other major effort, the Institutional Self-Assessment Project, managed by William Warren. *The Self-Study Assessment and Planning Guide,* published in 1984, was directed to senior administrators to help them assess how well they were serving adult learners and to help them plan improved or new services. Step by step, the guide took administrators through a series of questions about their outreach programs for adults; admissions, orientation and advising activities; curriculum and instruction; degree requirements, credit, and continuing education programs; support services; faculty and staff development and rewards; extracurricular activities; administrative structure and finances; and mission and objectives.

Institutions could take the guide and use it on their own, or they could get assistance from the commission on its use. The commission used its grant money to train twenty people to work with teams from colleges and universities. The grant subsidized twenty such teams, who were to monitor their self-assessment process and the initial impact of using the guide. In all, over 700 people from 210 institutions attended workshops about the guide between 1984 and 1986.

**Alternative Ways of Assessing Potential for College Work: The Student Potential Program.** Coordinated by Kathleen Gallay at CAEL Central, the Student Potential Program (SPP) was designed to identify students with the capacity for college work, even though their grades and test scores seemed to indicate otherwise. SPP developed rapidly during the second phase of LEARN. The behavioral event interview, a technique used by David McClelland and his associates at McBer and Company to select managers, was adapted for use in colleges and universities (Klemp, 1982). An hour-long structured interview asked high-risk applicants to college to tell four detailed stories about things they did in the past year that pleased them. CAEL trained faculty and staff members from colleges and universities to do the interviews and to code students' responses. The responses were then analyzed for capabilities which earlier research at McBer had shown to be related to success at work. After several iterations, eleven capabilities were coded from the stories: initiative, persistence, creativity, planning skill, critical thinking, restraint, leadership, influence skill, self-confidence, interpersonal diagnosis, and responsiveness.

With a pilot grant of $25,000 from the Lilly Endowment, a matching grant of $25,000 and then grants of $265,000 for implementation and $40,000 for research from the Ford Foundation, the SPP worked with twenty colleges and universities. An additional seven or so joined the project as observers. The colleges and universities were organized into three clusters, each coordinated by a CAEL regional representative. Each participating institution selected two people to be trained together. Over forty people were trained, some of whom were chosen to train other assessors. Altogether, the assessors administered the behavioral event interview to some 600 prospective or enrolled students between 1982 and 1986.[11]

An evaluation conducted by Alexander Astin and his colleagues showed that overall scores on the SPP interview were not related either to age or to sex. They were substantially correlated with SAT scores and more moderately related to high school grades. In other words, the behavioral event interview applied to a variety of populations and was measuring some qualities that overlapped with traditional academic measures, and others that were entirely different. High school grades and test scores were better in predicting college grades and how many courses students took, but interview scores helped improve their predictions. This was taken as an indication that the interview was tapping "relevant academic talents not measured by traditional" means (Astin, Inouye, and Korn, 1986, p. 14).

As the assessors began using the behavioral event interview,

---

11. For a full description of the program, see Kathleen Gallay, "Program on Student Potential for College Studies," Final Report to the Ford Foundation, 1985, and Council for Adult and Experiential Learning and McBer and Company, *Student Potential Program Assessor Training Manual*, February 1986.

other applications became apparent. It could be used to select students for programs and majors, to advise students, and to measure the "value added" by particular colleges and universities to their students' learning and development. The SPP seemed to demonstrate that the behavioral event interview and its accompanying coding scheme might help in screening students of particular interest to colleges and universities, such as athletes with poor academic skills or undergraduates wishing to become teachers.

Training for the SPP was demanding, and the coding stringent. The interview could be quite draining emotionally, and most assessors found that they could do only two a day. It was obvious that the SPP could not be run on the cheap, and that the assessors would have to be recertified and retrained. CAEL hoped to market the program after the grant ended, but an application to the Ford Foundation for a loan was turned down. In the business plan submitted to Ford, CAEL would have charged its institutional members $7,200 and non-members $7,800 to train, certify and monitor two people, provide unlimited consulting, and retrain them the second and third years after the initial training.[12] Making use of the regional system, Gallay and her colleagues from McBer traveled across the country with accounts of the interviews, materials, and a new videotape, "The Many Faces of Student Potential." It remained to be seen whether they would succeed in selling the program.

**Partnerships Between Higher Education and Other Sectors: The UAW-Ford College and University Options Program.** The SPP was modest, quiet, and slow to develop. There could be no greater contrast to it than the College and University Options Program for the United Automobile Workers (UAW)-Ford Motor Company National Development and

12. See Mary H. Ellis, Kathleen C. Gallay, and Morris T. Keeton, "Business Plan for the Student Potential Program" submitted to the Ford Foundation, no date.

Training Center (NDTC). The NDTC is the result of what is often called the "historic" collective bargaining agreement between UAW and Ford in 1982. In this agreement, the national leadership of the union accepted the company's argument that the labor force would have to contract. The company agreed to retrain workers displaced by plant closings or whose jobs were eliminated or changed by new technology. Ford agreed to put five cents an hour for every hour worked by every active UAW member into a special fund—the so-called "nickel fund"—for activities that would "promote training, retraining and development activities." This agreement created a fund which could accumulate close to $1 million a month when calculated for a work force of 114,000. As the original agreement phrased it, the activities covered by the fund would include training in "participative, cooperative techniques and concepts. In addition, training/educational courses can be made available to upgrade/sharpen present job skills, provide updating on the state-of-the-art technology. . . ."[13]

The NDTC was to help workers who would be displaced by the company or who chose to leave on their own to prepare themselves not only for another job, but for another life. Hence "development" as well as "training" in the title of the new center. The NDTC supported counseling programs, retraining projects, job search training, and relocation assistance. The center itself would not conduct training. It administered a tuition assistance program, which in 1985 allowed every eligible worker $1,500 a year in prepaid tuition for up to five years for credit and non-credit courses in existing educational institutions. Workers on permanent layoff with seniority could receive

13. The Ford-UAW Master Agreement in 1982, Letter of Agreement from Ernest Savoie, Director, Labor Relations and Employment Office, Ford Motor Company, to Donald F. Ephlin, Vice-President and Director of the National Ford Department, United Auto Workers, February 13, 1982.

between $3,000 and $5,000 in prepaid tuition in a four-year period.

The center was governed jointly by the UAW and Ford through a governing board headed by Ernest Savoie, director of the Labor Relations and Employment Office at Ford and principal architect of the program. Located next to the campus of Henry Ford Community College in Dearborn, the NDTC had a staff of approximately seventeen people. Director Thomas Pasco, a former rank-and-file member of the UAW with a master's degree from Western Michigan University, represented the union. Associate Director Richard Collins, who had worked in the Personnel Department at Ford, represented the company.

The funds kept growing. With additions for health, drug and alcohol counseling, and pre-retirement planning, the "nickel" fund grew to a 17½ cent fund in 1984. To this, 50 cents was added for every overtime hour worked by every active UAW member. In that year, the fund held more than $100 million. A UAW joint center with General Motors, with a larger work force, generated a fund that was worth two to three times more.

The NDTC had a large potential market for its services. Yet in 1984, when CAEL entered the picture, a fraction of union members was taking advantage of the NDTC's services. In 1983 and 1984, fewer than 2% of active workers used the tuition assistance plan, typically for much less than the full amount.[14] Staff at the NDTC were looking for ways of increasing its services when Collins encountered Pamela Tate, at that time a regional representative of CAEL and member of the Board of Trustees.

Tate had developed the Employee Action Plan seminars

14. For breakdowns on participation, see UAW-Ford Development and Training Program, "General Information Summary" (through 1984) and UAW-Ford National Development and Training Center, *Tuition Assistance: A Status Report on the UAW-Ford Plans*, Center Report 5.

under funding from the Mott Foundation. These seminars, first designed for managers and then adapted with a grant from FIPSE for unemployed workers, were offered through the Compact for Lifelong Educational Opportunities in Philadelphia, where Tate held a part-time appointment for several years. The Employee Action Plan seminars consisted of workshops on understanding personal change, self-assessment of skills, interests and values, exploring occupations and careers, job market research, resume writing, interviewing, goal setting and planning. The seminars also included a unit on understanding the changing economy.

The Employee Action Plan brought Tate in touch with other people working on education and training programs. The grant from FIPSE was part of a cluster of projects focused on different aspects of education and the economy. Jeanne Gordus, a researcher at the University of Michigan who directed a project on career change for displaced blue-collar workers, invited Tate in 1984 to a conference in Ann Arbor on unemployment. Collins, co-director of the NDTC, was on the same panel as Tate and, after hearing her, invited her to give a workshop at the NDTC. Tate's presentation on prior learning, as well as CAEL's other work, appealed to the staff at NDTC who were concerned about the low use of their programs and the unresponsiveness of colleges and universities to working-class adults. Collins offered Tate a job almost immediately.

Tate was working on a doctorate at the University of Pennsylvania at the time and could not accept a full-time position, but she agreed to work as a consultant. The NDTC wanted to see a plan right away. Tate sketched a preliminary design, which interested the NDTC staff, and then turned to Morris Keeton for help in fleshing it out. Working day and night, Keeton and Tate came up with a proposal in less than two weeks for the College and University Options Program (CUOP). The NDTC wanted CUOP to be targeted to employed workers. The program would put on workshops in the Ford plants for workers interested in returning to school. Each plant would have an on-site employee advisor to help guide workers in CUOP. Through its regional organization, CAEL would help identify the colleges and universities prepared to grant academic credit to Ford workers for prior learning and to offer courses in the plants. CAEL would then train faculty and staff in prior learning assessment. In addition, there would be seminars for administrators to support their institutions' activities in CUOP and adult education more generally.

As time passed, it became clear that CAEL would have to contend with more than time pressure in its dealings with the NDTC. CAEL was accustomed to dealing with grants from foundations and federal agencies, which give their grantees a good deal of leeway in how they do their work and when they must complete it. At NDTC, CAEL was under contract like any other vendor. The center was reluctant to pay CAEL the overhead rate it requested, a rate that was lower than those charged by most universities, and it took a year for the NDTC and CAEL to sign an official contract. The slowness of the NDTC in processing claims required CAEL to take out a loan for $100,000 to cover its expenses on CUOP until it collected from the center.

There was sharp competition for access to the center among friends and foes alike. Sam Baskin, a former colleague of Morris Keeton's at Antioch College and president of the Union for Experimenting Colleges and Universities, had presented a proposal to the NDTC, but withdrew when Pamela Tate entered the scene. David Novicki, a Project LEARN regional representative from Michigan State University, had worked with the NDTC before Tate met Collins.

The NDTC staff jealously guarded its own prerogatives, which caused some heartache for CAEL, especially Tate. Her original design for CUOP included a component centered on life and educational planning. The NDTC staff turned over responsibility for this component to Jeanne Gordus, with whom it had had a relationship before it began working with CAEL. Insisting that Gordus and the CAEL people not communicate with each other, the center built in a split which frustrated both sides. NDTC staff also prevented Tate and those working with her from communicating directly with workers and plants, which slowed down the implementation of the project.

Keeton and Tate pursued other venues for the expertise they were honing in CUOP. CAEL carried on negotiations with the UAW-General Motors center, along with the National Institute for Work and Learning (NIWL), an independent research and policy center founded in the early 1970s as the National Manpower Institute by former U.S. Secretary of Labor Willard Wirtz. NIWL had fallen on hard times in the Reagan administration. Its acting director Richard Ungerer, a friend and colleague of Pamela Tate's from the National Society for Internships and Experiential Education, was following the development of CUOP, which he hoped he could adapt for the UAW-General Motors center. Not much happened on this front as CAEL busied itself with CUOP, although NIWL later won a contract.

By June 1985, CAEL was operating a "pilot project" at forty plants. A few months later, the NDTC decided to expand the project to 72,000 workers, about two-thirds of the work force, in eight places where Ford plants were concentrated: Michigan, Chicago, Kansas City, St. Louis, Indianapolis, and three regions in Ohio. Pamela Tate as lead consultant, Diana Bamford-Rees in charge of training and publications, four regular CAEL regional representatives, and eight additional people hired especially for the project, sent out requests for proposals to over 200 colleges and universities, including proprietary schools, within a fifty-mile radius of the plants. The request for proposals emphasized that applicants should recognize the academic legitimacy of prior learning, be open to working with adult learners, have evening and weekend classes, and be willing to cooperate with other institutions in the region.

Some schools in the eight regions were reluctant to accept prior learning, but a sufficient number were not. From them, the NDTC selected sixty colleges and universities as "primary partners" (institutions that already accepted prior learning credits or were prepared to do so) and forty more as "preparatory partners" (institutions just beginning to focus on adults). Public comprehensive universities and public community colleges comprised the two largest groups among the primary partners, followed by private liberal arts colleges.

The partner schools in each region were joined together with unions and company educational committees in regional councils which met periodically. These councils were meant to give workers access to a variety of institutions through transfer agreements, joint acceptance of credits earned through prior learning, and coordinated courses and services offered at the plants. The regional councils put on learners' fairs at the plants, a practice pioneered at CLEO and carried to other CAEL regions. As they worked together, institutions in several of the regions began developing mechanisms for sharing the work of assessing prior learning.

CAEL first tried to mobilize the attention of senior administrators at the colleges and universities in the eight regions in which the Ford plants were located. A series of institutional leadership seminars coordinated with the Commission on Higher Education and the Adult Learner presented CAEL's case for taking adult learners seriously. Some 400 presidents and/or provosts and senior administrators from continuing education and student advising units in over one hundred institutions attended these seminars.

One hundred and twenty other administrators were involved in the regional councils and other meetings when CUOP was set up. As the regional councils were operating, CAEL trained over 700 faculty members, counselors, and administrators in prior learning assessment. These people represented sixty different fields and seventy-one institutions. Slightly over 300 workers interested in returning to school attended workshops, and 122 enrolled in nine portfolio development courses. 2,100 workers attended 100 sections of credit and non-credit on-site courses in a wide range of subjects. The most popular courses were in computers and business subjects.

The development and implementation of CUOP cost approximately $788,000 in 1984 and 1985 and $462,000 in 1986. Most of this money came from NDTC, with an additional $440,000 from the U.S. Department of Education for training activities (CAEL, 1986). After twenty-two months, the NDTC took over from CAEL Central the task of coordinating CUOP. CAEL regional representatives in five of the eight regions continued as consultants to CUOP as it was extended to all sixty Ford plants in 1986.

While the pressure of working in CUOP had been enormous, CAEL gained much from the experience. CAEL's role in the proposal process gave it visibility in the eight regions in which the program operated. As the NDTC's representative to colleges and universities in those regions, CAEL acquired greater leverage than it had ever had before to press colleges and universities to recognize prior learning. CUOP also put CAEL in touch with large numbers of working-class people, a group to which it had limited access. Finally, the program offered CAEL a common program and enough resources for the regional centers to carry it out.

CAEL learned to exploit its strengths quickly, whether it was the regional system, the "train the trainers" approach, or portfolio assessment. The experience with CUOP opened a new arena for CAEL, one it had been discussing for a long time—the provision of educational services for clients outside of higher education. Financial self-sufficiency and access to new groups of learners made programs like CUOP irresistible as a model for other potential ventures with the UAW-General Motors center, the Communications Workers of America, Mountain Bell, and other organizations. From some of its difficulties with CUOP, CAEL learned better how to administer, price and negotiate joint programs. As it was learning these lessons, CAEL began to articulate a "new agenda": experiential education was as important for the economy as for the individual, a line that the Commission on Higher Education and the Adult Learner had already taken.

## Accomplishments of the Third CAEL

In a report on the outcomes of LEARN, Morris Keeton asserted that the project had reached more than a million adult learners and at least 1500 institutions of higher education with twelve types of change. It had created 25 new products and had enhanced some 20 networks.[15] In making these statements, Keeton continued the practice he had begun with IDP of trying to quantify the effects of CAEL. Doing so was even more difficult with LEARN, given its increased scale and complexity.

His reasoning went this way: He divided the people CAEL reached into those who received educational services—the learners—and those who provided educational services or influenced policies affecting educational services—the providers. Services for learners included information, computer-assisted guidance and planning, and prior learning assessment. Every possible medium was used: not only courses and workshops but the telephone, computers, videotapes, television, slide/tape

15. "The Outcomes of Project LEARN," February 15, 1986, p. 1.

presentations, mailings, books, brochures, and advertisements. For example, Keeton included estimates of the number of people who used Betty Menson's WATS line and the number of people who were exposed to mentions of Susan Simosko's new student guide (1985) in *Family Circle* and *Glamour,* radio, and TV.

Table 1 summarizes Keeton's statistics about the reach of LEARN.

**TABLE 1**

**Keeton's Estimates of the Number of Learners and Education Providers Reached in Project LEARN (1983-1985)**

| **Learners** | | |
|---|---|---|
| Publications and Other Services to Identifiable People | | 55,872 |
| Computer-Assisted Guidance and Planning | | 366,858 |
| Improved Prior Learning Assessment | | 128,705 |
| Untargeted Direct Services | | 1,079,694 |
| | Total | 1,631,129 |
| **Education Providers** | **People** | **Institutions** |
| Institutions, Conferences, Workshops, etc. | 20,499 | 457 |
| Commission on Higher Education and the Adult Learner | 4,961 | 888 |
| Joint Ventures | 708 | 88 |
| International Networking Activities | 83 | 51 |
| Other Activities | 30,712 | 60 |
| Total | 56,963 | 1,544 |

Source: Recalculation and reorganization of Table 1, pp. 1-4 in "The Outcomes of Project Learn," February 15, 1986.

Between 1983 and 1985, 55,872 people had been reached by what Keeton called "major direct" services—publications and workshops for an identifiable group of people—while another 1,079,694 had been reached by "lesser direct" services like radio and TV, magazines, slide/tape presentations, and other sources of information without an identifiable audience. 366,858 people were exposed to computer-assisted guidance and counseling—primarily SIGI and DISCOVER—and another 128,705 had been helped by improved or expanded prior learning assessment. Altogether, then, Keeton's calculations yielded a total of 1.6 million learners reached by the second phase of LEARN.

Keeton's information from organizers of CAEL institutes, assemblies, conferences, training sessions and workshops turned up a cumulative attendance of 20,499 education providers at such events over the LEARN years. Efforts to reach colleges, universities, and other groups through the Commission on Higher Education and the Adult Learner's institutional self-assessments and public policy conferences around the country attracted 4,961 more people. The Joint Ventures program, which counted most on the College and University Options Program, produced another 708 people. An additional 83 people were drawn into various international networking activities. These figures, plus 30,712 people who wrote or edited a publication under CAEL auspices, participated in electronic conferences or networks, or received a mailing from CAEL, yielded a total number of 56,963 faculty members, administrators, and policy-makers drawn from some 1,544 institutions.

These numbers are nothing short of extraordinary. Even if we include only those who attended a CAEL workshop, were exposed to computer-assisted guidance and planning, and were reached by prior learning assessment—in other words, the more active modes of exposure—we come up with 500,000 learners exposed to CAEL's activities between 1983 and 1985. If we eliminate mailings from the tally of providers who were exposed to CAEL, we are still left with 44,000 people and 1,544 institutions with direct involvement in LEARN.

What do these numbers mean? It is difficult to know how reliable they are, since the regional managers and other sources generated them in a variety of ways. Even if the numbers are reliable, it is impossible to appraise the actual impacts of different events on the people or institutions exposed to them. On the provider side, most of the regional staff carried responsibilities besides their work for CAEL; they rarely separated other responsibilities from their work for CAEL. For many of the regional managers, work for CAEL was the same as work for LEARN. The distinction was not important.

Such ambiguities made it tricky to assess precisely the impacts of the different activities carried out under LEARN. This did not stop many people from trying. The first attempt was made by an evaluation firm appointed by Vice-President Kinsinger of the W.K. Kellogg Foundation in 1981. Formative Evaluation Research Associates (FERA) was hired on a retainer basis to help the foundation to evaluate some of the projects it funded. The second phase of LEARN included $75,000 for evaluation. In addition to this money, the foundation made FERA available to CAEL Central and the regions to help them design evaluation studies. If someone in CAEL also needed help in carrying out their studies, FERA could apply to the foundation for additional funding as needed.

Almost from the moment that the second phase of LEARN was funded, FERA began prodding the regional managers and CAEL Central for specific plans about how they would evaluate the project. At the beginning, Keeton encouraged the regional managers and his own staff to cooperate with FERA. As time passed, it became clear that Keeton and Margaret Talburtt, the representative of FERA who worked most closely with CAEL, disagreed about the scope of the evaluation. The regional managers, pressed as they always were for time, were loathe to take too much extra time for evaluation. Answering letters and telephone calls from Talburtt, submitting evaluation plans to her, and receiving her on visits were extra burdens they did not expect to bear. Three or four regional managers worked out agreements with FERA for special evaluation projects, and Keeton cooperated in a "reputational" survey of the perception of CAEL and LEARN among opinion leaders in higher education, but other regional managers limited their evaluation activities.

Keeton commissioned other assessments of LEARN. This history of CAEL, first conceived by FERA, was one. Keeton arranged for Valerie McIntyre, the regional manager from the Pacific Northwest, to do a survey of practices on prior learning assessment. Barry Sheckley, the regional manager from New England, was asked to carry out a survey of learners in programs for adults. Nancy Schlossberg of the University of Maryland was invited to write vignettes of individual learners. Later, the W.K. Kellogg Foundation contracted with Virginia Smith to evaluate LEARN and the foundation's funding strategies.

The question remained: What did LEARN add up to? If LEARN consisted of everything that CAEL did, as most participants felt, what accomplishments lay under the number of learners and providers it had reached through its myriad programs? In the conclusion to his evaluation of the first phase of LEARN, Harold Hodgkinson wrote that "success thus far has been more through the energy and entrepreneurial zeal of the parts rather than the collaborative effectiveness of the whole" (Hodgkinson, 1982, p. 9). The same could be said at the end of the second phase of LEARN—only more so. Instead of one primary focus shared by all of the regions, as in the first LEARN, the second LEARN began with many different activities and ended with even more. The "collaborative effectiveness of the whole" still seemed problematic.

## CHAPTER FOUR

In order to assess LEARN, it is necessary to analyze the kind of organization CAEL had become. One key to understanding CAEL as an organization is the regional system. Another is the temporary project mode of conducting activities. Viewed together, the regional system and the project mode meant that CAEL consisted of a series of spinning circles of activity. Some of the circles were based in the regions where CAEL operated; there might be several circles in a single region. Other circles were based in a program: the Commission on Higher Education and the Adult Learner, the College and University Options Program, and the Student Potential Program each generated sets of circles regionally and nationally. Other circles were based on common interests of one sort or another: administrators from black colleges, people working on telecommunications, counselors interested in working with adult learners, policy-makers in other countries attracted to the assessment of prior learning. The arrangement was synergistic. From the circles came ideas for new projects, new audiences, and new uses of old approaches and materials.

In her evaluation for Kellogg, Virginia Smith referred to the regional system as consisting of "change agent centers." These centers resembled local chapters of change-oriented voluntary organizations like the American Friends Service Committee. The effectiveness of the second phase of LEARN depended on the "simultaneous activity" of the regional representatives, CAEL Central programs, and the circles generated by them. In order to achieve the three major goals of LEARN—increased and improved learner services, institutional change, and an altered system of adult learning—CAEL needed to operate "on many fronts" which reinforced one another. Virginia Smith concluded that CAEL had succeeded "not only in theory but in results" (1987).[16]

---

16. Virginia Smith, who had recently completed a term as president of Vassar College, had been associate director of the Carnegie Commission on Higher

Many people did not accept a loose network like the one that CAEL had spawned. Instead of seeing CAEL as a voluntary organization, they saw it more as a franchise organization. On this view, if LEARN was to be "a network of adult learner systems," then it ought to be delivering a common program through an interconnected set of activities in different places. While they might appear to be chaotic, however, the circles had a certain coherence which derived from their connection to CAEL. They did not occur informally or accidentally. Rather, they were set spinning by CAEL, in a direction determined by CAEL, and with people helping them intersect with other CAEL circles. They usually drew on CAEL's resources—its money, people, access to the right people, publications, conferences, and training materials.

## CAEL's Future

Loose structure required that CAEL Central and the regions coordinate among themselves more than they had in the first and second versions of CAEL. LEARN made this possible, in very specific ways. Regional managers had begun meeting twice a year in 1979, but LEARN provided a way for the regional managers to influence each other. At meetings for regional managers in various parts of the country, Morris Keeton and the staff in Columbia set the agenda for the meetings, which were typically stuffed with items. Especially at the beginning of LEARN, the meetings were mainly occasions for Keeton to present information to the regional managers and for the managers to report on their activities. As time passed, the regional managers asked for more time to talk with each other.

---

Education and the founding head of the Fund for the Improvement of Postsecondary Education.

An unexpected source of coordination was a computer network for transmitting messages (electronic mail) and for more general discussions (computer conference). Under an additional grant from the Kellogg Foundation for a year, Herman Niebuhr ran a computer conference on the ''new paradigm'' (Niebuhr, 1984) and Barry Sheckley tried to stimulate a discussion of adult learning theories. Neither of these efforts got very far. While a few of the regional managers participated in the computer conferences, most were impatient with their abstractness and lack of relevance to the daily problems they faced.

Some of the regional managers did take to the electronic mail system. Since CAEL people moved around so much, the computer was often faster than playing ''telephone tag'' over a period of days and sometimes weeks. CAEL Central found the system convenient as a ''bulletin board'' for messages about meetings and other events, and for reviewing drafts of grant proposals. As they became more comfortable with the technology, the regional participants used the computer network to exchange private messages, as well as to issue general calls for information and help. Susan Simosko, for example, asked Urban Whitaker to help her with a handicapped person from San Francisco who had contacted her at Thomas A. Edison State College for advice about educational opportunities. Betty Menson sent out calls for help with her teleconferences. Others asked for recommendations of speakers at conferences they were organizing in their regions.

The effects of the computer network on the regional staff were subtle. Regional managers became more visible to one another between meetings than they would have been by telephone or mail. It became clearer who was doing what—and how hard they were or were not working. Because they were writing, they were forced to articulate what they were doing and to express themselves systematically. The electronic network rewarded people with ability in manipulating ideas and words, but it was clear from the response to the computer conferences that analytic virtuosity alone would have no impact if it did not help the regional staff get its work done.

The computer gradually helped to forge the regional managers into a more coherent, if not cohesive, group. They knew each other personally and were well enough acquainted with what they were doing to call on one another for information and help. Certain regional managers—Betty Menson and Urban Whitaker among the old-timers, and Susan Simosko among the newcomers—were more likely to initiate contacts. Different people would get together for different activities as they came up, but there did not appear to be any continuing subgroups or cliques. The first generation, mostly people who dated back to the original CAEL project but also others who had joined CAEL when it first became independent, were no longer dominant on the board and the regional staff. New people were more pragmatic in their attachment to CAEL and less likely to stay when their needs were no longer served. As CAEL grew more complex and the regions more active, Keeton observed that the familism of CAEL might interfere with its further development. The expansion of the regional system made it impossible for Keeton to relate to the regional managers as personally as he had in the past. CAEL would need a more formal basis for commitment.

This basis began to be laid with the appointment in 1985 of Mary Ellis as vice-president. The management of CAEL had vexed the Board of Trustees for many years; finding a vice-president who could handle CAEL's administration continued to be a high priority. CAEL seemed to have found the person it wanted in Mary Ellis. A native of Alabama, Ellis had a long association with black colleges in the South. She had taught English and theater, and then held a series of administrative positions at the New Orleans Consortium, St. Mary's Dominion College, and Xavier University. Ellis brought connections to rather different networks than CAEL and Keeton had cultivated: not only black colleges, Catholic institutions, and state systems, with which Keeton also had connections, but consortia, land grant universities, and arts organizations.

The division of labor the board had sought for so long began to take shape. Keeton handled the development and orchestration of new projects and represented CAEL around the country. Ellis handled management, the budget, the regional system, and planning. She set out immediately to rationalize the regional system. After reorganizing the regions into more manageable chunks, she recruited new regional representatives. She developed formal expectations for the regions, which included some common activities like regional conferences and newsletters. She also drafted written agreements for institutions' contributions to CAEL regional offices. These agreements included the provision of space, office and staff support, travel money, and quarter-time support or its equivalent for a senior regional staff person.

Another experienced manager, Anne Bryant, took over as chair of the Board of Trustees in 1985-86. Vice-President for professional education at P.M. Haeger Associates, a successful entrepreneurial organization whose primary clients are women financial executives, Bryant's doctorate in higher education from the University of Massachusetts-Amherst and her business experience made her an ideal chair for CAEL as it did business with organizations outside of higher education.

Bryant had served on the board since 1980 and knew her way around CAEL. She worked closely with Mary Ellis to design a long-range planning process, which the board had mandated as one of the first responsibilities of the new vice-president. After several rounds of discussion on the board and with some of the regional managers, Ellis circulated drafts of CAEL's first long-range plan, which was approved in 1986.

While Ellis settled in, Keeton was thinking through CAEL's

financial prospects. It was as clear in 1985 as in 1977 that CAEL needed grants. From 1980 through 1984, CAEL's annual income averaged a little over $1 million; close to 80% came from grants, the largest amount from the W.K. Kellogg Foundation. The foundation continued to press CAEL to find alternative sources of income. Until CAEL's work with the UAW-Ford National Development and Training Center (NDTC), efforts to raise non-grant money had not succeeded. For the twenty-two months between 1984 and 1986 that CAEL worked on CUOP, however, it received $469,000 as a service fee from the NDTC, in addition to direct costs. The service fee gave a big boost to CAEL's unrestricted fund. All told, close to 75% of CAEL's total income of $2.8 million during this period came from the CUOP program.

As CAEL's work with NDTC was winding down, Keeton reported to the board that institutes, assemblies, workshops and publications—the bulk of CAEL's "core program"—did not bring in enough money to pay their full cost. Membership in CAEL remained fairly stable, with some 277 institutional members and 254 individual members in 1985-86. Assembly attendance seemed to be rising, but revenues from assemblies were always modest.[17]

Joint ventures like the UAW-Ford program promised substantial sums of unrestricted revenues. The experience with CUOP, however, taught CAEL that contracts for service could be as unpredictable as getting grants. Further, Keeton wrote as CUOP was ending that, "[c]lients in Joint Ventures want to pay only for direct service to their constituencies and for the application of innovations already proved viable and useful."[18]

It appeared that money for innovation would have to come primarily from grants. This meant that CAEL would continue

17. See Appendix C for membership information and assembly attendance.

18. The President's Report to the Board of Trustees for the Fiscal Year 1985-1986, p. 4.

to live with great uncertainty from year to year, and with large fluctuations in its income. CAEL was less vulnerable to these fluctuations than traditional organizations because it did not have a large staff on salary; its staff in Columbia was small and willing to accept reductions and delays in their wages in hard times. The regional system was either funded by other organizations or by volunteers. Beyond the regional staff, much of CAEL's work was carried out by people hired for particular jobs—"adjuncts," in Keeton's lexicon. During LEARN, he estimated that approximately 200 adjuncts had been involved as trainers, consultants, authors, and editors.

Relations between Keeton and the board became smoother with the retirement of two persistent critics, Myrna Miller and Joan Knapp. Participants from the first days of the CAEL project, Miller and Knapp had argued forcefully that CAEL should adhere to its original goals—the use and assessment of experiential learning, research on it, and dissemination of information about it. Other members of the board disagreed. Finally, in 1985, the Board of Trustees unanimously agreed to ratify the broadening of CAEL into an organization focused generally on adults and to rename it.

Morris Keeton had been reaching for a broader view of CAEL's mission for a while. In an address delivered at Empire State College in October 1983, he traced the implications of non-traditional education's vision of higher education. This vision was to include individualization and flexibility of programs, learner self-directedness, and an emphasis on both cognitive and non-cognitive achievement. The increase in the number of adult learners and prior learning programs reinforced this vision and opened up the question of what a college education is for, who is capable of doing college work, when learning can occur, and where learning should take place.

Pursuing the question of where learning can take place, Keeton attacked the notion of the "ivory tower" and the "ivied walls,'' ''awe-inspiring symbols of the past.'' ''Who today,'' he asked, ''thinks that a monastic setting or a rural enclave is the most productive site for scholarly research and student development? Yet even though our old images of where best to learn are crumbling, we cling to the idea that the norm for the places for advanced learning is the campus cluster of classroom buildings, laboratories, libraries, and faculty offices.'' In their purposes as well, colleges and universities would have to shift from being ''agents of socialization,'' ''environments for transition from puberty to adulthood,'' and ''vehicles for transmitting from the past to the next generations a selection of the knowledge and habits of mind thought best by their faculties'' to the ''active fostering of maturation and self-development of their students'' (Keeton, 1983, pp. 2-3).

A few months later, in a report to the 1983 CAEL Assembly, Keeton related these ideas to CAEL's mission. No longer ''an enterprise of pre-adulthood,'' a college education is an adult institution. No organization other than CAEL was looking at the overall needs of adult learners, including experiential learning. Higher education needed to think much more seriously about the fact that many students were not studying to assume adult roles after college, but were already carrying out those roles while studying. What they needed were ''college-level competences and achievements'' to carry out those roles better in an information society (Keeton, 1984, p. 8).

The regional system made it possible for CAEL to mobilize a large number of people and organizations across the country quickly when a new project came along. The typical CAEL approach to problems—convene groups and panels of people who were likely to have the influence to move an agenda forward, assemble the trained people to carry out the agenda—allowed CAEL to move quickly and flexibly when opportunities arose. Indeed, this is probably the only way that an organization with so small a staff and with so insecure a financial base can operate.

The central office in Columbia had become at once more formalized and more entrepreneurial, the regions both more independent and more interdependent. Reaping the fruit of its ten years of experience, CAEL was enmeshed in a much more varied set of activities with more people and a larger budget than it had when it began the second phase of LEARN. No longer did CAEL have to choose between reaching learners vs. reaching institutions. It did both.

By 1985, CAEL had taken on the third goal of LEARN—"the transformation of the learning system." The wind seemed to be shifting in CAEL's direction as governors and pundits alike were arguing that education, including adult education, was a key to economic development. By working on public opinion, state and federal policy, leadership and skills in colleges and universities, and new technologies, CAEL was attempting to make not only higher education, but the larger society, more accepting of adult learners. Whether or not this would happen—and how much of a part CAEL would play in it—remains to be seen.

CHAPTER FIVE

# CAEL as a Social Movement Organization

CAEL is the responsible innovator.
CAEL is the conscience of higher education.
CAEL is an analogy.

CAEL began at a time of great ferment in higher education. The legitimacy of learning outside the classroom and the notion that content and pedagogy should be relevant to students' concerns went alongside the belief that more people—blacks and other minorities, women and adults—had a right to a higher education. This was the legacy the 1960s left for the 1970s. The task of the 1970s was to make some of these ideas work.

## The Emerging Movement for Change in Higher Education

There were resources to do it. Any college or university bent on starting a new program or improving existing ones stood a good chance of raising at least start-up money from the foundations or the federal government. Foundations, most prominently the Carnegie Corporation, the Lilly Endowment, the Ford Foundation, the W.K. Kellogg Foundation, the Exxon Education Foundation, the Rockefeller Foundation, the Danforth Foundation, and the Mellon Foundation were more than ready to support various improvement efforts.

The federal government was also encouraging improvement in higher education during this period. The passage of the Higher Education Act of 1965 and then the Education Amendments of 1972 expanded the federal role in improving higher education and increasing access to it. The greatest expenditures went to direct grants and loans to students, but there was also a variety of programs for institutions, special programs for minorities and underprepared students, and projects on particular subjects like science (Mayville, 1980).

Into this scene entered the Fund for the Improvement of Postsecondary Education (FIPSE), whose budget of $10 million when it was founded in 1973 did not match the resources of the foundations or other federal programs, but whose attention was squarely focused on reforming higher education. Its staff spent much time around the country carrying word of what was going on from innovator to innovator, people who were often geographically and socially isolated (Gamson, 1979; Fund for the Improvement of Postsecondary Education, 1983).

An infrastructure that would bring these scattered innovators together had already begun to emerge when the FIPSE staff began its travels. Some people, especially administrators, had already discovered *Change,* a bi-monthly magazine founded in 1969 by the Union of Experimenting Colleges and Universities, devoted entirely to higher education and its vicissitudes. *The Chronicle of Higher Education,* a weekly newspaper which began appearing in 1966, carried current news of higher education to every corner of the country. Jossey-Bass, a publishing house established in 1967 and specializing in higher education, became an outlet for current ideas.

While disciplinary associations and organizations representing prestigious institutions remained outside this growing infrastructure for change, other higher education associations were visibly active in the early 1970s. The American Association for Higher Education (AAHE), a department of the National Education Association which became an independent organization in 1969, served as a meeting ground for administrators and faculty members from a variety of disciplines. With support from FIPSE, AAHE sponsored a project called NEXUS, which operated a toll-free line for anyone with questions about what was going on in colleges and universities. The Council for the Advancement of Small Colleges (later, the Council for Independent Colleges) provided technical assistance to its members on ways of improving undergraduate education. The Association of American Colleges was a voice for liberal education. These three organizations set the tone for other higher education associations and regional consortia, which became increasingly active in the 1970s. They, in turn, could call on a myriad of consultants and experts who operated in and around colleges and universities.

The time was ripe for the formation of a movement for change in higher education. Much has been written about the conditions which are conducive to the formation of social movements (Jenkins, 1983; McCarthy and Zald, 1973): a combination of sentiments and ideologies in support of change, organizations ready to carry out programs for change, resources to help them do it, and the right opportunities for them to act. Several conditions for the formation of a social movement were already present in higher education when CAEL entered the scene. Non-traditional educators had a general ideology about improving higher education which received space in the higher education media. Through the higher education associations and regional consortia, a growing cadre of people had developed expertise in carrying out some of the change programs, with sufficient support from outside sympathizers in the foundations and federal government.

One critical element, however, was missing: a sense of collective identity among the advocates of change. There were several different sub-movements for change in higher education. Those concerned about increasing access for different groups—minorities, women, adults—pursued programs focused on those groups. The "sixties" innovators were disconnected from one another and culturally split off from the "seventies" innovators.

Those who were working on changes in curriculum did not communicate with those working on changes in the extra-curriculum. Individualistic and free-wheeling, people in the various sub-movements for change in higher education operated in different institutional sectors. This meant that they did not have a vehicle for mobilizing a potential constituency in the new programs and institutions already primed to respond to their change programs.

## CAEL as a Ringleader

CAEL became one of the vehicles for bringing the different sub-movements together. It took ideas from several social movements for change in higher education at the time it was founded and combined them in new ways. These ideas centered around increasing access to higher education for new populations, especially adults; legitimating learning which takes place outside of the classroom; changing traditional ideas and practices about admissions, counseling, and instruction; and becoming more explicit about articulating and assessing the outcomes of higher education.

With support from the emerging national infrastructure for change, CAEL attracted large pools of resources. Many of the foundations with an interest in higher education have given money to CAEL, some of them several times: the W.K. Kellogg Foundation, FIPSE, the Carnegie Corporation, the Lilly Endowment, and the Ford Foundation. What explains CAEL's appeal to foundations? The foundations actively seek innovation and promote their own agendas. As the "responsible innovator," Morris Keeton succeeded in articulating not only a practical program that was consistent with their agendas; he was also able to communicate a vision of success.

This vision drew support from the national higher education establishment. CAEL had enough resources to cultivate various members of the establishment by inviting them to work on its task groups, advisory committees, research projects, publications, or conferences. At one time or another, CAEL worked with most of the important higher education associations in Washington, most particularly the American Council on Education. In touch with campuses through its networks, CAEL itself was not bound by the constraints of a typical academic organization. It became, in many ways, a key link between the national infrastructure for change and campus-based innovators. Without the innovators, the infrastructure had no clients. Without the infrastructure, the innovators had no resources.

Throughout its history, CAEL operated as a social movement organization. A *social movement* occurs when a group of people want to change the social structure or the distribution of rewards in society at large or a segment of society (McCarthy and Zald, 1977). A social movement *organization* is a formal organization which tries to implement the goals of a social movement; it is not simply focused on doing something different for its members or on providing services to a clientele (McCarthy and Zald, 1977; Zald and Ash, 1966).

While CAEL certainly was an innovative organization in its own right and provided its members with a repertoire of experiences that were unusual in higher education, this was not its *raison d'etre*. Providing service—whether to colleges and universities, other organizations, or the public—was important to CAEL but, again, not its *raison d'etre*. Rather, CAEL was bent on changing colleges and universities. CAEL's history demonstrates how a social movement organization in higher education must operate.

# CHAPTER FIVE

## *Defining the Agenda: "Assessment" as an Organizing Framework*

CAEL took several ideas which were in the air when it was founded, applied them to a new domain, and used them to establish its own domain. It did this, first, by defining its collective agenda around the idea of assessment. "Assessment" turned out to be an extraordinarily robust tool. Ideologically, it put the first CAEL and its somewhat ragged troops on the high ground: they were for non-traditional approaches, to be sure, but with *discipline* and *quality*. Focusing on the assessment of learning from experience, as the first CAEL project did, was a fruitful entry point into many other aspects of higher education—admissions, counseling, teaching, curriculum, and faculty development.

"Assessment" was also subversive. If the basic premise of the first CAEL project was granted—that people learned outside of school settings and that this learning could be assessed for academic credit—then it followed that there should be ways of equating such learning with what went on within school settings. But the original CAEL project found that it was difficult to equate courses in the same subject taught at different schools or even by different instructors in the same school, let alone to compare course learning with learning from experience.

The only sensible way to award credit for learning from experience was to assess what was learned rather than how it was learned, i.e., to focus on outcomes.[1] The outcomes approach was particularly appealing to the schools in the original CAEL

1. CAEL commissioned Marvin Cook (1978a, 1978b, 1980) to develop techniques for mapping courses and programs, developing learning outcomes, and assessing learning outcomes. The state of Florida and, more recently, the vocational colleges in Scotland, have used Cook's work, but in general it has not received much attention in the United States.

project, many of which were operating without the resources taken for granted in traditional colleges and universities, such as well-stocked libraries and science laboratories. If it were true, as Morris Keeton claimed, that colleges and universities used "the same labels (Associate of Arts Degree or bachelor of arts degree, and so on) for enormously different outcomes," then quality was not only a problem for non-traditional education (Keeton, 1975, p. 3). What was sauce for the goose should be sauce for the gander. The argument that they were willing to be judged not on "inputs" but on "outcomes" had already been taken up by the movement for competence-based education (Grant, 1979) and would be raised under another guise a decade later under the banner of "value-added" education (Astin, 1985). By the time "value-added" came along, the point had been generalized to all of higher education.

CAEL's specific fix on assessment—the assessment of prior learning—became an important selling point when it began operating at the boundaries between higher education and other organizations. While portfolio assessment was a time-consuming technique, the idea of getting credit for what you learned in life was not complicated. It was an idea that appealed to housewives and insurance agents, employers and unions. It captured the attention of politicians and business people who were interested in education's effects on economic productivity. It became the center of CAEL's appeal in Great Britain and Quebec.

CAEL articulated its view of assessment in an extraordinary outpouring of publications, which began to appear the moment the first CAEL began operating. This literature itself signaled the reach of the assessment issue, and of CAEL's own ambitions.[2] Both the rate and the scope of CAEL's publications became mobilizing tools in their own right. As Morris Keeton

2. See Appendix B for a list of CAEL's publications from 1975 to 1985.

put it, "If you want to shape things in higher education, you need a literature."

*Broadening the Scope of Action: From Institutions to their Environment*

To what change would this literature point? Goals provide meaning and direction to organizations. They are the "shaping content of concern" (Zald, 1979, p. 21). Goals may be latent or explicit. They may be single or multiple. They may focus on ideas, practices, or structures. They may be directed at influencing those they wish to change, or they may aim at replacing them.

At the beginning, CAEL's goals were latent and rather limited. As time passed, they became more explicit. They also expanded to include new arenas and actors. Despite Keeton's claim that CAEL would become the "new establishment," CAEL was more interested in influencing authorities than in replacing them. Throughout its history, CAEL focused more on ideas and practices than on structures. Furthermore, CAEL did not challenge the fundamental structure of higher education or the resource base on which it rested. It did not question departmental structure, disciplinary specialization, or great inequalities in expenditures, facts of life in colleges and universities which affect much else.

From its founding in 1974, CAEL had multiple goals. These goals were enshrined in the very words in its title: cooperative, assessment, and experiential learning. As time passed some aspects of these initial preoccupations were heightened at the expense of others, but hardly anything in CAEL's original menu was dropped. Instead, new goals were added as new resources and interests became available.

Goals in social movement organizations change in response to the ebb and flow of sentiments and resources within larger social movements (Zald and Ash, 1966). When experiential learning stopped attracting the attention of educators and the support of foundations, CAEL broadened its scope to include a variety of programs to make higher education more accessible to adults—computer-based counseling, telecommunications, information services, work-site education, new ways of assessing potential for college-level work. CAEL's name changes signify its ever-broadening scope: from the *assessment* to the *advancement* of experiential learning to *adult* and experiential learning.

CAEL's ever-broadening scope was not accepted by all of its adherents. Several members of the Board of Trustees opposed extending CAEL beyond the assessment of experiential learning. They used terms like "protean" and "Arthurian" to describe CAEL's expanding horizon. Several objected to Keeton's zeal, as one person put it, to "fix what is wrong in higher education" and to "recreate the world according to his values."

This was an accurate reading of Keeton's intentions. CAEL's goals were implicit at the beginning because of the attention it gave to legitimating the assessment of prior learning, building a constituency, and gaining collective control over resources. But when CAEL became an independent organization, it focused on "institutionalizing" the systematic approach to experiential learning developed in the original CAEL project.

This point of attack was short-lived. CAEL shifted its tactics from working on colleges and universities directly to working instead on the environments which affect them. While to some core members of CAEL and to outside sympathizers as well, these new efforts looked like a shotgun approach, Keeton continued to argue that CAEL was still focused on changing higher education.

# CHAPTER FIVE

## *CAEL's Model of Education*

CAEL offered a new model of thinking about education, a "new paradigm" with a vivid populist tinge (Niebuhr, 1984).[3] CAEL framed the new model around its primary beneficiary, the "adult learner."[4] It offered an analysis of how higher education could serve the adult learner better, and then developed a set of procedures and practices to do so. CAEL emphasized that changes in work and family, as well as some of the recent work on life cycle development, implied that Americans needed to become lifelong learners.

Adults had full lives outside their studies. They had learned a lot from life, and what they learned should be honored and recognized by colleges and universities. Some might not appear to be "college material," but thoughtful and sensitive interviewing would show that many had great potential for college work. Many, indeed, had learned from life in ways that could be presented and documented in portfolios and systematically assessed for academic credit.

Colleges and universities, therefore, would have to accommodate themselves to adults more than they had in the past. Like all students, adults needed help in educational and life planning. They needed to get this help easily, at work sites and places near home as well as in formal educational settings. Computer-assisted guidance, carefully combined with face-to-face advising and information about educational programs suitable for them, was a promising tool for working with adults. Adults also needed courses taught at times and places that fit their situations—evenings and weekends, at work, through television. The content of these courses could be quite

3. Emily Schmeidler's work (1980) on civil rights organizations emphasizes the importance of models which guide change efforts. See also Snow et al. (1986).

traditional—CAEL rarely focused on content—but colleges and universities would have to respect individual differences in learning styles and treat students as "learners."[4]

For this to happen, it would not be enough to focus just on practices in colleges and universities. CAEL also attacked the policies of accrediting organizations, higher education associations, as well as state and federal agencies that made it difficult for adults to gain access to higher education. It worked on changing financial support for adult learners in states and in the federal government. And finally, it found new buyers of educational services among employers and labor unions.

CAEL could have set itself up as the provider of educational services directly to learners or to employers and labor unions. It could have joined forces with the training and education programs which grew up during its lifetime in the corporate sector (Eurich, 1985; Fenwick, 1983). Instead, it acted as an ambassador to the corporate sector from the nation of colleges and universities. Back home in higher education, CAEL acted as a goad and a broker.

## Mobilizing for Action

CAEL needed to make its agenda a collective project. There were simply not enough resources around to do the job without the help of many people. Even if there were enough resources, the very nature of U.S. higher education required a highly decentralized, grassroots approach. Social movement organizations must shape their structures and strategies to the nature of their targets. CAEL faced a large set of scattered, atomized

4. CAEL's use of the term "learners" immediately set it off from the dominant usage among academics of "students."

targets which operated in an extremely decentralized, disorganized manner. Reaching, let alone changing, such targets required enormous resources (Freeman, 1979). CAEL needed to find a way to identify and then mobilize the people who would carry out its program. This in itself takes time and money. Once mobilized, however, "people power" becomes a resource for change.

Mobilization for change is a complex process. It involves recruiting constituents, building cadres, taking collective control over resources, and building a collective identity based on the change agenda. CAEL dealt with each of these issues in one way or another.

### *Recruiting Constituents*

Even when they have resources, social movement organizations that cannot call for dramatic events like demonstrations or boycotts must put a good deal of energy into identifying their potential constituents. The original CAEL project had a tremendous advantage: it began with a core group of people who were doing things that were emblematic of many of the changes CAEL sought to bring about. Out of this group emerged the leaders who would define CAEL: Morris Keeton of Antioch, Arthur Chickering and Myrna Miller of Empire State College, George Ayers of Minnesota Metropolitan State, Urban Whitaker of San Francisco State, John Duley of Michigan State, Jane Szutu Permaul of UCLA, Sheila Gordon of LaGuardia Community College, Larraine Matusak of the University of Evansville, Diana Bamford-Rees and Joan Knapp of ETS. Some of these people were assigned to CAEL from the ETS staff. Others served as members of the Steering Committee of the CAEL project and then on the Board of Trustees when CAEL became an independent organization. Most also represented CAEL on its various projects.

Hundreds of people from colleges and universities across the country were drawn into the original CAEL's orbit. How were they attracted? It is easier to recruit members through pre-existing networks than to start from scratch (Jenkins, 1983). During the early 1970s, John Valley of ETS had carried on a correspondence with hundreds of people around the country engaged in innovative activities in colleges and universities. When the CAEL project began, Valley's contacts proved invaluable in identifying constituents. As some of them participated in the CAEL projects, they recruited others from their own institutions and regions.

From the wing of non-traditional education that was based in programs for adults, CAEL pulled in practitioners who were either unconnected to, or uncomfortable with, existing adult and continuing education organizations and offered them recognition and a sense of being in on something new. They were the faculty members, administrators, and staff in the new programs and institutions for non-traditional learners, as well as people in older programs, who were beginning to look for a professional home open to new ideas about adult development and degree programs for adults. This emerging professional group in higher education was CAEL's early and constant constituency—directors and staff members in programs for adults and other non-traditional programs located at the interstices of their institutions.[5]

### *Building Cadres*

Some of these people were ready to do more than receive materials and attend conferences. Constituents can vary in their degree of commitment, but it is essential that highly committed members—the "core," the "family"—share the central values

5. See Appendix C for the characteristics of CAEL's membership between 1974 and 1985.

of the organization. While they and less active members may receive material and social benefits from their connection to the social movement organization, a major basis for their participation must be shared values (Wilson, 1973; Fireman and Gamson, 1979). Even when members are attracted because of these values, their continuing commitment is always problematic. Social movement organizations, therefore, put much effort into building a sense of loyalty and collective identification among their constituents by using all of the means invented by human beings—rituals, symbols, emotional attachment, and control over several spheres of life.

People who become involved in decision-making and carry out tasks and programs are the "cadres" of social movement organizations (McCarthy and Zald, 1977). The development of cadres was built into the original CAEL project. In order to keep track of what was happening in its various projects, CAEL identified a contact person or coordinator of activities at each participating institution. This practice gave rise to the identification of unpaid "institutional liaisons" who were kept apprised of CAEL's activities.

The original CAEL project introduced the practice of gathering constituents in the same region at meetings and joint projects. When CAEL became an independent organization, it improvised a rough regional system. As time passed, the regional system became more elaborate and rationalized. The regional managers became the true cadres of CAEL, the foot soldiers who trudged through the trenches of academe. With their regional contacts, advisory committees, and conferences, the regional managers were in a position to mobilize the constituency and deploy CAEL's resources.

# CHAPTER FIVE

## *Taking Collective Control Over Resources*

Social movement organizations are dependent on outside sponsors and members' time to get their work done. But they cannot get their work done if they do not control the allocation and deployment of these resources. Conflicts between the institutional representatives and ETS during the first months of the original CAEL project were centered on the question of who controlled the project. The institutional representatives struggled to take collective control over whether ETS could be trusted not to use the project for its own gain, then over the governance of the project, and finally over the budget. In doing so, they had to renounce private gain; those who were unwilling to do so dropped away or reduced their commitment, leaving the more collectively oriented people to carry on. Thus sorted out, the institutional representatives and ETS staff learned how to work together toward their common ends.

## *Building a Collective Identity Based on the Change Agenda*

Americans, academics perhaps most of all, are not easily persuaded that the benefits of acting collectively are worth the costs. A key element in people's willingness to act collectively is trust in the others with whom they are to act, especially leaders (Fireman and Gamson, 1979; Wilson, 1973). Morris Keeton embodied the collective meaning of CAEL. Variously described as a "missionary," "preacher," and "evangelist," Keeton inspired great respect among people who came in contact with him. Essential to his impact was that he did not demand deference. Stories circulated among members about his penchant for ordering tuna fish sandwiches in fancy restaurants and for driving a battered old car to important appointments. When Keeton sold a cherished vacation home for personal reasons, the story was circulated that he had sacrificed it for CAEL when it fell on hard times.

Symbols, rituals, and distinctive styles are also important in building collective identity. So are incentives and frequent communication. Incentives can be material, solidary, or purposive (Wilson, 1973). CAEL relied on all three in different mixes for different kinds of members. CAEL offered rank-and-file members purposive incentives—the opportunity to be associated with an organization that stood for innovative ideas and respect for learners of all kinds. It held out material incentives as well, incentives based on its agenda for change—the opportunity to enhance their careers in their own institutions or to move to other jobs through their connections with CAEL.

Like rank-and-file members, the core group was drawn to CAEL because of what it stood for. Their involvement helped them to understand, more deeply than did less involved members, the implications of CAEL's model of education. The material benefits of their association with CAEL were also likely to be greater. While they donated much of their time to the organization, time that was only partly subsidized by another organization, they gained visibility in return. Some of this visibility could be converted to career advancement. Rather than conflicting with CAEL, however, personal gains often enhanced the collective agenda. When several CAEL activists became presidents of colleges and universities, for example, CAEL's status also rose.

CAEL held out powerful solidary incentives. Less involved members may have enjoyed interacting with others in CAEL, but it did not claim many aspects of their lives. Cadres and leaders, on the other hand, were connected to CAEL professionally, personally, and socially. CAEL claimed the core of perhaps a dozen people in the CAEL "family" seven days a week, year after year. Several had, in effect, "grown up" in CAEL. One was even married at a CAEL assembly!

CAEL also built collective identity through a unique style that conveyed the message that CAEL was innovative. . . effective, responsible, trustworthy. The cream and blue stationery bespoke dignity, while its lower-case logo indicated a certain playfulness. Before long, "CAELites" began speaking "CAELish." It is difficult to keep mobilization high in any social movement organization, and leaders look for opportunities to keep their constituencies "heated up" for collective action (Lofland, 1979). The assemblies—the term is itself a movement expression—were occasions for focusing the collective identity on change.

The content of change, however, shifted rapidly as the central staff took on new projects. The problem was how to mobilize the constituency around the new content. The solution was to present the new content as a solution to a new problem or as an extraordinary opportunity. Social movement organizations actively create the problems to which their programs are presented as solutions (McCarthy and Zald, 1973). CAEL's newsletter carried word of its new concerns throughout the year. Just before an upcoming assembly, it announced a theme which conveyed these concerns. The theme often emphasized newness—"Working at the New Frontiers," "Moving on to the Next Stage." Sessions playing off the theme featured new people or CAEL veterans who were involved in new activities. A palpable excitement charged these sessions, as participants waited to hear about the latest hot items.

The design of the national assemblies encouraged involvement. Waiting were large name tags, first names in large letters and color codes indicating special status. Participants could try out computer-assisted counseling programs, watch videos produced by various CAEL projects, and collect materials from programs across the country. They could leave notes or meet with colleagues. They could go to sessions in which members of the CAEL "family" and rising stars would be featured.

There, they would be likely to hear from Morris Keeton about CAEL's history and current status; then, they would be asked to give their reactions to options for the future.

The assemblies and newsletters were the primary means of communication between the central office and rank-and-file members, although many were in more direct communication with regional representatives. Constituents involved in particular projects, cadres, and staff were inundated with letters, idea papers, plans, and reports from the central office. The telephone and then the computer network also kept CAEL's collective identity live and on track.

## Organizational Structure

These efforts depended upon and helped elaborate CAEL as an organization. Social movement organizations must have instruments for mobilizing constituents for action, some notion of strategies and tactics for action, a program which roughly reflects strategies and tactics, and a way of coordinating constituents, strategies, tactics, and programs. An organizational structure is the main instrumentality for accomplishing these ends. Organizational structures vary according to the resources available and the environment in which a social movement organization operates. Structures can be centralized or decentralized, federated or isolated, bureaucratic or informal.

As an organization, CAEL mystified people. "I can't get a hold on it," one close observer declared. "It's schizoid," said another. "It is out there like the morning fog," said a third. The original CAEL project had laid down a plan for an independent organization that would be the envy of other social movement organizations. The second CAEL began with a formal transition process; a staff and a leader; cadres who were known quantities; a mobilized constituency; a name in good standing; organizational tools like the assembly and the newsletter; organizing techniques like training the trainers; relationships with key foundations and authorities—and a grant of close to $1 million.

Even so, the challenge of creating an independent organization for change in higher education was formidable. The new organization would have to permit the mobilization advantages of decentralization with the tactical advantages of centralization (Jenkins, 1983). It should have a broad reach into colleges and universities, associations and other non-governmental organizations, state agencies, and the federal government. It would need to keep its feet both in the world of non-traditional education and the mainstream of higher education. It should be able to move quickly, but in a systematic and organized fashion.

As time passed, CAEL evolved into an organization that was a fitting vehicle for achieving its agenda. In their influential discussion of social movements as networks, Luther Gerlach and Virginia Hine (1970) point out that social movement organizations typically do not have a single head the way other organizations do, although they often depend on the personal charisma of a single leader. They consist of a variety of localized cells, which operate quite independently of one another. Their organizational structures are simple and the division of labor in them rudimentary (Freeman, 1979).

It is often difficult to trace the reach of such a network, since the scope and nature of each cell's activities differ. What, then, holds them together? Gerlach and Hine (1970) argue that structures are less important than a complex web of personal ties and shared ideology. This characteriztion fits CAEL's regional structure quite closely. CAEL operated like a colonizer, either by attracting existing cells or by creating new ones. The regional cadres had some latitude to colonize within their own regions. While they differed in the complexity of their structures, most consisted of one or two part-time regional managers, a part-time secretary, and an advisory committee. At the same time that they operated relatively independently of one another, they were connected through personal relationships and shared beliefs.

The regional structure was a continuing feature of CAEL. CAEL also used more temporary forms of mobilizing new people and groups, such as *ad hoc* task groups and advisory committees, which also operated with much latitude. In many ways, CAEL perfected the "temporary organization," "project" or "team" approach that characterizes many innovative organizations (Bennis and Slater, 1968; McCarthy and Zald, 1977; Kanter, 1983; Lawler, 1986).

If that were all there was to CAEL, its significance would have been limited. Its interest in state and national policies, as well as the need to present a united front to foundations and other organizations, required more control and a more complex structure. "Control" is too strong, "coordination" too weak. "Orchestration" is perhaps more appropriate. While it did not possess the power of a typical hierarchical organization, CAEL acted more proactively and held more authority than a merely coordinative organization. Strong action was required to initiate the activities of the regions, projects, and *ad hoc* groups. Entrepreneurial effort was necessary to locate the resources and forge the relationships for them to do their work (Van de Ven and Walker, 1984).

By the time of this writing, CAEL's structure had become quite complex, and Morris Keeton's multiple organizational roles as entrepreneur, impresario, and manager had still not been decoupled. Two vice-presidents hired to take on the management of CAEL had not lasted long, and it was beginning to appear that this was a dynamic that had little to do with the particular people involved. Keeton's energy and charisma had built CAEL and continued to hold it together. What would happen when he was gone?

## Strategies for Change

This issue focused not only on the future of CAEL as an organization, but on whether it would remain committed to the social movement for change in higher education. While they benefited from Keeton's capacity to see connections among ideas and opportunities, members of the Board of Trustees, regional cadres, and staff did not always understand CAEL's larger strategies for change. In part, this was because they did not help shape them; in part, because Keeton acted intuitively and could not always articulate his strategies. When they experienced difficulties, especially in funding, CAEL activists often suggested solutions that could jeopardize the larger agenda. It is easy to go from success to success, but it takes skill to learn from failure. When others became upset with some of CAEL's problems, Keeton pointed out that successes are often built on failures. "[G]ood management" is "a matter of learning from mistakes" and "above all. . . a matter of constantly trying to learn," "trying new things and analyzing the interplay of forces and circumstances as the changes played themselves out" (Keeton, 1983, p. 3).

Keeton may have been thinking about his years at Antioch, when he and President Dixon lost control over the network of Antioch learning centers located across the country. In many ways, CAEL was Keeton's second chance to change higher education on a national scale. With CAEL, he could try almost every point of entry into higher education—senior administrators and public officials; students, faculty, counselors, and staff; associations and accrediting bodies.

CAEL proceeded with a mix of strategies, but followed four primary ones: the *hearts and minds* strategy, the *top-down* strategy, the *ripple* approach, and the *leverage* strategy. The hearts and minds strategy was built on the successes of the first CAEL, in particular the Faculty Development Program (FDP). An exemplar of CAEL's change goals, FDP identified a core group of interested faculty and staff from several colleges and universities, who helped design and then tried out training materials for the assessment of prior learning and related activities. They, in turn, trained others at their own and other institutions. What would happen next was never worked out, but presumably the faculty and staff trained in the CAEL approach would carve out a ''liberated area'' within their institutions, which would then serve as a launching pad for change.

This strategy worked when CAEL activists could link experiential learning to other important priorities in their institutions. For example, Sister Margaret Earley, who was associate professor of religious studies at Alverno College at the time of the FDP, coordinated the Valuing Department throughout this period. The Valuing Department is one among eight such departments, which exist alongside disciplinary departments, whose main purpose is to articulate and assess the generic abilities that an Alverno education promises to develop in its students. Along with its involvement in FDP, Alverno participated in other activities in the original CAEL project. This was happening at a time when Alverno was developing its unique approach to the assessment of outcomes (Ewens, 1979).

In less encouraging circumstances, there was rarely a critical mass of CAELites in any one institution. While CAEL undoubtedly had profound effects on individuals, the hearts and minds strategy did not have much institutional pay-off. Some people moved on to other institutions and other positions for which their connections to CAEL may not have been relevant. Those who remained often found themselves stranded. Norman Sundberg, for example, was a professor in the Wallace School of Community Service and Public Affairs at the University of Oregon when he was involved in FDP. The school was broken up in 1980 and, as of 1984, the university had neither accepted the assessment of prior learning, nor did it have a coordinated approach to field placement.

Urban Whitaker, a staunch CAEL cadre, offers another cautionary tale. While he was Dean of Undergraduate Studies at San Francisco State, several senior administrators in his institution and the California State University and Colleges supported him. As time passed, however, their interest in innovation and experiential learning began to wane. By the time Whitaker took an early retirement from San Francisco State, experiential learning had less support than when he began.

The Institutional Development Program (IDP), CAEL's first project as an independent organization, was designed to solve some of these problems. Instead of working from the bottom, as FDP had, IDP started at the top by asking senior administrators for a public commitment—an institutional plan for the introduction of experiential learning. These plans were slow in coming, if they ever did, and even slower to stick. Agreements from senior administrators about academic practices do not mean much without support from department chairs and rank-and-file faculty and staff. This support was thin, despite CAEL's strenuous efforts to reach all levels in the participating institutions. Without constant on-campus involvement, the effects of IDP would evaporate. Yet CAEL was not in a position to become deeply involved on campuses.

It was easier to go back to changing hearts and minds, but this time without assuming that individuals who came in contact with CAEL would necessarily change their own institutions. Rather, CAEL's emerging model of education would slowly begin to ripple outward. Like throwing a stone into a pond, people carrying CAEL's ideas into higher education would have effects on other people, who would have effects on others, and so on. In this view, anything CAEL did that was consistent with its agenda would add to its eventual impact. What might look like an unrelated scatter of activities could take on a certain logic when viewed in this way. It is impossible to catch ripples, but eventually the new consciousness takes hold—especially if it is reinforced by external circumstances.[6]

At this point, impelled by frustration with the inertia of colleges and universities and the need to find new funding, Keeton and the CAEL cadres looked outside to groups that might affect the resource base of higher education—learners, policy-makers, and non-educational institutions. The original CAEL project had published handbooks written for adult learners. A few years later, CAEL began offering services to learners through an information project and through computer-assisted counseling. The regions picked up these projects and elaborated them even further. The change strategy underlying these efforts was to use adult learners' interests as leverage on colleges and universities.

CAEL attempted to exert leverage more directly through federal and state policies. Its work in the policy arena was mediated by other organizations—the Coalition for Alternatives in Postsecondary Education at first and the Commission on Higher Education and the Adult Learner later. CAEL helped set the agenda for these organizations, whose primary focus was to increase financial aid for adult learners and funding for programs for adults. Making the resources available would, then, be a force for change.

Tentatively, and then with increasing momentum, CAEL became involved with non-educational institutions as a broker

6. This view of change comes close to the model associated with thinkers like Marilyn Ferguson (1980) and Erich Jantsch (1980).

of educational programs and services. The College and University Options Program developed for the UAW-Ford Training and Development Center held out strong incentives to colleges and universities for recognizing prior learning for adults and creating services that responded to adults' needs. These incentives would be multiplied as CAEL made agreements with other organizations. By this time, the line between a social movement organization and a service organization was becoming blurred. As long as finding the levers for changing higher education remained, CAEL would continue to be a social movement organization. When it stopped doing this, it would become a service organization.

## The Significance of CAEL

Evaluating CAEL's impact was always a sore point. Viewing CAEL as a social movement organization clarifies why this was so. Looking for effects on individual learners, faculty members or even institutions missed the mark. Rather, CAEL's significance was better tested in collective terms: Did it gain acceptance from influential people in higher education as a carrier of the agenda for change? Did it win new advantages for its constituents? Did it contribute to the larger social movement for change in higher education? (Gamson, 1975).

Results from a survey carried out in 1986 help to answer some of these questions. Talburtt and her colleagues at Formative Evaluation Research Associates (1986) conducted telephone interviews with fifty-five people from six general groupings: senior administrators in institutions, leaders of higher education associations, government representatives, foundation officers, researchers, and private sector representatives. These informants were selected because they were knowledgeable about adult learners and their needs, took a broad regional or national perspective on higher education, and had some knowledge of CAEL. The institutional informants typically came from less prestigious private colleges, regional state universities, and several research universities (Ohio State, American University, University of Maryland, and New York University).

Most of the associations important to CAEL's agenda were represented: general associations (the American Council on Education, the American Association for Higher Education, the American Association of University Professors), adult and continuing education associations (the National University Continuing Education Association, the American Association of Adult and Continuing Education), community college organizations (the American Association for Community and Junior Colleges), and several specialized groups (the National Society for Internships and Experiential Education, the Education Commission of the States, the National Association of Independent Colleges and Universities, and the American Society for Training and Development).

Government representatives came from several states, as well as from Quebec. Representatives from the Ford Foundation, the Lilly Endowment, the Carnegie Corporation, and the Fund for the Improvement of Postsecondary Education were interviewed. Researchers on higher education from UCLA, Harvard, the American College Testing Program, the Educational Testing Service, Pennsylvania State University, and California State University were included. Representatives from the Public Broadcasting Service, the AETNA Institute for Corporate Education, the Communication Workers of America, the Ford Motor Company, Charles River Consulting, and the Pentagon were also informants.

The informants, overall, represent one set of influentials in higher education—the infrastructure for change described at the beginning of this chapter. Absent are another set of influentials—representatives of elite colleges and universities and of disciplinary associations. It is unlikely that they would have met two of the three criteria for selection into the study: knowledge about adult learners and knowledge of CAEL.

*Gaining Acceptance*

Talburtt presented these people with a list of seventeen potential changes in postsecondary education that may have occurred in the past four to five years, especially those pertaining to adult learners, and asked them to rate the extent to which they had actually occurred. Then, she asked them to rate CAEL's influence on those changes.[7]

Among the changes in postsecondary education rated as having occurred rather extensively, CAEL was seen as having much influence. Informants rated CAEL as having a significant amount of influence even on changes which occurred less. CAEL was clearly important on any issue related to assessment, and pre-eminent when it came to the use of prior learning assessment.

These were the judgments of the whole group of informants. There were important differences, however, among the groups. Table 2 presents the average difference between the amount of change in postsecondary education and the amount of CAEL's influence on all of the items in the survey separately for the six groups of informants. A positive difference indicates what we might call an "influence surplus" for CAEL; CAEL was seen as exerting more influence than the extent of change overall. A negative difference indicates an "influence deficit"; CAEL was seen as exerting less influence than the extent of change.

While CAEL had a modest overall influence surplus, institutional leaders and government representatives saw CAEL

7. See Appendix E for the responses to these two questions.

**TABLE 2**

**Differences Between Changes in Postsecondary Education and CAEL's Influence Across All Statements, By Grouping**

| | Number | Total Minus | Total Plus | Difference (Column 2-Column 1) |
|---|---|---|---|---|
| Institutional Leaders | 16 | .11 | 3.47 | +3.36 |
| Association Leaders | 14 | 1.28 | .29 | − .99 |
| Government Representatives | 13 | .60 | 3.42 | +3.36 |
| Foundation Officers | 4 | 6.50 | 3.71 | −2.79 |
| Researchers | 6 | 1.36 | 3.09 | +1.73 |
| Private Sector Representatives | 6 | 2.14 | 3.70 | +1.56 |
| Total | 56 | .15 | .43 | + .28 |

as much more responsible for change in postsecondary education than association representatives and foundation officers did; researchers and private sector representatives fell in-between. In part, these differences reflect different judgments about how much higher education has changed. Institutional leaders reported more change in higher education than the other groupings; association leaders and private sector representatives saw less change.

The majority of the institutional leaders were from institutions that were members and constituents of CAEL; so were many of the government representatives. The associations were a mixture of competitors and coalition partners. Sponsors—foundation officers and private-sector representatives—did business with CAEL at one time or another. So did the researchers.

If we take a large influence surplus as indicating acceptance of CAEL, then it is clear that constituents and, to a lesser extent, experts on higher education accepted CAEL as a legitimate voice for certain change interests in higher education. Competitors and coalition partners, as well as foundation officers, were less willing to give such recognition to CAEL.

All, however, gave CAEL its due with respect to certain issues.[8] The assessment of prior learning was clearly CAEL's territory in the eyes of all groups; it held first or second place among all of them. Information and advocacy services, alliances with labor organizations and businesses, information and advocacy for adults, and greater sophistication among colleges and universities about assessment were the first or second choice among several of the groups, and were rated highly by the others (with the exception of foundation officers, who did not think CAEL had had much influence on colleges' and universities' general sophistication about assessment).

### *Winning New Advantages*

We have independent measures of the spread of prior learning assessment in colleges and universities from surveys conducted over CAEL's lifetime. In 1974, when CAEL began, there were just over forty such programs (Willingham, Burns, and Donlon, 1975). In 1978, a survey sponsored by CAEL turned up a total of 211 (Knapp and Davis, 1978). By 1980, when the American Council on Education did a survey, almost 1100 of 2000 institutions said they used portfolio assessment; almost all reported awarding credit for prior learning.[9]

8. See Appendix F for the areas of CAEL's greatest influence by grouping.

9. Office on Educational Credit and Credentials, American Council on Education, Memorandum to the Committee on Educational Credit and Credentials, September 9, 1980.

While it is difficult to document CAEL's impact on access to higher education, credit for prior learning must have brought more adults to colleges and universities. Certainly, some schools have found that recognizing prior learning has attracted more adults. This has been the case in the small private colleges, community colleges, and state colleges that have been CAEL's constituents. A follow-up study in 1986 of seventeen colleges and universities that participated in all three years of the Institutional Development Program turned up several examples.[10]

At Baldwin-Wallace College, a small private college in Ohio, adults now comprise more than 50% of the students. The CAEL training allowed Baldwin-Wallace to offer credit for prior learning through testing and portfolio assessment. Students may take a course to help them prepare portfolios, which are assessed by a committee composed of faculty members from different fields.

While these options are used by the college as a recruitment tool, the portfolio process is rigorous, and fewer than half of the eighty students in the course actually complete their portfolios and receive credit.

---

10. Richard Edelstein, a doctoral candidate at the University of California at Berkeley who had no prior knowledge of CAEL, conducted telephone interviews with representatives from a diverse set of institutions in 1986. About an hour in length, the interviews asked informants to describe the nature of their activities under the Institutional Development Program (IDP), the current status of activities initiated under it, the effects of IDP on the people who participated in it and on the institution, and continuing connections with CAEL. The institutions were: American University, Baldwin-Wallace College, Bunker Hill Community College, University of California at Los Angeles, Clackamas Community College, East Arkansas Community College, East Texas State University-Texarkana, the Florida Department of Education, the Kansas City, Kansas Community College, Mars Hill College, Marygrove College, Metropolitan State University (Denver), Neuman College, University of the Pacific, William Paterson College, Sangamon State College, and the University of South Dakota.

Two other examples. At East Texas State University at Texarkana, an institution with 1200 students which offers upper division and graduate programs, the student population is mostly adult. The university has an experience for credit program, in which students individually (and more recently, in a course) are assessed for credit. Some thirty to fifty students receive some credit this way each year. At Clackamas Community College in Oregon, which enrolls many part-time, adult students among its student population of over 20,000, students may enroll in alternative credit programs which allow them to receive advance credit, credit by examination, credit by telecourses, and credit for prior learning through portfolio. The examination option is most popular; about twenty students use the portfolio.

These schools are constrained by the amount of money they can spend on non-traditional programs. More affluent institutions like American University and Sangamon State have incorporated prior learning assessment into more ambitious programs for adults. At American University, the Apple adult re-entry program uses portfolio assessment techniques to grant up to thirty credits to older students with significant working experience and good writing skills. The seventy students in Apple take two courses when they enter: one on how to document field experience and develop a portfolio, and another on composition and reading comprehension. Faculty ''liaisons'' from departments assess portfolios.

Sangamon State, which was created in 1969 as a non-traditional college with an experiential emphasis in all of its programs, enrolls some 3000 students, of whom half are adults. A credit for prior learning program, with between 150 and 200 students a year, requires that students who wish to develop portfolios must take an assessment course, which also serves as an orientation course. Faculty assess the portfolios and may award up to thirty hours of credit. Adults may also enroll in an individualized experiential learning program, which allows students to design their own programs.

These institutions have made a commitment to substantial efforts in prior learning assessment. They typically have strong support from senior administrators and have involved a core group of faculty and staff. But even among the institutions which participated in all three years of the Institutional Development Program, there are many which have not made this commitment. Of seventeen interviewed in 1986, eight appeared to have strong prior learning or other experiential programs. The others had never been strong and had gotten weaker.

What about other items on CAEL's agenda? Sponsored experiential learning was equal to prior experiential learning when CAEL began. While there is little systematic information about the number of sponsored experiential learning programs in colleges and universities, the consensus among knowledgeable people is that internships, cooperative education, and other forms of non-classroom learning are more legitimate now than when CAEL began—though, like prior learning, they have a long way to go before most college faculty members become convinced of their value (Washington Center, 1984). CAEL has shared this territory with other organizations; it has probably brought greater legitimacy to all of their efforts.

### *Contributing to the Change Movement*

While CAEL is a unique organization in the history of higher education, there are two organizations that are close to it historically: the Center for the Study of Liberal Education for Adults (CSLEA) and the American Association for Adult Education (AAAE). CSLEA was founded in 1951. Established with a large grant from the Fund for Adult Education, itself created by the Ford Foundation, CSLEA encouraged innovation in the liberal education of adults. It helped with the development of special degree programs for adults at Brooklyn College,

Oklahoma University, and other institutions. It was also important in supporting the early stages of the College-Level Examination Program. Like CAEL, it produced many papers and study guides. It was also strategic in looking for levers of change, and it worked with continuing education organizations, professional organizations, and many colleges and universities across the country. CSLEA was not a membership organization and did not attract a cadre of dedicated constituents. When the Fund for Adult Education was disbanded by the Ford Foundation, CSLEA found it difficult to gain support and finally disbanded in 1968 (Grove, 1985; Hall, 1975).

Like CAEL, AAAE was a membership organization. It was also dependent on one source of funding, the Carnegie Corporation. Founded in 1926, it received a total of $5 million over its first fifteen years from Carnegie for research projects, conferences, publications, training programs for adult educators, demonstration projects, and international contacts. AAAE also advised the Carnegie Corporation on policies regarding adults. When funding from Carnegie was withdrawn, AAAE worked on attracting more members; at its height, membership reached 3000. Depending on membership fees limited what the organization could do; in any case, it was unable to redefine itself. It dissolved in 1951 to form a new organization, the Adult Education Association (Knowles, 1977).

CAEL's dependence on the W.K. Kellogg Foundation concerned many people, including some who had witnessed what had happened to CSLEA and AAAE. There is no guarantee that CAEL will avoid their fate. In contrast to them, however, CAEL parlayed the freedom it gained from foundation grants to act as a spearhead for change in higher education more generally. Influential figures on the national scene have been fascinated by CAEL. As two of them put it:

> CAEL can bridge the world of traditional institutions and organizations for adults. . . [It can] bring together traditional

> academic institutions, institutions that serve adults, and organizations comprised of adults, e.g., unions. Bridges and relationships are important among these groups. . . brokering and advocacy, creating a structure for new relationships (Talburtt, 1986, p. 27).

> CAEL is a seminal organization, a pioneering organization. It's the conscience of higher education, forging ahead and exploring areas that the higher education community has ignored or is unwilling to explore. . . CAEL is pushing out the frontiers, asking important questions we don't ask or are afraid to ask, or don't have time to ask (Talburtt, 1986, p. 17).

CAEL also encountered more than its share of critics. One national figure criticized CAEL because it had not reached prestigious universities. "People in higher education are snobbish," he said. "Judgments are based on who one associates with."

> CAEL says they have great response because [we] have gone from 40 to 1000 institutions using prior learning assessment in [only] four years. But, no Harvard or Ivy Leagues or Big 10 schools are in—no Berkeley, Stanford, Northwestern or Georgetown. [All we] have are small, struggling schools of middle size and state supported institutions, but these are not significant to those in the field. Get University of Chicago, University of Michigan, Stanford, or Harvard. CAEL doesn't have that kind of base yet, to its detriment. They only have those who are into the experimental mode as a survival. . . (Talburtt, 1986, p. 25).

CAEL ran into opposition at every stage in its history. In its early years, CAEL confronted the Council on Postsecondary Accreditation and the Council of Graduate Deans. Several organizations serving adults, as well as those focused on campus-based experiential education, competed with CAEL. CAEL was able to either neutralize or coopt many of these organizations. In some cases, as with the National Society for Internships and Experiential Education and the Coalition for Alternatives in Postsecondary Education, CAEL served as a senior partner. Indeed, as long as CAEL could raise foundation money, it could act as a patron of other groups which fell into its "dominant penumbra" (Zald, 1979).

CAEL could be the Common Cause of the higher education reform world. McCarthy and Zald (1973) describe Common Cause as a congolomerate in the ameliorative social movement industry. It speaks and acts for reform in general, picking up and losing supporters as it moves from issue to issue, problem to problem. As one problem is solved, it moves to another. As long as it can raise foundation money, it can support its less popular causes.

As time passed, CAEL shifted from running projects of its own to orchestrating multiple efforts. The first CAEL already set the stage for this role, as "the CAEL project" became a series of projects carried out by circles of people in colleges and universities across the country. With the growth of the regional system and its relationships with other organizations like the Coalition for Alternatives in Postsecondary Education and the American Council on Education, the second CAEL extended the model further. LEARN explicitly recognized CAEL as a kind of Common Cause: CAEL raised the money, defined a general agenda, and through its regional system and other relationship let other people carry it out.

Of all three measures of impact, then, CAEL's performance is mixed but impressive. CAEL *gained acceptance* from some influential people and organizations inside and outside of higher education as a legitimate—in some realms paramount—voice for the agenda it pursued. Acceptance of CAEL was quite high, especially for its work on the assessment of prior learning, among members of the national infrastructure for change in higher education. It was probably much lower among representatives of elite institutions and disciplinary bodies, which operate in a very different world from the one that CAEL inhabited.

CAEL did not penetrate the academic establishment—the selective private colleges, the research universities, and the disciplinary departments in many other colleges and universities. Senior administrators, staff in special programs for adults and experiential education, and maverick faculty members may have heard of CAEL. Some may have been involved in a CAEL project from time to time. Partly because of CAEL's work, but also because of the maturing of programs and the work of other organizations, experiential education became a more acceptable part of traditional higher education.

But these inroads did not put adult and experiential education at the core of academia. On the contrary, colleges and universities do not readily grant credit for life experience, and most continue to rely on traditional classrooms to educate students. The core is not easy to penetrate. Change in higher education is much more likely to occur through the addition of parallel structures.

Indeed, this is what happened during CAEL's lifetime. CAEL's base was in colleges and universities with large numbers of adult learners. Under pressure to maintain their enrollments when students of traditional age were less plentiful, these institutions received help from CAEL in reaching adults. Here CAEL played an important role in *winning new advantages* for adult learners. It also became involved with other organizations outside of higher education, such as Mountain Bell, the National Guard, and the UAW-Ford Training and Development Center, and won additional advantages for adult learners.

Not very long ago, these efforts could be dismissed as marginal to the enterprise of higher education. But as lifelong education, changes in the workplace, and the sheer increase in the enrollment of adults in colleges, universities and independent training programs have grown in the last decade, it is hard to call them marginal. They are part of a parallel framework for higher education, and CAEL was an active force in building it. It has contributed ideas, strategies, know-how, money and a sense of purpose to this *larger movement for change in higher education.* Indeed, at several points, CAEL was a ringleader.

# AFTERWORD

# Four Years Later

As I take a few days to reacquaint myself with CAEL, after four years, I feel as if I am among old friends. Much has happened in my own life and in the life of higher education since I completed my research on CAEL in 1985. I have taken a job that has deepened my understanding of colleges and universities in this country. I have become aware even more than I was four years ago of the sharp differences among them in wealth, students and working conditions. I have seen again and again their yearning to do a better job with their students—and how difficult it is to change the conditions that would allow them to do better.

The last four years have brought a deluge of reports and critiques of higher education from national higher education associations, the federal government, and governors. Hundreds of conferences and workshops have carried the ideas of the "reform movement" to college administrators and faculty members across the country. A central emphasis of the reform movement has been the assessment of student achievements and institutional performance.

CAEL has been noticeably absent from the reform movement in higher education, even in most discussions of assessment. In part, this may be due to the lack of serious attention in the reports and conferences to adult students, although now they constitute at least half of the enrollments in colleges and universities. But more importantly, it is because CAEL's trajectory has continued to take it farther away than it was four years ago from the current preoccupation of colleges and universities with general education requirements, faculty recruitment and scholarly publication. While CAEL continues to work with colleges and universities, it is likely to do so with senior administrators or with individual faculty or staff members who "deliver" educational "services" on one of CAEL's projects.

In many ways, CAEL is very like itself in 1985. It still has the quality of a social movement organization, with its calls for onward! and upward! The core group of staff, regional representatives and fellow travelers remains pretty much the same, although several people have withdrawn or changed jobs. The annual assembly is still a significant place for rallying troops and attracting new foot soldiers. Women, minorities and innovators of various kinds are still very much in evidence. Assessment continues to be a fertile—and subversive—idea as CAEL carries its word to new realms.

CAEL continues to be a membership organization whose budget is based on externally funded projects, carried out by hundreds of regional representatives, volunteers and short-term consultants. Its center of gravity has shifted to "joint ventures" with companies, government agencies and unions. CAEL has succeeded admirably in learning from its first experience in such a venture with the Ford-UAW National Development and Training Center in Michigan (NDTC). It has adapted the materials it developed for the NDTC and other projects into a comprehensive counseling and educational delivery program for workers in a variety of jobs. Its "Returning to Learning" workshops give adults the opportunity to assess their skills, decide what kind of work they want to do and how to prepare themselves to do it, and learn how to make their way in college. Other materials have been developed for unemployed workers and those facing lay-offs, for families and friends of adults returning to school, and for retirees. CAEL has organized numbers of colleges, universities and schools in different regions of the country to provide conveniently scheduled courses for workers who decide they want further study.

CAEL has always been good at exploiting its activities for several purposes, and it has done so to great effect in its joint ventures. The Student Potential Program, a structured interview to determine students' non-academic strengths and competencies, has been adapted for use with workers as the Employee Potential Program. CAEL's abiding interest in assessing learning acquired in settings other than school has attracted companies, unions, government agencies and workers alike. Its strategic use of joint ventures as a lever for change appears to have prodded some colleges and universities into accepting learning from experience through examination and certification of courses, although it has not succeeded in making its unique approach to assessment through portfolios more popular.

Since CAEL began its joint ventures, some 90,000 workers have been eligible for education and training benefits through U.S. West Communications (formerly Mountain Bell), the Communications Workers of America, the International Brotherhood of Electrical Workers, the Scott Paper Company, the United Food and Commercial Workers, Bell of Pennsylvania/Diamond State Telephone, the Food and Drug Administration and the Office of Personnel Administration of the federal government, AT&T, the International Union of Bricklayers and Allied Craftsmen, and the New York Department of Education. New programs are being explored all the time, not only in the United States but in other countries. In Great Britain, the Learning from Experience Trust, the "British CAEL" founded by CAEL's long-time associate, Norman Evans, is attracting leading companies, government agencies and universities. In Quebec, the Manpower Vocational Training Commission has used the Employee Potential Program to get single welfare mothers and displaced asbestos workers ready for further schooling.

The results for workers, and adult learners in general, have been extraordinary. CAEL has been instrumental in changing employer tuition payments from a reimbursement to a prepaid system; eliminating the necessity to seek reimbursement has dramatically increased worker participation in educational programs. It has legitimized the use of prepaid tuition for skills assessment, education and career counseling, and the assessment of prior learning. It has broadened the definition of eligible courses for employer support beyond narrowly defined job-related subjects.

Some 250 counselors and workshop leaders from colleges, universities, schools and other organizations, in addition to CAEL staff, have been trained to work with CAEL's projects, such as conducting the Employee Potential Program interview and assessment, Returning to Learning workshops, and counseling. Denver and Philadelphia have been centers for CAEL's joint ventures. In the U.S. West Communications/Communications Workers of America "Pathways to the Future" program directed by Elinor Greenberg, more than 1600 Mountain Bell employees attended "Returning to Learning" workshops, 7500 received career counseling, and as of this writing almost 6500 have enrolled in courses. In Philadelphia, Pamela Tate has directed the Philadelphia Joint Ventures Center, under whose auspices representatives from a network of forty colleges, universities and schools in the area have been trained to offer career and educational counseling and assessment. They have been able to conduct Returning to Learning workshops for employees at Scott Paper, Bell of Pennsylvania, Volkswagen, and the United Food and Commercial Workers.

Joint ventures have put CAEL on a more solid financial footing. Keeton estimates that colleges, universities and other postsecondary institutions have received $5 million from CAEL for tuition, career counseling, assessment fees, other fees and books from its joint ventures. CAEL itself has nearly doubled its budget and reduced its dependency on grants from 80% of its budget in the 1977 to 1984 period, to less than 6% in 1989. There is no reason to think that CAEL's success will diminish. It has very little competition, and even if more competitors enter the field, its track record with non-educational institutions, access to colleges and universities, and credibility with opinion leaders in higher education is likely to keep it dominant.

Thus, it appears that CAEL has discovered a formula for survival as an independent organization. CAEL has been able to convince employers and policy-makers within and outside of higher education that the future of the economy and the workforce depends on education approached in ways that it pioneered: experiential, linked to adult learners' needs and potentials, physically and temporally flexible, and sophisticated about how adults learn. CAEL designed impressive materials and procedures for carrying out its approach to education. As opportunities for joint ventures arose, CAEL refined its materials and procedures. Building on its membership base, the commitment of its core group, and a regional ''movement'' structure, CAEL identified, trained and deployed hundreds of people to carry out its projects as new opportunities arose. This cadre, with a few exceptions, does not require that CAEL carry a large, expensive central staff.

CAEL will move into other hands in January, 1990, as Morris Keeton retires as president and Pamela Tate succeeds him. This is a fateful move not only in the presidency; it will also involve a shift of setting from a quiet planned community in a border state to a seething Rust Belt city. As Tate moves CAEL from Columbia to Chicago, she will work with a more integrated, financially independent and mature organization than CAEL was when I first began studying it. As the person who is most responsible for bringing employer-supported and employee-based education to CAEL, Tate's presidency will carry CAEL further along this path. In so doing, CAEL will become a central player in the rapidly growing parallel framework for higher education.

Zelda F. Gamson
Chilmark, Massachusetts
July, 1989

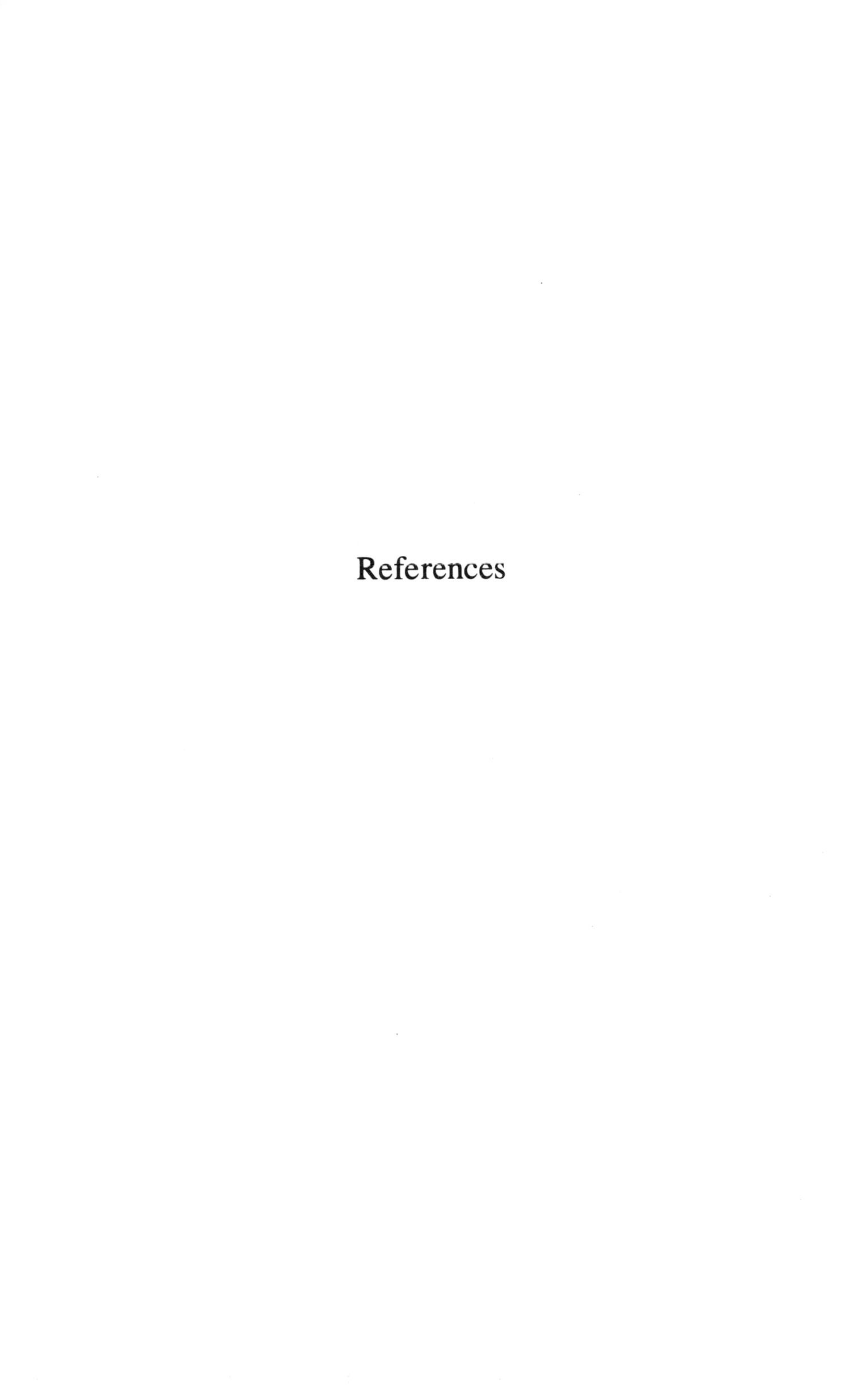

# References

# References

Adler, Paul. "Technology and Us." *Socialist Review*, 1986, *16*, 67-98.

Astin, Alexander W. *Achieving Educational Excellence*. San Francisco: Jossey-Bass, 1985.

Asti, Alexander W., Carolyn J. Inouye, and William S. Korn. *Preliminary Evaluation of the CAEL Student Potential Program*. Columbia, Md.: CAEL, 1986.

Barzun, Jacques. *The American University: How It Runs, Where It is Going*. New York: Harper and Row, 1969.

Baskin, Sam (Ed.). *Higher Education: Some Newer Developments*. New York: McGraw-Hill, 1965.

Bennis, Warren and Philip Slater. *The Temporary Society*. New York: Harper and Row, 1968.

Berg, Ivar. *Education and Jobs*. New York: Praeger, 1970.

Bloland, Harlan G. *Associations in Action: The Washington, D.C. Higher Education Community*. ASHE-ERIC Higher Education Report No. 2, 1985.

Boyd, Joseph L., Jr. and Benjamin Shimberg. *Handbook of Performance Testing: A Practical Guide for Test Makers*. Princeton: N.J.: Educational Testing Service, 1974.

Breen, Paul, Thomas Donlon, and Urban Whitaker. *The Learning and Assessment of Interpersonal Skills: Guidelines for Administrators and Faculty*. Working Paper No. 4. Columbia, Md.: CAEL, 1975a.

Breen, Paul, Thomas Donlon, and Urban Whitaker. *The Learning and Assessment of Interpersonal Skills: Guidelines for Students*. Working Paper No. 5. Columbia, Md.: CAEL, 1975b.

CAEL, "The UAW Ford College and University Options Program." Manuscript report prepared for the United States Department of Education, May 1986.

Carnegie Commission on Higher Education. *Less Time, More Options: Education Beyond the High School*. New York: McGraw-Hill, 1971a.

Carnegie Commission on Higher Education. *New Students and New*

*Places: Policies for the Future Growth and Development of American Higher Education.* New York: McGraw-Hill, 1971b.

Carnegie Commission on Higher Education. *The Fourth Revolution: Instructional Technology in Higher Education.* New York: McGraw-Hill, 1972.

Carnegie Commission on Higher Education. *Digest of Reports of the Carnegie Commission on Higher Education.* New York: McGraw-Hill, 1974.

Carnevale, Anthony Patrick. *Human Capital: A High Yield Corporate Investment.* Washington, D.C.: American Society for Training and Development, 1982.

Carp, Abraham, Richard Peterson, and Pamela Roelfs. "Adult Learning Interests and Experiences." In K. Patricia Cross, John R. Valley and Associates. *Planning Non-Traditional Programs.* San Francisco: Jossey-Bass, 1974.

"Change in America." *The Chronicle of Higher Education,* September 17, 1986, *XXXIII* (3), 1.

Cheren, Mark. *The Self-Directed Educator: A CAEL Syllabus.* Columbia, Md.: CAEL, 1979.

Chickering, Arthur W. *Education and Identity.* San Francisco: Jossey-Bass, 1969.

Chickering, Arthur W. *The Modern American College: Responding to the New Realities of Diverse Students and a Changing Society.* San Francisco: Jossey-Bass, 1981.

Christenson, Frank. *Guidelines and Procedures for the Assessment of Experiential Learning and for the Selection and Training of Field Experts.* Institutional Report No. 5. Columbia, Md.: CAEL, 1975.

Cleveland, Harlan. "Educating for the Information Society." *Change,* July/August 1985, *17* (4), 13-21.

Collins, Randall. *The Credential Society: An Historical Sociology of Education and Stratification.* New York: Academic Press, 1979.

Commission on Higher Education and the Adult Learner. *Adult Learners: Key to the Nation's Future.* Columbia, Md.: CAEL, 1984.

Commission on Non-Traditional Study. *Diversity by Design.* San Francisco: Jossey-Bass, 1973.

## REFERENCES


Cook, Marvin J. *Developing Learning Outcomes, Module 1.* Columbia, Md.: CAEL, 1978a.

Cook, Marvin J. *Developing Learning Outcomes, Module 2.* Columbia, Md.: CAEL, 1978b.

Cook, Marvin J. *Samples—Program Maps, Learning Outcomes, and Assessment Tasks—Module 4.* Columbia, Md.: CAEL, 1981.

Cook, Marvin J. and Henry R. Walbesser. *Developing Assessment Tasks, Module 3.* Columbia, Md.: CAEL, 1980.

"Cooperative Assessment of Experiential Learning." A Proposal to the Carnegie Corporation of New York. Princeton, N.J.: Educational Testing Service, 1973.

Cornell Center for Improvement in Undergraduate Education. *The Yellow Pages of Undergraduate Innovations.* Ithaca, New York: Cornell University, 1974.

Crooks, Lois A. *The Selection and Development of Performance Measures for Assessment Center Programs.* Princeton, N.J.: Educational Testing Service, 1974.

Cross, K. Patricia. *Beyond the Open Door: New Students to Higher Education.* San Francisco: Jossey-Bass, 1971.

Cross, K. Patricia. *Adults as Learners.* San Francisco: Jossey-Bass, 1981.

Cross, K. Patricia, John R. Valley, and Associates. *Planning Non-Traditional Programs.* San Francisco: Jossey-Bass, 1974.

Eurich, Nell P. *Corporate Classrooms: The Learning Business.* Princeton, N.J.: The Carnegie Foundation for the Advancement of Teaching, 1985.

Evans, Norman. *The Knowledge Revolution: Making the Link Between Learning and Work.* London: Grant McIntyre Ltd., 1981.

Evans, Norman. "Degree of Flexibility: Earn Credit Where It's Due." *CAEL News,* May/June 1986, *9*(4), 3.

Ewens, Thomas. "Transforming a Liberal Arts Curriculum: Alverno College." In Gerald Grant (Ed.). *On Competence: A Critical Analysis of Competence-Based Reforms in Higher Education.* San Francisco: Jossey-Bass, 1979.

Feasley, Charles E. *Serving Learners at a Distance: A Guide to Program Practices.* ASHE-ERIC Higher Education Research Report No. 5, 1983.

# REFERENCES

Fenwick, Dorothy C. *Directory of Campus-Business Linkages: Education and Business Prospering Together.* New York: Macmillan, 1983.

Ferguson, Marilyn. *The Aquarian Conspiracy: Personal and Social Transformation in the 1980's.* New York: St. Martin's, 1980.

Fireman, Bruce and William A. Gamson. "Utilitarian Logic in the Resource Mobilization Perspective." In Mayer N. Zald and John D. McCarthy (Eds.). *The Dynamics of Social Movements.* Cambridge: Mass.: Winthrop, 1979.

Forrest, Aubrey. *A Student Handbook for Preparing a Portfolio for the Assessment of Prior Experiential Learning.* Working Paper No. 7. Columbia, Md.: CAEL, 1975.

Freeman, Jo. "Resource Mobilizaion and Strategy: A Model for Analyzing Social Movement Organization Actions." In Mayer N. Zald and John D. McCarthy (Eds.). *The Dynamics of Social Movements.* Cambridge, Mass.: Winthrop, 1979.

Fund for the Improvement of Postsecondary Education. *A Decade of Improvement.* Washington, D.C.: Fund for the Improvement of Postsecondary Education, 1983.

Gamson, William A. *The Strategy of Social Protest.* Chicago: Dorsey, 1975.

Gamson, Zelda F. "Understanding the Difficulties of Implementing a Competence-Based Curriculum." In Gerald Grant (Ed.). *On Competence: A Critical Analysis of Competence-Based Reforms in Higher Education.* San Francisco: Jossey-Bass, 1979.

Gamson, Zelda F. "Notes on Collaborative Work and Multi-Institutional Projects." Unpublished Paper, 1983.

Gamson, Zelda F. "What is CLEO and What Can We Learn from It?" Unpublished report available from Formative Evaluation Research Associates, Ann Arbor, Michigan, 1984.

Gamson, Zelda F. "An Academic Counter-Revolution: The Roots of the Current Movement to Reform Undergraduate Education. *Educational Policy,* 1987, *1* (4), 429-444.

Gamson, Zelda F. and Associates. *Liberating Education.* San Francisco: Jossey-Bass, 1984.

Gamson, Zelda F. and Richard A. Levey. *Structure and Emergence: Proceedings of an Institute on Innovations in Undergraduate*

*Education.* Ann Arbor, Michigan: Center for the Study of Higher and Postsecondary Education, School of Education, University of Michigan, 1977.

Gerlach, Luther P. and Virginia H. Hine. *People, Power, Change: Movements of Social Transformation.* Indianapolis: Bobbs- Merrill, 1970.

Gould, Samuel B. and K. Patricia Cross (Eds.). *Explorations in Non-Traditional Study.* San Francisco: Jossey-Bass, 1972.

Grant, Gerald (Ed.). *On Competence: A Critical Analysis of Competence-Based Reforms in Higher Education.* San Francisco: Jossey-Bass, 1979.

Grant, Gerald and David Riesman. *The Perpetual Dream: Reform and Experiment in the American College.* Chicago: University of Chicago Press, 1978.

Greenwood, Phyllis. "Comments on CAEL Materials." Unpublished paper, 1984.

Gross, Edward and Paul V. Grambsch. *University Goals and Academic Power.* Washington, D.C.: American Council on Education, 1968.

Grove, Judith. "A History of the Center for the Study of Liberal Education for Adults." Unpublished doctoral dissertation, Northern Illinois University, 1985.

Hall, James C. "A History of Special Baccalaureate Programs for Adults, 1945-1970." Unpublished doctoral dissertation, University of Chicago, 1975.

Hall, Lawrence. *New Colleges for New Students.* San Francisco: Jossey-Bass, 1974.

Harrington, Fred Harvey. *The Future of Adult Education.* San Francisco: Jossey-Bass, 1981.

Hartle, Terry W. and Mark A. Kutner. "Federal Policies: Programs, Legislation, and Prospects." In Richard E. Peterson and Associates. *Lifelong Learning in America.* San Francisco: Jossey-Bass, 1980.

Hartnett, Rodney T., Mary Jo Clark, Robert A. Feldmesser, Margaret L. Gieber, and Neal M. Soss, *The British Open University in the United States.* Princeton, N.J.: Educational Testing Service, 1974.

Hefferlin, J.B. Lon. *Dynamics of Academic Reform.* San Francisco: Jossey-Bass, 1969.

## REFERENCES


Hefferlin, J.B. Lon. "Avoiding Cut-Rate Credits and Discount Degrees." In K. Patricia Cross, John R. Valley, and Associates. *Planning Non-Traditional Programs.* San Francisco: Jossey-Bass, 1974.

Heffernan, James M., Francis U. Macy, and Donn F. Vickers. *Educational Brokering: A New Service for Adult Learners.* Syracuse, N.Y.: Regional Learning Service of Central New York, 1976.

Heiss, Ann. *An Inventory of Academic Innovation and Reform.* New York: McGraw-Hill, 1974.

"The Higher Education Amendments of 1986: What They Mean for Colleges and Students." *The Chronicle of Higher Education,* October 8, 1986, *XXXIII* (6), 28-29.

Hirschhorn, Larry. *Beyond Mechanization: Work and Technology in a Postindustrial Age.* Cambridge: MIT Press, 1984.

Hodgkinson, Harold. *Assessment of Phase I—Project LEARN.* Columbia, Md.: CAEL, 1982.

Houle, Cyril O. *The External Degree.* San Francisco: Jossey-Bass, 1973.

Houle, Cyril O. "Deep Traditions of Experiential Learning." In Morris T. Keeton and Associates. *Experiential Learning: Rationale, Characteristics, and Assessment.* San Francisco: Jossey-Bass, 1976.

Houle, Cyril O. *Patterns of Learning: New Perspectives on Life-Span Education.* San Francisco: Jossey-Bass, 1984.

Jacobs, Frederic and Richard J. Allen. (Eds.). *Expanding the Missions of Graduate and Professional Education.* New Directions in Experiential Learning No. 15. San Francisco: Jossey-Bass, 1982.

Jantsch, Erich. *The Self-Organizing Universe: Scientific and Human Implications of the Emerging Paradigm of Evolution.* Oxford: Pergamon, 1980.

Jencks, Christopher and David Riesman. *The Academic Revolution.* New York: Doubleday, 1968.

Jenkins, J. Craig. "Resource Mobilization Theory and the Study of Social Movements." *Annual Review of Sociology,* 1983, *9,* 527-553.

Kanter, Rosabeth Moss. *The Change Masters: Innovation for*

*Productivity in the American Corporation.* New York: Simon & Schuster, 1983.

Keeton, Morris T. *Models and Mavericks: A Profile of Private Liberal Arts Colleges.* New York: McGraw-Hill, 1971a.

Keeton, Morris T. *Shared Authority on Campus.* Washington, D.C.: American Association for Higher Education, 1971b.

Keeton, Morris T. "Dilemmas in Accrediting Off-Campus Learning." In Dyckman W. Vermilye (Ed.), *The Expanded Campus: Current Issues in Higher Education 1972.* San Francisco: Jossey-Bass, 1972.

Keeton, Morris T. *Reflections on Experiential Learning and Its Uses.* Working Paper No. 3. Columbia, Md.: CAEL, 1975.

Keeton, Morris T. "A Challenge from Within Our Own Ideas", *CAEL News,* November 1983, *7* (3), 2-3.

Keeton, Morris T. and Associates. *Experiential Learning: Rationale, Characteristics, and Assessment.* San Francisco: Jossey-Bass, 1976.

Keeton, Morris T. and Conrad Hilberry. *Struggle and Promise: A Future for Colleges.* New York: McGraw-Hill, 1969.

Klemp, George O., Jr. "Assessing Student Potential: An Immodest Proposal." In Clark Taylor (Ed.), *Diverse Student Preparation: Benefits and Issues.* New Directions in Experiential Learning No. 17. San Francisco: Jossey-Bass, 1982.

Knapp, Joan E. *Assessing Prior Learning—A CAEL Handbook.* Columbia, Md.: CAEL, 1977.

Knapp, Joan E. (Ed.). *Financing and Implementing Prior Learning Assessment.* New Directions in Experiential Learning No. 14. San Francisco: Jossey-Bass, 1981.

Knapp, Joan and Leta Davis. "Scope and Varieties of Experiential Learning." In Morris T. Keeton, and Pamela J. Tate, (Eds.). *Learning by Experience—What, Why, How.* New Directions in Experiential Learning No. 1. San Francisco: Jossey-Bass, 1978.

Knapp, Joan and Amiel Sharon. *A Compendium of Assessment Techniques.* Working Paper Paper No. 2. Columbia, Md.: CAEL, 1975.

Knowles, Malcolm S. *The Adult Education Movement in the U.S.* Malabar, Fla.: Robert E. Krieger, 1977.

## REFERENCES


Knox, Alan B. *Adult Development and Learning.* San Francisco: Jossey-Bass, 1977.

Kolb, David A. *Experiential Learning: Experience as the Source of Learning and Development.* Englewood Cliffs, N.J.: Prentice-Hall, 1984.

Lawler, Edward E. *High-Involvement Management.* San Francisco: Jossey-Bass, 1986.

Lewis, Robert, Elaine Comegys, Loraine Shepard, and Shannon Groves. *The Use of Expert Judgment in the Assessment of Demonstrated Learning in the Antioch College Yellow Springs Adult Degree Completion Program.* Institutional Report No. 1. Columbia, Md.: CAEL, 1975.

Lindquist, Jack. *Strategies for Change.* Berkeley, Calif.: Pacific Soundings Press, 1979.

Lofland, John. "White-Hot Mobilization Strategies of a Millenarian Movement." In Mayer N. Zald and John D. McCarthy (Eds.). *The Dynamics of Social Movements.* Cambridge: Mass.: Winthrop, 1979.

MacTaggart, Terrence (Ed.). *Cost-Effective Assessment of Prior Learning.* New Directions in Experiential Learning No. 19. San Francisco: Jossey-Bass, 1983.

Mayville, William V. *Federal Influence on Higher Education Curricula.* AAHE-ERIC Higher Education Research Report No. 1, 1980.

McCarthy, John D. and Mayer N. Zald. *The Trend in Social Movements in America: Professionalization and Resource Mobilization.* Morristown, N.J.: General Learning Press, 1973.

McCarthy, John D. and Mayer N. Zald. "Resource Mobilization and Social Movements." *American Journal of Sociology,* 1977, *82* (6), 1212-1214.

McIntosh, Naomi E. with Judith A. Calder and Betty Swift. *A Degree of Difference: A Study of the First Year's Intake of Students to the Open University of the United Kingdom.* Society for Research into Higher Education, University of Surrey, 1976.

Meyer, Peter. *Awarding College Credit for Non-College Learning.* San Francisco: Jossey-Bass, 1976.

Morse, Nancy W. *Employee Educational Programs: Implications for*

*Industry and Higher Education.* ASHE-ERIC Higher Education Report No. 7, 1984.

Munson, Fred and Donald D. Pelz. *Innovating in Organizations: A Conceptual Framework.* Ann Arbor: Institute for Social Research, University of Michigan, 1981.

Nash, Nancy S. and Elizabeth M. Hawthorne. *Formal Recognition of Employer-Sponsored Instruction.* ASHE-ERIC Higher Education Report No. 3, 1987.

National Center for Educational Statistics. *Digest of Educational Statistics.* Washington, D.C.: U.S. National Center for Education Statistics, 1976.

Nesbitt, Hadley S. and Warren W. Willingham. (Eds.). *Implementing a Program for Assessing Experiential Learning.* Columbia, Md.: CAEL, 1976.

Newman, Frank. *Report on Higher Education.* Washington, D.C.: Office of Education, Department of Health, Education and Welfare, 1971.

Newman, Frank and Special Task Force. *The Second Newman Report: National Policy and Higher Education.* Cambridge, Mass.: MIT Press, 1973.

Niebuhr, Herman, Jr. *Revitalizing American Learning: A New Approach That Just Might Work.* Belmont, Calif.: Wadsworth, 1984.

Nisbet, Robert. *The Degradation of the Academic Dogma: The University in America 1945-1970.* New York: Basic Books, 1971.

Office of Technology Assessment. *Computerized Manufacturing Automation: Employment, Education and the Workplace.* Washington, D.C.: U.S. Congress, OTA-CIT-235, April 1984.

Permaul, Jane, Joan Steele, Marina Miko, and Laird Hayes. *Evaluation and Expert Judgment.* Institutional Report No. 3. Columbia, Md.: CAEL, 1975.

Peters, Thomas J. and Robert H. Waterman, Jr. *In Search of Excellence: Lessons from America's Best-Run Companies.* New York: Harper & Row, 1982.

Peterson, Marvin W. (Ed.). *Black Students on White Campuses: The Impacts of Increased Black Enrollments.* Ann Arbor, Mich.: Survey Research Center, Institute for Social Research, University of Michigan, 1978.

## REFERENCES


Peterson, Richard E. and Associates. *Lifelong Learning in America.* San Francisco: Jossey-Bass, 1979.

Pifer, Alan. "Has the Time Come for an External Degree?" Speech at the Annual Meeting of the College Entrance Examination Board, October 27, 1970.

Powell, Susan A. "State Policies: Plans and Activities." In Richard E. Peterson and Associates. *Lifelong Learning in America.* San Francisco: Jossey-Bass, 1980.

Reilly, Richard, et al. *The Use of Expert Judgment in the Assessment of Experiential Learning.* Working Paper No. 10. Columbia, Md.: CAEL, 1975.

Reinharz, Shulamit. "Some Problems Associated with Service/Learning or Experiential Education." In Thomas Sherman and Walter Saunders, Jr. *Proceedings: Roles of Colleges and Universities in Volunteerism.* Blacksburg, Va.: Virginia Polytechnic Institute and State University, 1977.

Riesman, David. *On Higher Education: The Academic Enterprise in an Era of Rising Student Consumerism.* San Francisco: Jossey-Bass, 1981.

Riesman, David, Joseph Gusfield, and Zelda Gamson. *Academic Values and Mass Education: The Early Years of Oakland and Monteith.* New York: McGraw-Hill, 1975.

Rogers, Everett M. "Reinvention During the Innovation Process." In Michael Radnor, Irwin Feller, and Everett Rogers. (Eds.). *The Diffusion of Innovations: An Assessment.* Evanston, Ill.: Center for the Interdisciplinary Study of Science and Technology, Northwestern University, 1978.

Ruyle, Janet and Lucy Ann Geiselman. "Non-Traditional Opportunities and Programs." In K. Patricia Cross, John R. Valley and Associates. *Planning Non-Traditional Programs.* San Francisco: Jossey-Bass, 1974.

Schmeidler, Emily. "Shaping Ideas and Actions: CORE, SCLC, and SNCC in the Struggle for Equality, 1960-1966". Unpublished doctoral dissertation, University of Michigan, 1980.

Schon, Donald A. *Beyond the Stable State.* New York: Random House, 1971.

Sharon, Amiel. *A Task Based Model for Assessing Work Experience.*

Working Paper No. 8. Columbia, Md.: CAEL, 1975.

Silverman, Paul and Pamela J. Tate. "The Accrediting Process as an Aid to Quality Assurance." In Keeton, Morris T. (Ed.). *Defining and Assuring Quality in Experiential Learning.* New Directions in Experiential Learning No. 9. San Francisco: Jossey-Bass, 1980.

Simosko, Susan. *Earn College Credit for What You Know.* Washington, D.C.: Acropolis Books, 1985.

Smith, Virginia. "Report on W.K. Kellogg Foundation Project LEARN." Battle Creek, Mich.: W.K. Kellogg Foundation, 1987.

Snow, David A., Burke E. Rockford, Jr., Steven K. Worden, and Robert D. Benford. "Frame Alignment and Mobilization." *American Sociological Review,* 1986, *51* (4), 464-481.

Sosdian, Carol P., *External Degrees: Program and Student Characteristics.* Washington, D.C.: National Institute of Education, 1978.

Spenner, Kenneth I. "Deciphering Prometheus: Temporal Change in the Skill Level of Work." *American Sociological Review,* 1983, *48,* 824-837.

Spitzer, Kurt and Sue Smock. *The Refinement and Modification of an Instrument for Assessing the Achievement of Interpersonal Skills of Social Work Students.* Institutional Report No. 4. Columbia, Md.: CAEL, 1975.

Stewart, David W. "Trendlines." *Adult and Continuing Education Today,* November 24, 1986, *XVI* (23), 180.

Talburtt, Margaret. *A Question of Transformation: Post-Secondary Education's Responses to Adult Learners and CAEL's Role in These Changes.* Ann Arbor, Mich.: Formative Evaluation Research Associates, 1986.

Tatzel, Miriam and Lois Lamdin. *Interpersonal Learning in an Academic Setting: Theory and Practice.* Institutional Report No. 2. Columbia, Md.: CAEL, 1975.

Taylor, Harold. *Students Without Teachers: The Crisis in the University.* New York: McGraw-Hill, 1969.

U.S. Bureau of the Census. *Historical Statistics of the United States—Colonial Times to 1970,* Part 1. Washington, D.C.: U.S. Department of Commerce, Bureau of the Census, 1975.

## REFERENCES


Van de Ven, Andrew and Gordon Walker. "The Dynamics of Interorganizational Coordination." *Administrative Science Quarterly*, 1984, *29* (4), 598-621.

Vermilye, Dyckman W. (Ed.). *Relating Work and Education.* San Francisco: Jossey-Bass, 1977.

Washington Center. *Preparing Humanists for Work: A National Study of Undergraduate Internships in the Humanities.* Washington, D.C.: The Washington Center, 1984.

Weathersby, George and Armand J. Henault, Jr. "Cost-Effectiveness of Programs." In Keeton, Morris T., and Associates. *Experiential Learning: Rationale, Characteristics, and Assessment.* San Francisco: Jossey-Bass, 1977.

Wegmann, Robert G. "Looking for Work in a New Economy." *Change,* July/August 1985, *17* (4), 41-47.

"Who's Who in Higher Education?" *Change,* February 1975, *7,* 24-31.

Willingham, Warren W. *Principles of Good Practice in Assessing Experiential Learning.* Columbia, Md.: CAEL, 1977.

Willingham, Warren W. and Associates. *The CAEL Validation Report.* Columbia, Md.: CAEL, 1976.

Willingham, Warren W., Richard Burns, and Thomas Donlon. *Current Practices in the Assessment of Experiential Learning.* Working Paper No. 1. Columbia, Md.: CAEL, 1975.

Willingham, Warren W., John R. Valley, and Morris T. Keeton. *Assessing Experiential Learning—A Summary Report of the CAEL Project.* Columbia, Md.: CAEL, 1977.

Wilson, James Q. *Political Organizations.* New York: Basic Books, 1973.

Wolff, Robert Paul. *The Ideal of the University.* Boston: Beacon, 1969.

Zald, Mayer N. "Macro Issues in the Theory of Social Movements." Paper delivered at the annual meeting of the American Sociological Association, Boston, Mass., 1979.

Zald, Mayer N. and Roberta Ash. "Social Movement Organizations: Growth, Decay and Change." *Social Forces,* 1966, *44* (3), 327-341.

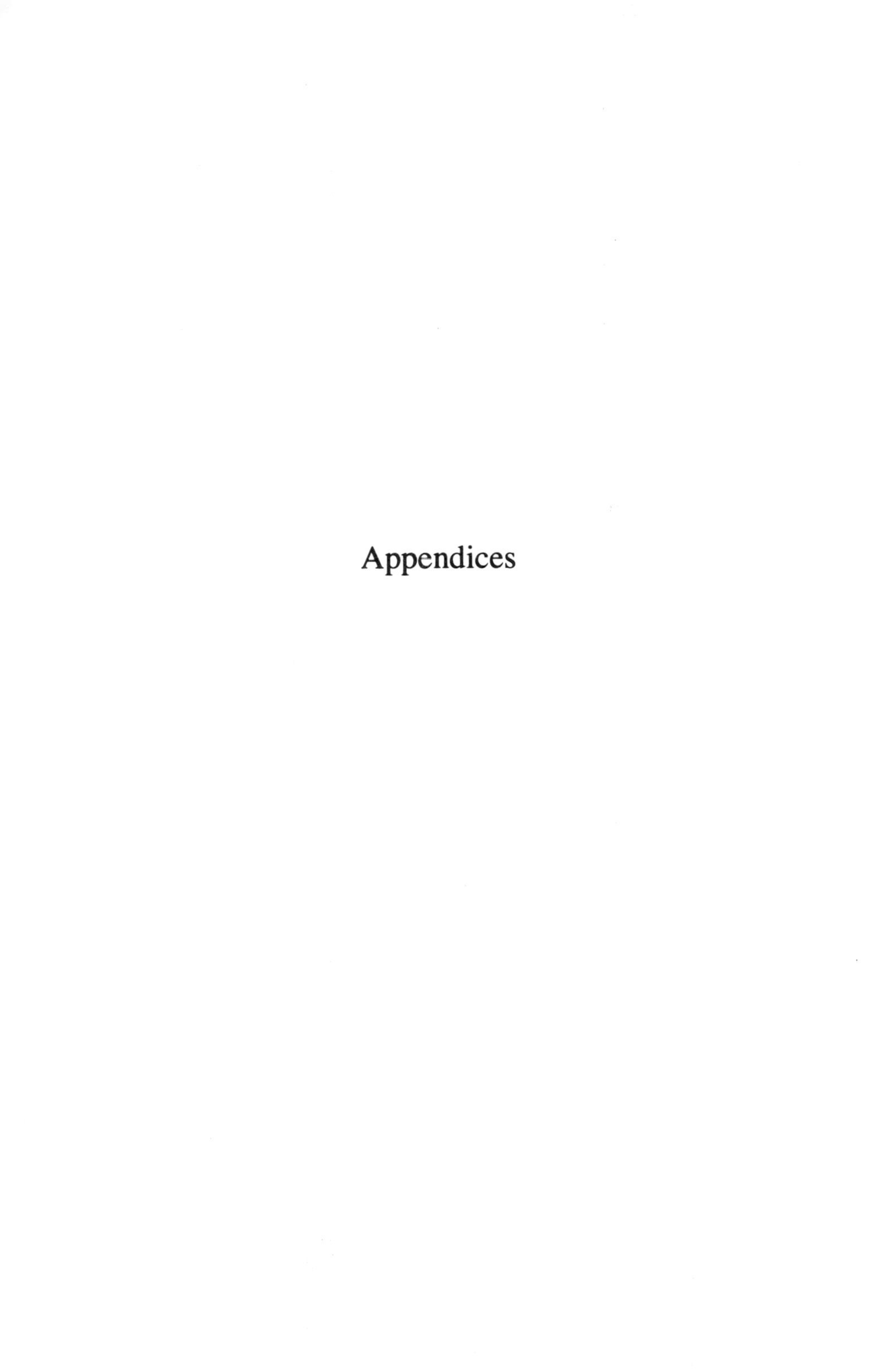

# Appendices

# Appendix A

## Institutions Participating in CAEL 1 Projects

| Institution | Site Visits/ Surveys, 1974-75 | Resource Panel 1974-75 | Tryout for Validation | Field Research for Validation Studies* | Faculty Development Program | Operational Models | Contributors to Annotated Literature Guide, 1977 | Contributors to Annotated Literature Guide—Supplement, 1978 | Total for Each Institution |
|---|---|---|---|---|---|---|---|---|---|
| Adelphi University | x | | | | | | | | 1 |
| Akron, Univ. of | | | x | x | x | | | | 3 |
| Alabama, Univ. of | | | | | | | x | | 1 |
| Alabama, Univ. of, New College | x | x | x | x | | | | | 4 |
| Alverno College | x | | x | x | x | | | | 4 |
| American Association of State Colleges and Universities | | | | | | | x | | 1 |
| American College | | | x | | | | | | 1 |
| Amer. Medical Assn. | | | | | | | | x | 1 |
| Antioch | | x | x | x | | x | | | 4 |
| Antioch, Minneapolis Center | x | | | | | | | | 1 |

# APPENDIX A

| Institution | Site Visits/ Surveys, 1974-75 | Resource Panel 1974-75 | Tryout for Validation | Field Research for Validation Studies* | Faculty Development Program | Operational Models | Contributors to Annotated Literature Guide, 1977 | Contributors to Annotated Literature Guide—Supplement, 1978 | Total for Each Institution |
|---|---|---|---|---|---|---|---|---|---|
| Antioch, San Francisco Center | x | | | | | | | | 1 |
| Armstrong College | x | | | | | | | | 1 |
| Augustana College | | | x | | | | | | 1 |
| Berea College | | | x | | | | | | 1 |
| Bethany College | | | x | | | | | x | 2 |
| Bethel College | x | | | | | | | | 1 |
| Black Hawk College | | | x | | | | | x | 2 |
| Brevard College | | | x | | | | | | 1 |
| Butler University | x | | | | | | | | 1 |
| Calif. State College, Bakersfield | | | x | | | | | | 1 |
| Calif. State College, Dominguez Hills | x | | | | | | | | 1 |
| Calif. State College, Los Angeles | | | x | | | | | | 1 |
| Calif. State Univ. and Colleges, Consortium of | | | | | | x | | | 1 |

| | | | | | | | | |
|---|---|---|---|---|---|---|---|---|
| California, Univ. of, Los Angeles | | | x | x | | x | x | 4 |
| Capital Higher Educ. Service | x | | | | | | | 1 |
| Central Michigan U. | x | | x | | | | x | 3 |
| Cincinnati, Univ. of | | | x | | | | | 1 |
| CUNY Bacc. Program | x | | | | | | | 1 |
| Dayton, Univ. of | | | x | | | | | 1 |
| Delaware County Community College | x | x | x | x | x | x | x | 7 |
| Delta College | | | x | | | | | 1 |
| DePaul University | x | | | | | | | 1 |
| Eastern Illinois Univ. | x | | | | | | | 1 |
| Eckerd College | | | x | | | | | 1 |
| Edinboro State Coll. | x | | | | | | | 1 |
| Education Develop. Center | | x | | | | | | 1 |
| Educational Testing Service | | | | | | x | x | 2 |
| El Paso Community College | | | x | | | | | 1 |
| Embry-Riddle Aeronautical Univ. | x | | | | | | | 1 |
| Empire State College | x | | x | x | | | | 3 |

# APPENDIX A

| Institution | Site Visits/ Surveys, 1974-75 | Resource Panel 1974-75 | Tryout for Validation | Field Research for Validation Studies* | Faculty Development Program | Operational Models | Contributors to Annotated Literature Guide, 1977 | Contributors to Annotated Literature Guide—Supplement, 1978 | Total for Each Institution |
|---|---|---|---|---|---|---|---|---|---|
| Evansville, Univ. of | | | x | | x | | x | | 3 |
| Everett Community College | x | | x | | | | | | 2 |
| Florida Int. Univ. | x | x | x | | | x | | | 4 |
| Fordham Univ. | x | | | | | | | | 1 |
| Fort Lewis College | x | | | | | | | | 1 |
| Fort Wright College | | | x | | | | | | 1 |
| Framingham State College | x | | | | | | | | 1 |
| Georgetown Univ., Career Planning Ctr | | | | | | | | x | 1 |
| Goddard College | x | | | | | | | | 1 |
| Golden West College | | | x | | | | | | 1 |
| Governors State U. | x | | x | x | x | | x | | 5 |
| Great Lakes Colleges Assn., Philadelphia Urban Semester | | | | | | | | x | 1 |
| Hampshire College | x | | | | | | | | 1 |

| | | | | | | | | | |
|---|---|---|---|---|---|---|---|---|---|
| Hartwick College | | | x | x | x | | | | 3 |
| Johns Hopkins Univ. | | | x | | | | | | 1 |
| Kansas State Univ. | | | x | | | | | | 1 |
| Kent State Univ. | | | x | | | | | x | 2 |
| Kentucky State Univ. | | | x | | | | | | 1 |
| Kentucky, Univ. of | | x | | | | x | x | x | 4 |
| Kings College | | | x | | | | | | 1 |
| LaGuardia Community College | | x | x | x | | | x | | 4 |
| Lone Mountain College | | | x | | | | | | 1 |
| Luzerne County Community College | | | x | | | | | | 1 |
| Macalester College | | | x | x | | | | | 2 |
| Madonna College | x | | x | | | | | | 2 |
| Maryland, Univ. of | | | x | | | | | | 1 |
| Massachusetts, U. of | x | | x | | | | | | 2 |
| Massachusetts, U. of, U. Without Walls | | | | | | | | x | 1 |
| Memphis State Univ. | x | | | | | x | x | | 3 |
| Metropolitan State U. | x | x | x | x | x | x | x | | 7 |
| Miami-Dade Community College | | | x | | | | | | 1 |
| Michigan State Univ. | | | | | | | x | | 1 |

| Institution | Site Visits/ Surveys, 1974-75 | Resource Panel 1974-75 | Tryout for Validation | Field Research for Validation Studies* | Faculty Development Program | Operational Models | Contributors to Annotated Literature Guide, 1977 | Contributors to Annotated Literature Guide—Supplement, 1978 | Total for Each Institution |
|---|---|---|---|---|---|---|---|---|---|
| Michigan State U., Justin Morrill College | | x | x | | x | | | | 3 |
| Minnesota, Univ. of | | | x | | | | | | 1 |
| Missouri, Univ. of | | | x | x | | | | | 2 |
| Missouri, Univ. of, Columbia, | | | | | | | x | x | 2 |
| Moorehead State College | x | | | | | | | | 1 |
| Mount Mary College | | | x | | | | | | 1 |
| Mount Union College | | | x | | x | | | | 2 |
| New Hampshire, University of | x | | | | | | | | 1 |
| New Rochelle, College of | x | | | | | | | | 1 |
| New York, State Univ. of | | | | | | | | x | 1 |
| New York, State Univ. of, Brockport | x | | x | | | | | | 2 |

| | | | | | | | | | |
|---|---|---|---|---|---|---|---|---|---|
| North Carolina Agric & Tech State Univ. | | | x | x | x | | | | 3 |
| North Dakota State School of Science | x | | | | | | | | 1 |
| Northeastern Illinois University | x | | | | | | | | 1 |
| Northeastern Univ. | | | | | | | | x | 1 |
| Northern Virginia Community College | | | | | | | | x | 1 |
| Northwest Regional Educ. Lab. | | | | | | | | x | 1 |
| Notre Dame College | | | x | x | | | | | 2 |
| Oregon, Univ. of | | | x | x | x | x | x | | 5 |
| Our Lady of Angels College | | | x | | | | | | 1 |
| Our Lady of the Lake College | x | | x | | | | | | 2 |
| Pace Univ. | x | | | | | | | | 1 |
| Pennsylvania State Univ. | | | | | | | x | | 1 |
| Queens College | x | | | | | | | | 1 |
| Ramapo College of New Jersey | x | x | | | | | | | 2 |
| Redlands, Univ. of, Johnston College | x | | x | | | | | | 2 |

| Institution | Site Visits/ Surveys, 1974-75 | Resource Panel 1974-75 | Tryout for Validation | Field Research for Validation Studies* | Faculty Development Program | Operational Models | Contributors to Annotated Literature Guide, 1977 | Contributors to Annotated Literature Guide—Supplement, 1978 | Total for Each Institution |
|---|---|---|---|---|---|---|---|---|---|
| Rochester Institute of Technology | | | x | | | | | | 1 |
| Roosevelt Univ. | x | | x | | | | | | 2 |
| Sacred Heart Univ. | x | | x | | | | | | 2 |
| Saint Benedict, College of | | | x | | | | | | 1 |
| Saint Louis Univ., Metropolitan College | | | x | x | | | | | 2 |
| Saint Mary of the Woods College | x | | | | | | | | 1 |
| Saint Rose, College of | x | | x | | | | | | 2 |
| Saint Thomas Aquinas College | | | x | | | | | | 1 |
| San Francisco State Univ. | x | x | x | x | | x | x | | 6 |
| San Francisco, Univ. of | x | | | | | | | | 1 |
| Sinclair Community College | | | | | | | | x | 1 |

| | | | | | | | | | |
|---|---|---|---|---|---|---|---|---|---|
| Southern Illinois University | x | | x | | | | | | 2 |
| Southern Oregon State College | | | x | | | | | | 1 |
| State Tech. Institute of Memphis | x | | | | | | | | 1 |
| Staten Island Community College | | | x | x | x | | | | 3 |
| Stephens College | | | x | x | | | x | x | 4 |
| Sterling College | x | | | | | | | | 1 |
| Temple Univ. | | | | | x | | | | 1 |
| Texas Christian Univ. | | | x | x | | | | | 2 |
| Texas Southern Univ. | | | x | | | | | | 1 |
| Thomas A. Edison College | x | x | x | x | | | x | | 5 |
| Towson State College | | | x | | | | | | 1 |
| Tri-County Tech College | | | | | | | | x | 1 |
| Union College | | | x | | | x | | | 2 |
| Upsala College | x | | | | | | | | 1 |
| Utah, Univ. of | | | | | | | | x | 1 |
| Vermont, Community College of | x | x | x | x | | x | | | 5 |

| Institution | Site Visits/ Surveys, 1974-75 | Resource Panel 1974-75 | Tryout for Validation | Field Research for Validation Studies* | Faculty Development Program | Operational Models | Contributors to Annotated Literature Guide, 1977 | Contributors to Annotated Literature Guide—Supplement, 1978 | Total for Each Institution |
|---|---|---|---|---|---|---|---|---|---|
| Virginia Polytechnic Institute & State U. | | | x | | | | | | 1 |
| Washington International College | | | | | | | | x | 1 |
| Webster College | x | | | | | x | | | 2 |
| Whatcom Community College | | | x | | | | | | 1 |
| Wichita State Univ. | | | x | x | | | | | 2 |
| Winona State Univ. | | | x | | | | | | 1 |
| Wisconsin, Univ. of, Greenbay | | | | | | | | x | 1 |
| TOTALS | 54 | 13 | 76 | 24 | 12 | 12 | 18 | 23 | |

TOTAL NUMBER OF PARTICIPANTS = 232

TOTAL NUMBER OF INSTITUTIONS Involved in One or More Projects** = 132

*Institutions Involved in Field Research were automatically included in Tryout.

**Each institution is only counted once in this summary.

# Appendix B

CAEL Publications,
1975-1985

## 1975

*CAEL Resource Book* includes annotated bibliographies, institutional annotations, agency annotations, a CAEL Assembly Directory, and condensed versions of the special project reports.

### Working Papers

Willingham, Warren, Richard Burns, and Thomas Donlon, Working Paper No. 1, *Current Practices in the Assessment of Experiential Learning,* 1975.

Knapp, Joan and Amiel Sharon, Working Paper No. 2 initially; later reprinted as a CAEL special report, *A Compendium of Assessment Techniques,* 1975.

Keeton, Morris, Ed., Working Paper No. 3, *Reflections on Experiential Learning and Its Uses.* Commissioned Papers were published in 1976 in *Experiential Learning: Rationale, Characteristics, and Assessment* (Morris Keeton, Ed.).

Breen, Paul, Thomas Donlon and Urban Whitaker, Working Paper No. 4, *The Learning and Assessment of Interpersonal Skills: Guidelines for Administrators and Faculty,* 1975.

Breen, Paul, Thomas Donlon, and Urban Whitaker, Working Paper No. 5, *The Learning and Assessment of Interpersonal Skills: Guidelines for Students,* 1975.

Knapp, Joan, Working Paper No. 6, *A Guide for Assessing Prior Experience Through Portfolios,* 1975.

Forrest, Aubrey, Working Paper No. 7, *A Student Handbook for Preparing a Portfolio for the Assessment of Prior Experiential Learning,* 1975.

Sharon, Amiel, Working Paper No. 8, *A Task-Based Model for Assessing Work Experience,* 1975.

Nesbitt, Hadley, Working Paper No. 9, *A Student Guide to Learning Through College-Sponsored Work Experience,* 1975.

Reilly, Richard, Ruth Churchill, John Clark, Arnold Fletcher, Myrna Miller, Judith Pendergrass, and Jane Porter, Working Paper No. 10, *The Use of Expert Judgment in the Assessment of Experiential Learning,* 1975.

# APPENDIX B

## Institutional Reports*

Lewis, Robert, Elaine Comegys, Loraine Shepard, and Shannon Groves, Institutional Report No. 1, *The Use of Expert Judgment in the Assessment of Demonstrated Learning in the Antioch College Yellow Springs Adult Degree Completion Program,* 1975.

Tatzel, Miriam and Lois Lamdin, Institutional Report No. 2, *Interpersonal Learning in an Academic Setting: Theory and Practice,* 1975.

Permaul, Jane, Joan Steele, Marina Miko, and Laird Hayes, Institutional Report No. 3, *Evaluation and Expert Judgment,* 1975.

Spitzer, Kurt and Sue Smock, Institutional Report No. 4, *The Refinement and Modification of an Instrument for Assessing the Achievement of Interpersonal Skills of Social Work Students,* 1975.

Christensen, Frank, Institutional Report No. 5, *Guidelines and Procedures for the Assessment of Experiential Learning and for the Selection and Training of Field Experts,* 1975.

## Special Project Reports**

Angus, Edward L., *Identification and Articulation of Specific Learning Outcomes of Different Types of Experiential Education,* Mars Hill College, 1975.

Barbato, Barbara Ann, *The Use of Portfolios in the Assessment of Prior Learning,* Webster College, 1975.

Clark, John L.D., *A Diagnostic Approach to the Assessment of Experiential Learning (Interim Report),* Thomas A. Edison College, 1975.

Daloz, Laurent, *Student Self-Assessment of Non-Sponsored Learning,* Community College of Vermont, 1975.

Edwins, Steven B. *The Panel Review of Architectural Education,* University of Kentucky, 1975.

Galson, Nirelle J. and L. Richard Oliker, *Assessment of Work Outcomes in Business Administration,* Syracuse University, 1975.

Harvey, Leah and Aubrey Forrest, *Use of Portfolios in the Assessment of Prior Experiential Learning,* Minnesota Metropolitan State College, 1975.

---

*Condensed versions of Institutional Reports, except for Tatzel and Lamdin, appear in the *CAEL Resource Book,* 1975.

**Institutional Reports were originally Special Project Reports.

Laramee, William A., *Educational Debriefing*, Berea College, 1975.

McQueen, Lila, Richard Fehnel, Janet Moursund, Ricardo Munoz, and Norman Sundberg, *Assessing Interpersonal Skills in the Human Services*, University of Oregon, 1975.

Nickse, Ruth S., *Home Management and Human Service Competencies*, Regional Learning Service of Central New York, 1975.

O'Neil, Edward H. and Bernard J. Sloan, *Awarding Credit for Prior Learning Experiences: A Manual for More Traditional Institutions of Higher Education*, New College, University of Alabama, 1975.

Palladino, Joseph R., *Development of a Resume/Portfolio, Student Assessment Handbook, and a Student Training Institute*, Framingham State College, 1975.

Park, Dabney and Nancy Wylie, *A Taxonomy of Basic Competencies in the World of Work*, Florida International University, 1975.

Rivera, Jose, *Exploring Alternative Learning Methods at El Paso Community College*, El Paso Community College, 1975.

Whitaker, Urban and Paul Breen, *Interpersonal Skills: Their Identification, Classification and Articulation to Student Goals*, San Francisco State University, 1975.

## Tape/Slide Presentations

Breen, Paul and Urban Whitaker, *Interpersonal Skills: An Analytical Framework*, 160 color slides and 32-minute synchronized audio tape, 1975.

Breen, Paul and Urban Whitaker, *Interpersonal Literacy*, 90 color slides and 14-minute synchronized audio tape, 1975.

## 1976

Keeton, Morris (Ed.), *Experiential Learning: Rationale, Characteristics, and Assessment*, Jossey-Bass, 1976, includes the following chapters:

Smith, Virginia, "The Search for an Integrating Logic"
Keeton, Morris, "Credentials for the Learning Society"
Houle, Cyril O., "Deep Traditions of Experiential Learning"
Gartner, Alan, "Credentialing the Disenfranchised"
Tumin, Melvin, "Valid and Invalid Rationales"

Coleman, James S., "Differences Between Experiential and Classroom Learning"

Chickering, Arthur W., "Developmental Change as a Major Outcome"

Gordon, Sheila, "Campus and Workplace as Arena"

Barton, Paul E., "Learning Through Work and Education"

Weathersby, George B. and Armand Henault, "Cost Effectiveness of Programs"

Kirkwood, Robert, "The Importance of Assessing Learning"

Aubrey Forrest, Joan Knapp, and Judith Pendergrass, "Tools and Methods of Evaluation"

Whitaker, Urban G., "Assessors and Their Qualifications"

Willingham, Warren W., "Critical Issues and Basic Requirements for Assessment"

*An Individualized Competence-Based Assessment Model*, 1976.

*Analyzing Costs in the Assessment of Prior Learning*, 1976.

*Coordinating Educational Assessment Across College Centers*, 1976.

*Implementing a Program for Assessing Experiential Learning*, 1976.

*Implementing and Financing Portfolio Assessment in a Public Institution*, 1976.

*Implementing Competency-Based Assessment of Prior Learning*, 1976.

*Initiating Experiential Learning Programs: Four Case Studies*, 1976.

*Standard Setting by Students and Community—How Much is Enough?*, 1976.

Nesbitt, Hadley S. and Warren W. Willingham (Eds.), *Implementing a Program for Assessing Experiential Learning*, 1976.

Warren W. Willingham and Associates, *The CAEL Validation Report*, 1976.

**1977**

Breen, Paul, Thomas F. Donlon and Urban Whitaker, *Learning and Assessing Interpersonal Competence—A CAEL Student Guide*, 1977.

Breen, Paul, Thomas F. Donlon and Urban Whitaker, *Teaching and Assessing Interpersonal Competence—A CAEL Handbook*, 1977.

Duley, John and Sheila Gordon, *College-Sponsored Experiential Learning—A CAEL Handbook*, 1977.

Forrest, Aubrey, *Assessing Prior Learning—A CAEL Student Guide*, 1977.

Knapp, Joan, *Assessing Prior Learning—A CAEL Handbook*, 1977.

Nesbitt, Hadley, *College-Sponsored Experiential Learning—A CAEL Student*

*Guide,* 1977.

Permaul, Jane Szutu and Marina Buhler Miko, *Documentation and Evaluation of Sponsored Experiential Learning,* CAEL Institutional Report No. 3 from University of California at Los Angeles—Revised Edition, 1977.

Reilly, Richard, Ruth Churchill, Arnold Fletcher, Myrna Miller, Judith Pendergrass, Jane Porter Stutz, and John Clark, *Expert Assessment of Experiential Learning—A CAEL Handbook,* 1977.

Sharon, Amiel T., *Assessing Occupational Competences—A CAEL Handbook,* 1977.

Tatzel, Miriam, *Prospects and Methods for Interpersonal Studies,* CAEL Institutional Report No. 2 from Empire State College—Revised Edition, 1977.

Willingham, Warren W., *Principles of Good Practice in Assessing Experiential Learning,* 1977.

Willingham, Warren W., John R. Valley and Morris T. Keeton, *Assessing Experiential Learning: A Summary Report of the CAEL Project,* 1977.

## Other Publications

Rees, Diana Bamford, (Ed.), *The CAEL Newsletter.*

## 1978

Cook, Marvin, *Developing Learning Outcomes, Module 2,* 1978.

Cook, Marvin, *Developing Program Maps, Module 1,* 1978.

Davis, Leta and Joan Knapp, *The Practice of Experiential Education: A CAEL Status Report,* 1978.

Keeton, Morris T. and Pamela J. Tate, (Eds.), *Learning by Experience—What, Why, How, (NDEL***)* 1978.

Stutz, Jane Porter and Joan Knapp, *CAEL Literature Guide,* 1978.

Stutz, Jane Porter and Joan Knapp, *CAEL Literature Guide Supplement,* 1978.

Wilson, James W., (Ed.), *Developing and Expanding Cooperative Education,* (NDEL), 1978.

Yelon, Stephen and John S. Duley, *Efficient Evaluation of Individual Performance in Field Placement,* 1978.

---

***"NDEL" indicates that the publication is part of the New Directions for Experiential Learning Series published by Jossey-Bass, San Francisco, CA

APPENDIX B

Other Publications

*CAEL Directory,* 1977-78.

Rees, Diana Bamford, (Ed.), *The CAEL Newsletter.*

Breen, Paul and Urban Whitaker, *The CAEL Story* (Tape/slide show), 1978.

**1979**

Beechem, Kathleen, *Opportunities for Prior Learning Credit: An Annotated Directory,* 1979.

Brooks, Stevens E. and James E. Athof, (Eds.), *Enriching The Liberal Arts Through Experiential Learning,* (NDEL), 1979.

Cheren, Mark, *The Self-Directed Educator: A CAEL Syllabus,* 1979.

Cross, K. Patricia, *Lifelong Learning: Purposes and Priorities,* 1979.

Knapp, Joan, *The Assessor: A CAEL Syllabus for Professionals,* 1979.

MacTaggart, Terrence, *Cost-Effectiveness: A CAEL Syllabus for Professionals,* 1979.

Martorana, S.V. and Eileen Kuhns, (Eds.), *Transferring Experiential Credit,* (NDEL), 1979.

Pottinger, Paul S. and Joan Goldsmith, (Eds.), *Defining and Measuring Competence,* (NDEL), 1979.

*Proceedings: CAEL National Assembly—November 7-9, 1979, Minneapolis, MN*

van Aalst, Frank D., (Ed.), *Combining Career Development with Experiential Learning,* (NDEL), 1979.

Other Publications

*CAEL Directory,* 1978-79.

Tate, Pamela, (Ed.), *CAEL Newsletter.*

**1980**

Byrne, Eugene T. and Douglas E. Wolfe, (Eds.), *Developing Experiential Learning Programs for Professional Education,* (NDEL), 1980.

Cabell, Harriet W., edited by Ruth Cargo, Introduction by Henry Spille, *Using Licenses and Certificates as Evidence of College-Level Learning,* 1980.

Cook, Marvin and Henry H. Walbesser, *Developing Assessment Tasks, Module 3,* 1980.

Keeton, Morris T., (Ed.), *Defining and Assuring Quality in Experiential Learning,* (NDEL), 1980.

Moon, Rexford G. Jr. and Gene R. Hawes, (Eds.), *Developing New Clienteles of Adult Students,* (NDEL), 1980.

Stack, Hal and Carroll M. Hutton, (Eds.), *Building New Alliances: Labor Unions and Higher Education,* (NDEL), 1980.

### Other Publications

*CAEL Directory,* 1979-1980.

Tate, Pamela, (Ed.), *The CAEL Newsletter.*

## 1981

Cook, J. Marvin, *Samples—Program Maps, Learning Outcomes, and Assessment Tasks—Module 4,* 1981.

Duley, John and Associates, *Field Experience Education: A Casebook,* 1981.

Gold, Gerard G., (Ed.), *Business and Higher Education: Toward New Alliances,* (NDEL), 1981.

Hayenga, Adams, and Rowe, *How to Choose: A Consumer's Guide to Understanding Colleges,* 1981.

Knapp, Joan, (Ed.), *Financing and Implementing Prior Learning Assessment,* (NDEL), 1981.

Knapp, Joan and Paul Jacobs, *Setting Standards for Assessing Experiential Learning,* 1981.

McIntyre, Valerie, edited by Ruth Cargo, *Wherever You Learned It: A Directory of Opportunities for Educational Credit,* 1981.

Neff, Charles B., (Ed.), *Cross-Cultural Learning,* (NDEL), 1981.

Loacker, Georgine, and Ernest G. Palola, (Eds.), *Clarifying Learning Outcomes in the Liberal Arts,* (NDEL), 1981.

Warren, Jonathan R. and Paul W. Breen, *The Educational Value of Portfolio and Learning Contract Development,* 1981.

*You Deserve The Credit: A Guide to Receiving Credit for Non-College Learning,* CAEL, 1981.

### Other Publications

*CAEL Directory,* 1980-81.

Hayenga, E. Sharon, (Ed.), *The CAEL News.*

# APPENDIX B

## 1982

Greenberg, Elinor Miller, (Ed.), *New Partnerships: Higher Education and the Non-Profit Sector,* (NDEL), 1982.

Jacobs, Frederic and Richard J. Allen, (Eds.), *Expanding the Missions of Graduate and Professional Education,* (NDEL), 1982.

Menson, Betty, (Ed.), *Building on Experiences in Adult Development,* (NDEL), 1982.

Rydell, Susan, edited by Judith Irwin, *Creditable Portfolios: Dimensions in Diversity,* 1982.

Taylor, Clark, (Ed.), *Diverse Student Preparation: Benefits and Issues,* (NDEL), 1982.

### Other Publications

Cockey, Patricia, (Ed.), and Rees, Diana Bamford, (Managing Ed.), *The CAEL News.*

## 1983

Breen, Paul and Urban Whitaker, *Bridging the Gap: A Learner's Guide to Transferable Skills,* 1983.

Little, Thomas C., (Ed.), *Making Sponsored Experiential Learning Standard Practice,* (NDEL), 1983.

MacTaggart, Terrence, (Ed.), *Cost Effectiveness in Experiential Learning,* (NDEL), 1983.

### Other Publications

Cockey, Patricia, (Ed.), and Rees, Diana Bamford, (Managing Ed.), *The CAEL News.*

## 1984

Commission on Higher Education and the Adult Learner, *Postsecondary Education Institutions and the Adult Learner: A Self-Study Assessment Guide,* 1984.

### Other Publications

Cockey, Patricia, (Ed.), and Rees, Diana Bamford, (Managing Ed.), *The CAEL News.* (There were also several other editors during the course of 1984.)

# APPENDIX B

## 1985

Simosko, Susan, *Earn College Credit for What You Know (Student Guide)*, 1985.

### Other Publications

Kushner, Phyllis, (Ed.), *The CAEL News.*

# Appendix C

## Biennial Membership and Assembly Information, 1974-1986

### Table C-1: Schools and Organizations with a Membership Connection

| | 1974-75 | 1977-78 | 1979-80 | 1981-82 | 1983-84 | 1985-86 |
|---|---|---|---|---|---|---|
| Number of Institutional Members | 157 | 313 | 329 | 251 | 208 | 277 |
| Number of Schools and Organizations with at Least One Associate Member* | n/a | n/a | 118 | 169 | 190 | 191 |
| Total Number of Schools and Organizations with Some Type of CAEL Membership | 157 | 313 | 447 | 420 | 398 | 468 |

# APPENDIX C

## Table C-2: Consistency in CAEL Institutional Membership, 1974-1986**

| | Schools | Organizations | Totals |
|---|---|---|---|
| Were Members for Only 1 Year | 40% | 60% | 42% |
| Were Members for 2 or 3 Years | 34 | 31 | 33 |
| Were Members for 4 or 5 Years | 21 | 8 | 19 |
| Were Members for all 6 Years | 5 | 2 | 5 |
| | 100% | 100% | 100% |
| N | 578 | 65 | 643 |

*In a few cases, a school or organization had both Institutional Membership and a person with Associate Membership. Such cases are not included in this category. (In 1979-80 there were 21 schools or organizations with Institutional Membership which also had one or more Associate Members; in 1981-82 there were 15; in 1983-84 there were 20; in 1985-86 there were 18.)

**Years included are 1974-75, 1977-78, 1979-80, 1981-82, 1983-84, and 1985-86.

# APPENDIX C

## Table C-3: Individuals with Associate Membership

| | 1974-75 | 1977-78 | 1979-80 | 1981-82 | 1983-84 | 1985-86 |
|---|---|---|---|---|---|---|
| Number of Associate Members (i.e., Number of Individuals) | n/a | n/a | 205 | 229 | 271 | 254 |

## Table C-4: Attenders at National Assembly

| | 1974-75 | 1977-78 | 1979-80 | 1981-82 | 1983-84 | 1985-86 |
|---|---|---|---|---|---|---|
| Number of Schools and Organizations with at Least One Assembly Attender | 145 | 189 | 189 | 162 | 141 | 208 |
| Number of Assembly Attenders* | 214 | 301 | 317 | 244 | 240 | 362 |

*In years when two assemblies were held, only the fall assembly was counted.

## APPENDIX C

### Table C-5: Associate Members' Positions*

| | 1979-80 | 1981-82 | 1983-84 | 1985-86 |
|---|---|---|---|---|
| President, Academic V.P., Academic Dean | 7% | 15% | 15% | 11% |
| Dean (Other Than Academic) | 5 | 8 | 13 | 11 |
| Other Administrator | 47 | 52 | 52 | 56 |
| Faculty | 6 | 7 | 8 | 6 |
| Staff | 5 | 4 | 3 | 7 |
| Other & Unspecified | 30 | 15 | 9 | 10 |
| | 100% | 100% | 100% | 100% |
| N | 138 | 151 | 181 | 189 |

*This table includes only Associate Members from academic institutions.

# APPENDIX C

## Table C-6

Institutional Control of CAEL Member Schools, (with National Comparisons)

| Control | | 1974-75 | 1977-78 | 1979-80 | 1981-82 | 1983-84 | 1985-86 |
|---|---|---|---|---|---|---|---|
| Public | | | | | | | |
| | Institutional Members | 81 | 182 | 192 | 140 | 106 | 151 |
| | Associate Members | n/a | n/a | 27 | 53 | 68 | 53 |
| | Total | 81 | 182 | 219 | 193 | 174 | 204 |
| (National: 45%)* | | 58% | 64% | 60% | 55% | 54% | 53% |
| Private—Affiliated With Religious Group: | | | | | | | |
| | Institutional Members | 31 | 52 | 54 | 55 | 45 | 44 |
| | Associate Members | n/a | n/a | 18 | 30 | 33 | 44 |
| | Total | 31 | 52 | 72 | 85 | 78 | 88 |
| (National: 24%) | | 22% | 18% | 20% | 24% | 24% | 23% |
| Private—Independent, Nonprofit: | | | | | | | |
| | Institutional Members | 28 | 50 | 46 | 39 | 36 | 47 |
| | Associate Members | n/a | n/a | 29 | 31 | 31 | 41 |
| | Total | 28 | 50 | 75 | 70 | 67 | 88 |
| (National: 25%) | | 20% | 17% | 20% | 20% | 21% | 23% |

# APPENDIX C

## Table C-6 (continued)

Institutional Control of CAEL Member Schools (with National Comparisons)

| Control | 1974-75 | 1977-78 | 1979-80 | 1981-82 | 1983-84 | 1985-86 |
|---|---|---|---|---|---|---|
| Private—Organized as Profitmaking: | | | | | | |
| Institutional Members | 0 | 2 | 0 | 0 | 2 | 2 |
| Associate Members | n/a | n/a | 2 | 3 | 1 | 1 |
| Total | 0 | 2 | 2 | 3 | 3 | 3 |
| (National: 6%) | 0% | 1% | 1% | 1% | 1% | 1% |

*National figures indicate the percentage of all U.S. schools which were under each type of control during 1983-84. These percentages are taken from the *Education Directory 1983-84,* Table 3.

## APPENDIX C

### Table C-7

Enrollment of CAEL Member Schools, (with National Comparisons)

| Enrollment Category | | 1974-75 | 1977-78 | 1979-80 | 1981-82 | 1983-84 | 1985-86 |
|---|---|---|---|---|---|---|---|
| Less than 500 | Institutional Members | 7 | 9 | 14 | 7 | 7 | 8 |
| | Associate Members | n/a | n/a | 9 | 9 | 8 | 11 |
| | Total | 7 | 9 | 23 | 16 | 15 | 19 |
| (National: 22%)* | | 5% | 3% | 6% | 5% | 5% | 5% |
| 500-2,499 | Institutional Members | 26 | 70 | 73 | 66 | 61 | 66 |
| | Associate Members | n/a | n/a | 34 | 53 | 50 | 62 |
| | Total | 26 | 70 | 107 | 119 | 111 | 128 |
| (National: 42%) | | 19% | 25% | 29% | 34% | 34% | 33% |
| 2,500-9,999 | Institutional Members | 58 | 114 | 119 | 104 | 70 | 103 |
| | Associate Members | n/a | n/a | 25 | 36 | 52 | 38 |
| | Total | 58 | 114 | 144 | 140 | 122 | 141 |
| (National: 25%) | | 42% | 40% | 39% | 40% | 38% | 37% |
| 10,000-19,999 | Institutional Members | 27 | 55 | 54 | 32 | 29 | 40 |
| | Associate Members | n/a | n/a | 6 | 8 | 11 | 16 |
| | Total | 27 | 55 | 60 | 40 | 40 | 56 |
| (National: 7%) | | 19% | 19% | 16% | 11% | 12% | 15% |

## APPENDIX C

### Table C-7 (continued)

Enrollment) of CAEL Member Schools,
(with National Comparisons)

| Enrollment Category | | 1974-75 | 1977-78 | 1979-80 | 1981-82 | 1983-84 | 1985-86 |
|---|---|---|---|---|---|---|---|
| More than 20,000- | Institutional Members | 21 | 37 | 32 | 26 | 23 | 27 |
| | Associate Members | n/a | n/a | 3 | 11 | 12 | 12 |
| | Total | 21 | 37 | 35 | 37 | 35 | 39 |
| (National: 4%) | | 15% | 13% | 9% | 11% | 11% | 10% |

*National figures indicate the percentage of all U.S. schools which were in each enrollment category in 1981. These percentages were taken from the *Digest of Educational Statistics 1983-84*, p. 4.

## APPENDIX C

### Table C-8

Level of Academic Competitiveness of CAEL Member Schools, with National Comparisons*

| Competitiveness | 1974-75 | 1977-78 | 1979-80 | 1981-82 | 1983-84 | 1985-86 |
|---|---|---|---|---|---|---|
| Most Competitive: | | | | | | |
| Institutional Members | 3 | 0 | 0 | 0 | 0 | 1 |
| Associate Members | n/a | n/a | 2 | 1 | 2 | 1 |
| Total | 3 | 0 | 2 | 1 | 2 | 2 |
| (National: 2%)** | 2% | 0% | 1% | .3% | 1% | 1% |
| Highly Competitive: | | | | | | |
| Institutional Members | 4 | 2 | 2 | 1 | 1 | 1 |
| Associate Members | n/a | n/a | 3 | 5 | 3 | 2 |
| Total | 4 | 2 | 5 | 6 | 4 | 3 |
| (National: 5%) | 3% | 1% | 1% | 2% | 1% | 1% |
| Very Competitive: | | | | | | |
| Institutional Members | 13 | 15 | 22 | 15 | 9 | 12 |
| Associate Members | n/a | n/a | 4 | 7 | 12 | 9 |
| Total | 13 | 15 | 26 | 22 | 21 | 21 |
| (National: 11%) | 10% | 6% | 8% | 7% | 7% | 6% |
| Competitive: | | | | | | |
| Institutional Members | 64 | 107 | 102 | 96 | 71 | 95 |
| Associate Members | n/a | n/a | 28 | 50 | 59 | 66 |
| Total | 64 | 107 | 130 | 146 | 130 | 161 |
| (National: 45%) | 50% | 40% | 38% | 44% | 43% | 45% |

## Table C-8 (continued)

| Competitiveness | 1974-75 | 1977-78 | 1979-80 | 1981-82 | 1983-84 | 1985-86 |
|---|---|---|---|---|---|---|
| Less Competitive: | | | | | | |
| Institutional Members | 19 | 56 | 54 | 46 | 38 | 44 |
| Associate Members | n/a | n/a | 10 | 15 | 18 | 23 |
| Total | 19 | 56 | 64 | 61 | 56 | 67 |
| (National: 27%) | 15% | 21% | 19% | 18% | 19% | 19% |
| Non-Competitive: | | | | | | |
| Institutional Members | 26 | 85 | 94 | 66 | 55 | 73 |
| Associate Members | n/a | n/a | 22 | 29 | 32 | 28 |
| Total | 26 | 85 | 116 | 95 | 87 | 101 |
| (National: 7%) | 20% | 32% | 34% | 29% | 29% | 28% |
| Special: | | | | | | |
| Institutional Members | 0 | 0 | 0 | 0 | 0 | 0 |
| Associate Members | n/a | n/a | 1 | 1 | 0 | 0 |
| Total | 0 | 0 | 1 | 1 | 0 | 0 |
| (National: 4%) | 0% | 0% | .3% | .3% | 0% | 0% |

*Data are missing for some 4-year schools which were not listed in *Barron's Profiles of American Colleges.* Competitiveness categories are defined by the level of academic standing and test scores a student needs for admission to a school and the percentage of applicants typically accepted.

**National percentages are from *Barron's Profiles of American Colleges* for 1983-84.

## APPENDIX C

### Table C-9

Highest Degree Offered in CAEL Member Schools

| Highest Degree | 1974-75 | 1977-78 | 1979-80 | 1981-82 | 1983-84 | 1985-86 |
|---|---|---|---|---|---|---|
| Two but Less Than Four Years | 17% | 26% | 28% | 25% | 24% | 23% |
| Bachelor's and/or First Professional Degree | 20 | 16 | 20 | 22 | 23 | 21 |
| Master's and Beyond, but Less Than Doctorate | 30 | 32 | 31 | 32 | 32 | 34 |
| Doctor of Philosophy and Equivalent | 33 | 26 | 21 | 21 | 21 | 22 |
| | 100% | 100% | 100% | 100% | 100% | 100% |
| N | 140 | 286 | 368 | 351 | 322 | 383 |

### Table C-10

Percentage of Part-Time Students in CAEL Member Schools

| | 1974-75 | 1977-78 | 1979-80 | 1981-82 | 1983-84 | 1985-86 |
|---|---|---|---|---|---|---|
| | 30% | 36% | 35% | 33% | 35% | 33% |

# Appendix D

## Participating Institutions in the Institutional Development Program 1977-1980

| | Year I 1977-78 | Year II 1978-79 | Year III 1979-80 |
|---|---|---|---|
| **Alabama** | | | |
| Birmingham Southern College | x | x | x |
| Community College of the Air Force, Montgomery | | | x |
| Council for Institutional Leadership | | | x |
| Spring Hill College, Mobile | | x | x |
| Troy State University, Montgomery | | | x |
| University of Alabama, Birmingham | x | x | x |
| University of Alabama, New College | x | x | x |
| University of South Alabama, Mobile | | | x |
| **Alaska** | | | |
| Inupiat University, Barrow | | | x |
| University of Alaska, Fairbanks | | | x |
| **Arizona** | | | |
| Northland Pioneer College, Show Low | x | x | x |
| Prescott Center College, Prescott | | | x |
| Western International University, Phoenix | | | x |
| **Arkansas** | | | |
| Arkansas College, Batesville | | | x |
| Arkansas State University, Beebe | | | x |
| Arkansas Dept. of Higher Education | | | x |
| East Arkansas Community College, Forrest City | x | x | x |
| Garland County Community College, Hot Springs | | | x |
| Harding College, Searcy | | | x |
| Hendrix College, Conway | | | x |
| Mississippi County Community College, Blytheville | | | x |
| North Arkansas Community College, Harrison | | | x |
| Phillips County Community College, Helena | x | x | x |
| Westark Community College, Fort Smith | | | x |

# APPENDIX D

| | Year I 1977-78 | Year II 1978-79 | Year III 1979-80 |
|---|---|---|---|
| **California** | | | |
| American Baptist Seminary West, Berkeley | | | x |
| California Christian University, Adelanto | | | x |
| California Community College, Sacramento | | | x |
| California State College/Bakersfield | x | x | x |
| California State College/Dominquez Hills | x | x | x |
| California State University/Long Beach | x | x | x |
| California State University/Los Angeles | x | x | x |
| Cerritos College, Norwalk | x | | x |
| Coastline Community College, Fountain Valley | x | | x |
| Community College of San Diego | | x | x |
| Consortium of California State Colleges & Universities, Los Angeles | x | x | x |
| Golden West College, Huntington Beach | x | x | x |
| Humboldt State University, Arcata | | x | x |
| Los Angeles Community College, Los Angeles | x | | |
| Jesuit School of Technology, Berkeley | | | x |
| National University, San Diego | | x | x |
| Orange Coast College, Costa Mesa | x | x | x |
| Rancho Santiago Community College District, Santa Ana | x | | |
| Saddleback Community College, Mission Viejo | | | x |
| St. Mary's College at California, Moraga | x | x | x |
| San Francisco State University, San Francisco | | | x |
| Santa Ana College, Santa Ana | x | x | x |
| University of California/Berkeley | | | x |
| University of California/Davis | | | x |
| University of California/Irvine | | x | x |
| University of California/Los Angeles | x | x | x |
| University of California/San Diego | x | | x |
| University of California/Santa Cruz | | | x |
| University of Humanistic Studies, San Diego | | | x |
| University of La Verne | x | x | x |
| University of San Francisco | x | x | x |
| University of Southern California, Los Angeles | | x | x |
| University of the Pacific, Stockton | x | x | x |
| Vista College, Berkeley | | | x |

# APPENDIX D

| | Year I 1977-78 | Year II 1978-79 | Year III 1979-80 |
|---|---|---|---|
| **California (continued)** | | | |
| Westmont College, Santa Barbara | | | x |
| University of the Redlands, Whitehead College | x | x | x |
| **Canada** | | | |
| British Columbia Institute of Technology, B.C. | | x | x |
| Georgian College, Barrie, Ontario | x | x | x |
| Lambton College, Sarnia, Ontario | x | x | x |
| Mohawk College, Stoney Creek, Ontario | x | x | x |
| Ryerson Technical | | | x |
| St. Clair College, Windsor, Ontario | x | x | x |
| Sault College, Sault Ste Marie, Ontario | x | x | x |
| Simon Fraser University, B.C. | | x | x |
| Southern Alberta Institute of Technology | | | x |
| **Colorado** | | | |
| Arapahoe Community College, Littleton | x | x | x |
| Colorado State College, Ft. Collins | x | x | x |
| Community College of Denver | x | x | x |
| Denver Association | | | x |
| Loretto Heights College, Denver | | | x |
| Metropolitan State College, Denver | x | x | x |
| Mile High Girl Scouts, Denver | | | x |
| Regis College, Denver | | x | x |
| University of Northern Colorado, Greeley | | x | x |
| **Connecticut** | | | |
| Eastern Connecticut State College, Willimantic | | | x |
| Fairfield University | | | x |
| Manchester Community College | | | x |
| Mohegan Community College, Norwich | | x | x |
| Northwestern Connecticut Community College, Winsted | | x | x |
| Sacred Heart University, Bridgeport | x | | x |
| South Central Community College, New Haven | | x | x |
| University of Hartford | | x | x |
| **Delaware** | | | |
| Delaware State College, Dover | | | x |
| University of Delaware | | | x |

# APPENDIX D

| | Year I 1977-78 | Year II 1978-79 | Year III 1979-80 |
|---|---|---|---|
| **District of Columbia** | | | |
| American Association for Higher Education | | | x |
| The American Red Cross | | | x |
| American University | x | x | x |
| Center for Human Services | | | x |
| Clearinghouse for CBFSEI | | | x |
| Federal Acquisitions Institute for Employee Education | | | x |
| University of D.C., Mt. Vernon | | x | x |
| Washington Center for Learning Alternatives | x | | x |
| Washington International College | x | | x |
| Youthwork, Inc. | | | x |
| **Florida** | | | |
| Biscayne College-University Without Walls, Miami | | x | x |
| Brevard Community College, Cocoa | x | x | x |
| Broward Community College, Ft. Lauderdale | x | x | x |
| Daytona Beach Community College | | x | x |
| Eckerd College, St. Petersburg | | x | x |
| Florida Board of Regents State University System | x | | x |
| Florida Department of Education | x | x | x |
| Florida International University, Miami | x | x | x |
| Florida Junior College, Jacksonville | | x | x |
| Florida Southern College, Orlando | x | x | x |
| Florida State University, Tallahassee | | | x |
| Florida Theological University, Orlando | x | x | |
| Heed University, Hollywood | x | x | x |
| Hillsborough Community College, Tampa | x | x | x |
| Luther Rice Seminary, Jacksonville | | x | x |
| Manatee Junior College, Bradenton | | | x |
| Miami-Dade Community College | x | x | x |
| Rollins College, Winter Park | | | x |
| Southern Florida Junior College, Avon Park | | | x |
| State University System Board of Regents | | x | |
| University of Central Florida, Orlando | | | x |
| University of North Florida, Jacksonville | | | x |
| University of South Florida, Tampa | | | x |
| University of Tampa | | | x |

# APPENDIX D

| | Year I 1977-78 | Year II 1978-79 | Year III 1979-80 |
|---|---|---|---|
| **Florida (continued)** | | | |
| Valencia Community College, Orlando | x | x | x |
| World University of Miami, Miami | | x | |
| **Georgia** | | | |
| Atlanta Junior College, Atlanta | | | x |
| Georgia State University, Atlanta | | x | x |
| Savannah State College | | x | x |
| U.S. Dept. of Labor, Atlanta | | x | x |
| **Idaho** | | | |
| Lewis-Clark State College, Lewiston | | | x |
| North Idaho College, Coeur D'Alene | | | x |
| **Illinois** | | | |
| Barat College, Lake Forest | | | x |
| Board of Governors, State of Illinois | x | x | x |
| Central Y.M.C.A. Community College, Chicago | | | x |
| Chicago City-Wide College | x | x | x |
| Chicago State University | x | x | x |
| College of DuPage, Glen Ellyn | x | x | x |
| College of Lake County, Grayslake | | | x |
| DePaul University, Chicago | x | x | x |
| Eastern Illinois University, Charleston | x | x | x |
| Elmhurst College | | | x |
| Governors State University, Park Forest | x | x | x |
| National College of Education, Chicago | | | x |
| North Central Assn.'s Commission on Institutions of Higher Education, Evanston | | | x |
| Northeastern Illinois University, Chicago | x | x | x |
| Roosevelt University, Chicago | x | x | x |
| Sangamon State University, Springfield | x | x | x |
| Southern Illinois University, Edwardsville | | | x |
| Southern Illinois University, Chicago | | | x |
| University of Illinois, Chicago | | | x |
| Western Illinois University, Macomb | x | x | x |
| William Rainey Harper College, Palatine | x | x | x |
| **Indiana** | | | |
| Calumet College, Whiting | | x | x |
| Indiana University, Indianapolis | x | x | x |
| Indiana Vocational Technical College, Kokomo | | x | x |

# APPENDIX D

| | Year I 1977-78 | Year II 1978-79 | Year III 1979-80 |
|---|---|---|---|
| **Indiana (continued)** | | | |
| Martin Center College, Indianapolis | | | x |
| University of Evansville | x | x | x |
| **Iowa** | | | |
| American College Testing Program | | | x |
| Drake University, Des Moines | x | x | x |
| Loras College, Dubuque | | | x |
| Mount Mercy College, Cedar Rapids | | | x |
| North Iowa Area Community College, Mason City | | | x |
| Saint Ambrose College, Davenport | | | x |
| University of Iowa, Iowa City | | x | x |
| University of Northern Iowa, Cedar Falls | | | x |
| Westmar College, Lemars | | x | x |
| **Kansas** | | | |
| Kansas City, Kansas Community College | x | x | x |
| Kansas State University, Manhattan | x | x | x |
| Ottawa University | | | x |
| St. Mary College, Leavenworth | | | x |
| Wichita State University | | | x |
| **Kentucky** | | | |
| Berea College | | | x |
| Kentucky State University, Frankfort | | | x |
| Spalding College, Louisville | | | x |
| Union College, Barbourville | | x | x |
| University of Kentucky, Lexington | | | x |
| **Louisiana** | | | |
| Delgado College, New Orleans | x | x | x |
| **Maine** | | | |
| University of Maine, Augusta | | x | x |
| University of Maine, Orono | | x | x |
| **Maryland** | | | |
| Hood College, Frederick | x | x | x |
| Johns Hopkins University, Evening College | x | x | x |
| Morgan State University, Baltimore | x | | |
| University of Maryland, University College | x | x | x |
| **Massachusetts** | | | |
| Berkshire Community College, Pittsfield | | | x |

# APPENDIX D

| | Year I 1977-78 | Year II 1978-79 | Year III 1979-80 |
|---|---|---|---|
| **Massachusetts (continued)** | | | |
| Boston Six | | x | x |
| Bristol Community College, Fall River | | | x |
| Bunker Hill Community College, Charlestown | x | x | x |
| Greenfield Community College | | | x |
| Hampshire College, Amherst | | x | |
| Institute for Open Education, Cambridge | x | x | x |
| Lesley College, Cambridge | x | | |
| Massachusetts Bay Community College, Wellesley | | | x |
| Massachusetts Board of Regional Community Colleges, Boston | | | x |
| Massasoit Community College, Brockton | | | x |
| Northeastern University, Boston | | | x |
| Northern Essex Community College, Haverhill | | x | x |
| North Adams State College | | | x |
| Quinsigamond Community College, Worcester | | | x |
| Simon's Rock College, Great Barrington | | | x |
| Southeastern Massachusetts University, North Dartmouth | x | x | x |
| University of Massachusetts, Amherst | x | | x |
| University of Massachusetts, Boston | x | x | x |
| **Michigan** | | | |
| Alma College | | | x |
| Central Michigan University, Mt. Pleasant | x | x | x |
| Delta College, University Center | | x | x |
| Detroit Institute of Technology | x | x | x |
| Ferris State College, Big Rapids | x | x | x |
| Grand Valley State College, Allendale | | x | x |
| Jackson Community College | | | x |
| Jordan College, Cedar Springs | | | x |
| Kalamazoo Valley Community College, Rochester | | x | x |
| Madonna College, Livonia | x | x | x |
| Marygrove College, Detroit | x | x | x |
| Mercy College, Detroit | | | x |
| Michigan Christian College, Rochester | | | x |
| Michigan State University, East Lansing | x | x | x |
| Oakland University, Rochester | | | x |
| Siena Heights College, Adrian | x | | |
| Washtenaw Community College, Ann Arbor | | | x |
| Wayne State University, Detroit | x | x | x |

# APPENDIX D

| | Year I 1977-78 | Year II 1978-79 | Year III 1979-80 |
|---|---|---|---|
| **Minnesota** | | | |
| College of Saint Benedict, St. Joseph | x | x | x |
| College of Saint Scholastica, Duluth | | x | x |
| Inver Hills Community College, Inver Grove Heights | | x | x |
| Lakewood Community College, White Bear Lake | x | | x |
| Metropolitan State University, Saint Paul | x | | x |
| Normandale Community College, Bloomington | | x | x |
| Saint Cloud State University, Saint Cloud | | | x |
| Saint Mary's College, Wionna | | x | x |
| Southwest State University, Marshall | | | x |
| University of Minnesota, Minneapolis | | | x |
| Vermillion Community College, Ely | | | x |
| **Mississippi** | | | |
| Itawamba Junior College, Fulton | | | x |
| Northwest Mississippi Junior College, Senatobia | | | x |
| **Missouri** | | | |
| American International Open University, St. Louis | x | | |
| Clayton University, St. Louis | | x | x |
| Columbia College, Columbia | | | x |
| Metropolitan Community College, Kansas City | | | x |
| Park College, Parkville | | | x |
| Stephens College, Columbia | x | x | x |
| Univerity of Missouri, Columbia | | x | x |
| Webster College, St. Louis | x | x | x |
| **Montana** | | | |
| Montana State University, Bozeman | x | x | x |
| University of Montana, Missoula | x | | |
| **Nebraska** | | | |
| Central Technical Community College, Hastings | x | x | |
| Chadron State College | | x | x |
| Metropolitan Community College, Omaha | | x | |
| **Nevada** | | | |
| University of Nevada, Reno | | | x |

# APPENDIX D

| | Year I 1977-78 | Year II 1978-79 | Year III 1979-80 |
|---|---|---|---|
| **New Hampshire** | | | |
| University System of New Hampshire, Durham | | | x |
| **New Jersey** | | | |
| Bergen Community College, Paramus | | | x |
| Bloomfield College, Bloomfield | x | x | x |
| Burlington Community College, Pemberton | x | x | |
| Caldwell College | | | x |
| Educational Testing Service, Princeton | | | x |
| Glassboro State College | x | x | x |
| Gloucester County College, Sewell | | | x |
| Jersey City State College | x | | x |
| Kean College, Union | x | x | x |
| Mercer County Community College, Trenton | | | x |
| Middlesex County College, Edison | x | x | x |
| Montclair State College | | | x |
| Ramapo College, Mahwah | | x | x |
| Stockton College, Pomona | x | x | x |
| Rutgers University, New Brunswick | | x | x |
| Somerset County College, Somerville | | | x |
| Thomas A. Edison College, Trenton | x | x | x |
| Trenton State College | x | x | x |
| William Paterson College, Wayne | x | x | x |
| **New Mexico** | | | |
| University of Albuquerque | | x | x |
| **New York** | | | |
| Adelphi University, Garden City | | | x |
| College of New Rochelle | | x | x |
| College of Saint Rose, Albany | | | x |
| Corning Community College | | | x |
| Council for International Education, New York | x | | |
| Empire State College, Saratoga Springs | x | x | x |
| Girl Scouts of the U.S.A., New York | | | x |
| LaGuardia Community College, Long Island City | x | x | x |
| New York Institute of Technology, Old Westbury | | | x |
| Pace University, Pleasantville | x | x | x |
| Rochester Institute of Technology | | | x |
| Rockland Community College, Suffern | x | x | x |

# APPENDIX D

| | Year I 1977-78 | Year II 1978-79 | Year III 1979-80 |
|---|---|---|---|
| **New York (continued)** | | | |
| State University College, Buffalo | | | x |
| State University College, Cortland | | | x |
| State University College, Fredonia | | | x |
| State University College, Oneonta | | | x |
| State University College, Plattsburgh | | | x |
| State University College, Potsdam | | | x |
| State University of New York, Albany | | | x |
| State University of New York System | | x | x |
| State University of New York, Agricultural and Technical College, Delhi | | | x |
| State University of New York at Brockport | | | x |
| **North Carolina** | | | |
| Mars Hill College, Mars Hill | x | x | x |
| Shaw University, Raleigh | | | x |
| **North Dakota** | | | |
| Dickinson State College, Dickinson | | | x |
| Lake Region Junior College, Devil Lake | | x | |
| Mary College, Bismarck | x | x | x |
| Standing Rock Community College, Ft. Yates | | x | x |
| Valley City State College | | | x |
| **Ohio** | | | |
| Antioch College, Yellow Springs | | x | x |
| Antioch International, Yellow Springs | x | x | x |
| Baldwin-Wallace College, Berea | x | x | x |
| Capital University, Columbus | x | x | x |
| Cincinnati Technical College | | x | x |
| Cleveland State University | | | x |
| College of Mount St. Joseph | | | x |
| Cuyahoga Community College, Cleveland | | | x |
| Dyke College, Cleveland | | x | x |
| East Central College Consortium, Alliance | x | | |
| Findlay College | | | x |
| Franklin University, Columbus | | x | x |
| Heidelberg College, Tiffin | x | | |
| Hiram College | x | x | |
| Hocking Technical College, Nelsonville | x | x | x |
| Kent State University | | | x |
| Lake Erie College, Painesville | x | x | x |
| Lorian County Comm. College, Elyria | | x | x |

# APPENDIX D

| | Year I 1977-78 | Year II 1978-79 | Year III 1979-80 |
|---|---|---|---|
| **Ohio (continued)** | | | |
| Michael Owens Technical College, Toledo | x | x | x |
| North Central Technical College, Mansfield | | | x |
| Ohio State University, Columbus | | | x |
| Ohio University, Athens | x | x | x |
| Sinclair Community College, Dayton | x | x | x |
| Union for Experimenting Colleges and Universities, Cincinnati | x | x | x |
| University of Akron | | | x |
| University of Cincinnati | x | x | x |
| University of Dayton | | x | x |
| Wright State University, Dayton | x | x | x |
| **Oklahoma** | | | |
| Flaming Rainbow University, Tahlequah | | x | x |
| University of Oklahoma, Norman | | x | x |
| **Oregon** | | | |
| Blue Mountain Community College, Pendleton | | | x |
| Central Oregon Community College, Bend | | x | x |
| Chemeketa Community College, Salem | | | x |
| Clackamas Community College, Oregon City | x | x | x |
| Clatsop Community College, Astoria | | | x |
| Colegio Cesar Chevez, Mount Angel | | x | x |
| Eastern Oregon State College, La Grande | x | x | x |
| Institute for Managerial Women | | | x |
| Lane Community College, Eugene | x | x | x |
| Linfield College, McMinnville | | x | x |
| Marylhurst Education Center, Marylhurst | x | x | x |
| Oregon/CAEL, Portland | | | x |
| Oregon College of Education, Monmouth | | x | x |
| Oregon Consortium for the Advancement of Experiential & Lifelong Learning/ McMinnville | | x | |
| Oregon Education Coordinating Commission, Salem | | | x |
| Oregon Institute of Technology, Klamath Falls | | | x |
| Oregon State University, Corvallis | x | x | x |
| Portland State University, Portland | | | x |
| Roque Community College, Grants Pass | | | x |

# APPENDIX D

| | Year I 1977-78 | Year II 1978-79 | Year III 1979-80 |
|---|---|---|---|
| **Oregon (Continued)** | | | |
| Southern Oregon College, Ashland | x | x | x |
| Treasure Valley Community College, Ontario | | | x |
| Umpqua Community College, Roseburg | | | x |
| University of Oregon, Eugene | x | x | x |
| Warner Pacific College, Portland | | | x |
| **Pennsylvania** | | | |
| Allegheny County Community College, Pittsburgh | | | x |
| American College, Bryn Mawr | | | x |
| Antioch/Philadelphia | | | x |
| Bloomsburg State College | x | x | x |
| Bucks County Community College, Newton | x | x | x |
| Cabrini College, Radnor | | x | x |
| Carlow College, Pittsburgh | | | x |
| CLEO, Philadelphia | | | x |
| Community College of Philadelphia | | | x |
| Delaware County Community College, Media | x | x | x |
| East Stroudsburg State College | x | x | |
| Erie College | | | x |
| King's College, Wilkes Barre | | | x |
| Lincoln University-Eagleville | | x | x |
| Luzerne County Community College, Nanticoke | x | x | x |
| Millersville State College, Millersville | x | x | x |
| Moravian College, Bethlehem | | | x |
| Neuman College, Aston | x | x | x |
| Northampton County Community College, Bethlehem | | | x |
| Pennsylvania Department of Education | x | x | x |
| Reading Area Community College | x | x | x |
| Temple University, Philadelphia | x | x | x |
| University of Scranton | x | x | x |
| Westminster College, New Wilmington | x | x | x |
| Westmoreland County Community College, Youngwood | | x | x |
| Widener University, Chester | | x | |
| **Rhode Island** | | | |
| Rhode Island College, Providence | | | x |
| Rhode Island Junior College, Warwick | | x | x |

# APPENDIX D

| | Year I 1977-78 | Year II 1978-79 | Year III 1979-80 |
|---|---|---|---|
| **South Carolina** | | | |
| College of Charleston, Charleston | | | x |
| Instructional Action Center, Pendleton | | x | x |
| North Greenville College, Tigerville | | x | x |
| South Carolina State Board of Technical and Comprehensive Education | | | x |
| State Department of South Carolina | | x | x |
| Voorhees College, Denmark | | x | x |
| Winthrop College, Rock Hill | | | x |
| **South Dakota** | | | |
| Augustana College, Sioux Falls | x | x | x |
| Black Hills State College, Spearfish | | x | x |
| Mount Marty College, Yankton | | x | x |
| National College of Business, Rapid City | x | x | x |
| University of South Dakota, Vermillion | x | x | x |
| **Tennessee** | | | |
| Dyersburg State Community College | x | x | x |
| East Tennessee State University, Johnson City | | | x |
| Jackson State Community College | x | x | x |
| Lincoln Memorial University, Harrogate | x | x | x |
| Memphis State University | x | x | x |
| Middle Tennessee State University, Murfreesboro | | x | x |
| Shelby State Community College, Memphis | x | x | x |
| Trevecca Nazarene College, Nashville | x | x | x |
| University of Tennessee, Memphis | | | x |
| Volunteer State Community College, Gallatin | | | x |
| **Texas** | | | |
| Austin College, Sherman | x | x | x |
| Dallas Baptist College, Dallas | | x | x |
| East Texas State University, Commerce | | | x |
| East Texas State University, Texarkana | x | x | x |
| Mountain View College, Dallas | | x | x |
| Our Lady of the Lake University, San Antonio | | x | x |
| Saint Edward's University, Austin | | x | x |
| Schreiner College, Kerrville | | | x |
| Southwest Texas State University, San Marcos | | x | x |

# APPENDIX D

| | Year I 1977-78 | Year II 1978-79 | Year III 1979-80 |
|---|---|---|---|
| **Texas (continued)** | | | |
| University of Houston | | x | x |
| **Utah** | | | |
| Westminster College, Salt Lake City | | x | x |
| **Vermont** | | | |
| Community College of Vermont Montpelier | x | x | x |
| School for International Training, Brattleboro | | x | |
| Trinity College, Burlington | x | x | x |
| **Virginia** | | | |
| George Mason University, Fairfax | | x | x |
| Hampton Institute | | x | x |
| James Madison University, Harrisonburg | | x | x |
| J. Sargeant Reynolds Community College, Richmond | | x | x |
| Mary Baldwin College, Staunton | | x | x |
| Mary Washington College, Fredericksburg | | x | x |
| Northern Virginia Community College, Annandale | | | x |
| Piedmont Virginia Community College, Charlottesville | | x | x |
| Thomas Nelson Community College, Hampton | | x | x |
| Virginia Commonwealth University, Richmond | | x | x |
| Virginia State University, Petersburg | | x | x |
| **Washington** | | | |
| Bellevue Community College, Bellevue | | | x |
| City College, Seattle | x | x | x |
| Eastern Washington State College, Cheney | x | x | x |
| Edmonds Community College, Lynnwood | | x | x |
| Everett Community College | | x | x |
| Evergreen State College, Olympia | x | x | x |
| Fort Steilacoom Community College, Tacoma | | x | x |
| Fort Wright College, Spokane | x | x | x |
| Northwest Program Development and Coordination Center, Seattle | | | x |

# APPENDIX D

| | Year I 1977-78 | Year II 1978-79 | Year III 1979-80 |
|---|---|---|---|
| **Washington (continued)** | | | |
| Olympic College, Bremerton | | | x |
| Pacific Lutheran College, Tacoma | | | x |
| Seattle Pacific University, Seattle | | | x |
| Seattle University | | | x |
| Skagit Valley College, Mount Vernon | | | x |
| Western Washington State College, Bellingham | x | x | x |
| Whatcom Community College, Bellingham | x | x | x |
| **West Virginia** | | | |
| Bethany College | x | x | |
| Marshall University, Huntington | | x | x |
| Wheeling College | | x | x |
| **Wisconsin** | | | |
| Alverno College, Milwaukee | x | x | x |
| Gateway Technical Institute, Kenosha | | x | x |
| Milwaukee Area Technical College | | | x |
| University of Wisconsin/Green Bay | x | x | x |
| University of Wisconsin/Lacrosse | x | x | x |
| University of Wisconsin/Oshkosh | x | x | x |
| University of Wisconsin/Parkside | x | x | x |
| University of Wisconsin/Platteville | x | x | x |
| University of Wisconsin/River Falls | x | x | x |
| University of Wisconsin/Stevens Point | x | x | x |
| University of Wisconsin/Stout, Menomonie | | | x |
| University of Wisconsin/Superior | x | x | x |
| University of Wisconsin System | x | x | x |
| University of Wisconsin/Whitewater | x | x | x |
| Waukesha County Technical Institute, Pewaukee | x | x | x |
| TOTAL | 176 | 258 | 437 |

Number of Institutions Involved for One Year Only: 200
Number of Institutions Involved for Two Years Only: 112
Number of Institutions Involved for Three Years Only: 149
Total Number of Institutions Involved in IDP: 461

# Appendix E

## Mean Scores* on Changes in Postsecondary Education and CAEL's Influence on Them**

| | Overall Change | CAEL's Influence | Difference (Column 2 – Column 1) |
|---|---|---|---|
| An increased awareness has developed among adults that learning is on-going throughout life | 3.8 | 3.5 | –.3 |
| Information and advocacy services for adults have become wide-spread | 3.6 | 3.7 | +.1 |
| Alliances between educational institutions and labor organizations and/or businesses have been developed | 3.4 | 3.7 | +.3 |
| Institutions of higher education have examined their mission and roles relative to adult learners | 3.3 | 3.3 | 0 |
| The use of prior learning assessment has increased | 3.3 | 4.2 | +.9 |
| The number of flexibly delivered degree programs for adults has expanded | 3.2 | 3.3 | +.1 |
| The use of sponsored experiential learning in higher education has increased (e.g., internships, practica, cooperative education | 3.2 | 3.4 | +.2 |
| Alliances between educational institutions and voluntary service groups and/or community agencies have been developed | 2.9 | 3.2 | +.3 |
| Faculty have become more competent in the use of computers and telecommunications to provide educational services | 2.9 | 2.1 | –.8 |
| Colleges and universities are more sophisticated in their use of various assessment techniques | 2.9 | 3.6 | +.7 |

| | Overall Change | CAEL's Influence | Difference (Column 2 – Column 1) |
|---|---|---|---|
| The primary place of learning has shifted from schools or colleges to such places as the home, the workplace, churches, professional associations and the military | 2.9 | 2.8 | –.1 |
| The use of telecommunications to inform adults about available educational opportunities has increased | 2.8 | 2.6 | –.2 |
| There is greater use by adults of computer-assisted guidance software | 2.8 | 3.2 | +.4 |
| Colleges and universities have adapted their admissions practices to better assess the potential of adults returning to school | 2.7 | 3.4 | +.7 |
| Colleges and universities have placed more emphasis on looking at the outcomes of education | 2.7 | 3.0 | +.3 |
| More cost-effective learning options for both learners and institutions have been developed | 2.6 | 2.5 | –.1 |
| New credentials other than college degrees have been developed to reflect the outcomes of experiential learning | 2.4 | 2.7 | +.3 |
| | | N=55 | |

* Adapted from Talburtt (1986).
** Ratings were on a five-point scale, with 1 = "None at all," 3 = "Somewhat" and 5 = "A great deal."

# Appendix F

Areas of CAEL's Greatest Influence,
By Location of Correspondents*

| | Inst | Assoc | Govt | Edn | Res | PriSec |
|---|---|---|---|---|---|---|
| The use of prior learning assessment has increased | 4.5 | 3.8 | 4.0 | 4.6 | 4.3 | 4.3 |
| Alliances between educational institutions and labor organizations and/or businesses have been developed | 4.9 | 3.6 | 3.6 | 3.5 | 4.0 | 3.5 |
| Information and advocacy services for adults have become more widespread | 4.3 | 3.1 | 3.7 | 3.6 | 4.1 | 3.6 |
| Colleges and universities are more sophisticated in their use of various assessment techniques | 4.1 | 3.4 | 4.1 | 2.3 | 3.1 | 3.4 |

*Location of correspondents is abbreviated as follows: Inst = Institutions, Assoc = Associations, Govt = Government, Edn = Educational Organizations, Res = Research Organizations, PriSec = Private Sector.

# Index

# Index

# INDEX

# INDEX

INDEX

## INDEX

INDEX

# INDEX

INDEX